A Short History of Quebec:

A Socio-Economic Perspective

Brian Young
McGill University

John A. Dickinson
Université de Montréal

Copp Clark Pitman Ltd.
A Longman Company
Toronto

ISBN: 0-7730-4756-5

Care has been taken to trace ownership of copyright material
contained in this text. The publishers will gladly take any
information that will enable them to rectify any reference or
credit in subsequent editions.

Executive Editor: Brian Henderson
Copy Editor: Jane Lind
Cover/Text Design: Catherine Aikens
Typesetting: Attic Typesetting Inc.

Canadian Cataloguing in Publication Data

Young, Brian J., 1940–
  A short history of Quebec

Bibliography: p.
Includes index.
ISBN 0-7730-4756-5

1. Quebec (Province) – History. 2. Quebec
(Province) – Economic conditions. 3. Quebec
(Province) – Social conditions. I. Dickinson,
John Alexander, 1948–   . II. Title.

FC2911.Y68 1988   971.4   C88-093258-9
F1052.Y68 1988

Copp Clark Pitman Ltd.
2775 Matheson Blvd. E.
Mississauga, Ontario
L4W 4P7

Associated companies:
  Longman Group Ltd., London
  Longman Inc., New York
  Longman Cheshire Pty., Melbourne
  Longman Paul Pty., Auckland

Printed and bound in Canada

Preface

This book originated in 1984 with the authors' perception that Quebec history as represented in English-language literature had a traditional political orientation that neglected important elements in Quebec society. Emphasizing socio-economic relations, we reshaped the periodization of Quebec history and within this framework integrated recent research.

Akin to jury duty, reading a colleague's manuscript calls for patience, wisdom, attention to detail, and ultimately, judgment. Three of our colleagues at the University of Montreal and McGill University—Bettina Bradbury, Robert Sweeny, and Pierre Tousignant—read all or parts of this manuscript, and their comments sent us scurrying to rethink elements of our interpretation, periodization, and presentation. While their suggestions led to important improvements, they have no responsibility for the final text.

Writing in partnership over a three-and-a-half-year period involves important but endless debate over theory, method, content, and style. While we hope these debates led to a better book, they did have implications for our families and it is to them—Béatrice Kowaliczko, Julien Leloup, Louise Tremblay-Dickinson and Brigitte and Michael Dickinson—that we affectionately dedicate this book.

cover: McCord Museum of Canadian History, McGill University, Montréal.

VIEW OF QUEBEC, CANADA, FROM THE RAILWAY STATION
OPPOSITE QUEBEC, THE CITY
C. Krieghoff 1856

Table of Contents

Introduction

There are few histories of Quebec in English and fewer yet that are short. In the 1950s Mason Wade's massive narrative, *The French Canadians*, inserted Quebec into what he called Canada's "ancient ethnic conflict". Francophones, or the Sinn Feiners of North America, as he described them, used nationalism and politics to overcome their "basic loneliness and insecurity".

Much research and historiographical re-evaluation has gone under the bridge since Wade's work. In particular, graduate schools have produced significant numbers of scholars whose work concentrates on Quebec. Much of this scholarship, published and unpublished, is in French, but given the nature of Canadian "bilingualism", it is inaccessible to many anglophone readers. For example, the most important historical journal treating Quebec *Revue d'histoire de l'Amérique française*, reflects a range of professionalism and ideologies that give a measure of change in Quebec since Lionel Groulx founded the *Revue* in 1947; its articles are often virtually unknown to anglophone students, even those in Quebec's English language universities.

As university teachers of Quebec history, we are concerned by the limited means anglophone readers have of understanding Quebec society. While historians like Ramsay Cook and Susan Mann Trofimenkoff have done much to interpret Quebec to the rest of Canada, important works in French—from scholars like Louise Dechêne, Jean Hamelin, Serge Courville, and Jean-Pierre Wallot—have not been translated. Many anglophones' knowledge of Quebec can be summarized as slim pickings based on a few clichés about Roman Catholic Church spires and the social significance of Montreal's outside staircases, mixed with a rudimentary knowlege of Quebec political history, particularly as it intrudes upon larger Canadian crises. We have also shaped our book with a view toward the growing body of readers outside Canada who are interested in Quebec society.

An important school of Quebec historiography—and one of particular significance in the period of the Parti Québécois government and the referendum—has emphasized Quebec's ideological traditions. An example of this school is Susan Trofimenkoff's *The Dream of Nation* (1983). Also of importance and with greater social and economic emphasis is the two-volume synthesis of contemporary Quebec by Paul-André Linteau, René Durocher, Jean-Claude Robert, and François Ricard. However, their work does not treat pre-Confederation Canada and, at present, only one volume is available in English. In our short book, we try to complement these works by treating Quebec from its origins to the present by evaluating different interpretations of Quebec history, and by proposing a different theoretical and time frame.

Although we do not neglect the relationship of Quebec to larger Canadian and North American realities, it must be emphasized that this is a socioeconomic history of Quebec and its people. Francophones outside Quebec are not treated systematically. The geographical frame is the province as defined in 1912 and confirmed by the Privy Council in 1927: from Ungava Bay and Hudson Bay to the Appalachians, and from the Ottawa Valley to Labrador (Figure 1).

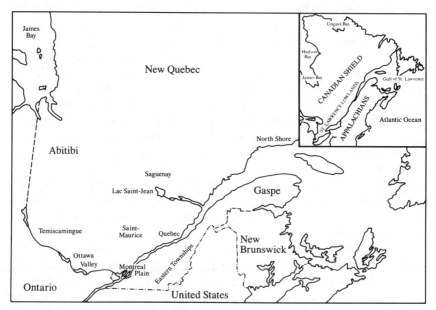

Figure 1 Quebec: Physical Characteristics and Regions

At the same time, we avoid treating Quebec as a monolithic whole and have been careful to highlight regional, class, and ethnic diversity: for example, life in the Gaspé and in the Montreal plain has always been very different. Variations in dialect, economy, and social structure differentiate the franco-phone populations of the Saguenay, the Eastern Townships, and the Ottawa Valley. At the same time, the worker at the snowmobile factory in Valcourt is separated by profound class differences from members of the Bombardier family, although they share a similar cultural heritage. In this century, ethnic differences and the particular structure of capitalism have set Montreal apart from the other regions of the province.

Periodization is, of course, a crucial task for the historian with profound interpretative and structural implications. In subordinating political events such as the Conquest and Confederation, our concept of "period" in Quebec history differs from most syntheses of Canadian history. Our periodization is much closer to recent Quebec scholarship, for example that outlined by Gilles Paquet and Jean-Pierre Wallot (Paquet et Wallot, 1982: 491). While agreeing with their concept of process, our time periods are different and we relate our periodization closely to the passage of Quebec through distinct modes of production and exchange: until 1650, a barter society in which native peoples play a dominant role; from 1650 to 1815, a preindustrial society based on a peasant economy and commercial capitalism; from 1816 to 1885, the crucial period of Quebec's transition from preindustrial to industrial society; we characterize Quebec from 1886 to 1933 as a mature industrial capitalist economy dominated by monopolies. Somewhat unsure of the present economic direction, we date contemporary Quebec from 1933.

Periodization, as Paquet and Wallot and Louise Dechêne have pointed out, is never clearcut and our chronological frames are only bench-marks. Change takes place over time and at varying rates; we can discern overlapping and the co-existence of different economic stages in the same period. In isolated regions, for example, elements of the preindustrial peasant economy persisted into the twentieth-century, a period of mature industrial capitalism.

Like our concept of periodization, the decision to concentrate on a socio-economic perspective has ideological implications. Property and other forms of economic power, the law, social structure, institutions, and gender are central to our book and predominate over questions of politics, culture, and nationalism. The latter are, of course, elements of the former, but are not the determinants of our periodization or our interpretation.

Native peoples, their life, their occupation of the territory of Quebec, and the evolution of their societies are central before 1650. Colonization was incidental to the history of Quebec in this period and the European experience was subordinate to that of native peoples who provided the labour, barter systems, and often the technology and support essential for successful European adaptation to North America. This concentration on the society of native peoples emphasizes our view that while staples are important in explaining the linkage between Quebec and the larger Atlantic economy, the staple theory is inadequate to explain overall economic and social development. Local economies and local exchange were important from the time of the barter economy and they form a major and ongoing focus of Quebec history.

Instead of treating New France as an ethnic and religious entity that was then inextricably altered by the British Conquest in 1760, we have united the period from the mid-seventeenth to the early nineteenth century into Quebec's preindustrial experience. From this perspective, the Conquest, while it marked a fundamental change in metropolis and set the stage for the "national question", left intact the fundamental institutions and ideology of preindustrial society.

This emphasis on economic and social change leads to the subordination of Confederation (a traditional division in political histories of Canada) into the transition in Quebec to industrial capitalism. This transition to industrial production, across the period from the end of the Napoleonic Wars in 1815 to the completion of the Canadian Pacific Railway in 1885, was characterized by fundamental transformation in work and the work place, by changing technology, by an expanding market economy, and by new forms and roles for capital.

This placing of the transition in Quebec near the beginning of the nineteenth century has parallels in other parts of Canada. Gerald Friesen, for example, sees Lord Selkirk's Red River settlement (1812) as "the harbinger of British and European industrial capitalist conventions" (Friesen, 1984: 66).

This process was accompanied in Quebec by the modernization of the state after the rebellions of 1837-38, by the rise to dominance of a conservative bourgeois ideology that gave prominence to parliamentary institutions, by individualism, and by the freedom of property. In this society, the emerging capitalists and the francophone bourgeoisie formed a common front. The Roman Catholic Church was a central force in industrializing Quebec by assuming new ideological and social functions through the parish newspapers, libraries, and publishing, and particularly through education, and national, social, and voluntary associations.

The transformation of the state, the reinforcing of social-control institutions, and the rise to dominance of bourgeois ideology was not accomplished without strong resistance. Labour formed unions and fraternal organizations. Iroquois on reserves resisted their missionaries by burning the church at Oka and by rejecting the sacraments. Peasants attacked schools and the central state's other intrusions into preindustrial communities. And women used particular female institutions such as the convent to protect their autonomy and power.

Given the ideological and institutional power of these forces, Quebec's response to maturing industrial capitalist society in the period 1886 to 1933 is not surprising. Conservatism was expressed in political and social life, institutions, and unions. A contributing factor to this conservatism was a deepening insecurity in the face of mounting evidence of Quebec's and French Canada's minority status in the Canadian federal state. Riel, the various school crises across Canada, and the drama of conscription in the First World War emphasized that the ideological and political values of the Canadian majority would prevail in periods of crisis.

It was in the early twentieth century, in the face of the ideological and institutional power of the elite in industrial capitalist society, that Quebec labour, women, native peoples, and other social groups found their means of resistance most limited. Conservative unionism, the increasing dependence of native peoples on the state and market economy, and the dominance of the symbol of the Virgin as a model of female behaviour were signs of this weakness.

The Depression brought new forces to the fore. Signs of the shift in capitalist power were evident by the strength of the Toronto Stock Exchange. And given the church's inability to cope with the social dimensions of the Depression, state authorities at the federal, provincial, and municipal levels entered more directly into Quebec's economic and social life.

At the same time, frustrations with the federal system and with the reality of increasing American and Anglo-Canadian domination of the Quebec economy led to a more introspective nationalism and demands for a francophone state. Provincial autonomy was increasingly posited against the centralization policies of successive federal governments through the Depression, the Second World War, and postwar periods. On the other hand, we can discern the emergence of changing social forces. Progressive clergy challenged traditional Catholic attitudes to unionism and social action. Unions, and particularly Catholic unions, grew in size and adopted strike action and broadening social and political measures. Women obtained not only the provincial vote, but began, in both the work place and home, to successfully combat the oppression of the gross gender inequalities of Quebec society.

Elements of social democracy, nationalism (both progressive and conservative), provincial autonomy, and the successful statism of the Liberal government of the early 1960s culminated in the formation of the Parti Québécois, a party committed to an independent Quebec. In the last three decades, expanded provincial government intervention in the economy, a growing francophone presence in the federal government, the creation of the welfare state, and growing accumulation of capital by francophones provided the means for the local bourgeoisie to obtain political and economic power.

In our interpretation, ethnicity in Quebec can be understood only in tandem with socio-economic development. The transition to industrial capitalism in Quebec was accompanied by an increasing synonymity between ethnicity and capital. This must not obscure the ongoing importance of significant anglophone elements in the popular classes: fishermen in the Gaspé, farmers in the Eastern Townships, and artisans and labourers in Montreal and Quebec City.

However, from the early nineteenth century, capital in Quebec and the power accompanying it increasingly fell into the hands of anglophones. This process accelerated after 1885 with the union of industrial and financial capital, with the growing significance of concentration, with new forms of corporate organization, and with the new role of capital-based resource industries in the Quebec economy. Accompanying this concentration of capital was an increasing isolation of the anglophone bourgeoisie. Whereas the Prices and Redpaths of transition Quebec had an awareness of Quebec society, the owners of Sun Life and the Canadian Pacific Railway ignored Quebec.

Frustration with this economic and social reality was an important factor in the nationalist movement, in the statism of contemporary Quebec, and in the push for increased cultural, political, and economic sovereignty. Given these factors, it is not surprising that Quebec nationalism had its base among emerging elements in the Quebec bourgeoisie and that its strongest roots were in Montreal.

In addition to the importance we give to socio-economic process, we have emphasized gender, class, and groups largely invisible in traditional histories of Quebec. From their place at centre stage in the first part of the book, we try to follow the passage of native peoples through the subsequent periods.

Women are absent in elitist history since they were not formal players in politics, the army, or journalism and most historians have not asked about or conceptualized the place of women in Quebec society. However, when we use parish, notarial, or judicial records to look at population, work, the family, and social relations, a different perspective emerges. Servants, for example, were the largest paid occupation in eighteenth- and nineteenth-century urban Quebec, and most of these were women. While domestics represented 22.4 percent of Montreal's "active" labour force in 1825, the liberal professions, who shaped our political history and memory, represented 2 percent of the "active" population.

Consideration of women's experience is fundamental to our periodization and socio-economic perspective. However, the debate over whether women's history should be separated from traditional history presented an organizational dilemma. Should gender questions be integrated into the general text under headings such as labour or financial institutions, or should women be treated separately? After trying to weigh the paucity of research (and, therefore, the absence of women in certain key areas) against the obvious dangers of ghettoization, we have attempted both approaches.

Not all aspects of Quebec history can be treated in a short work. For some important issues, such as protoindustrialization, research is so preliminary that viable conclusions cannot be presented. We see this book's vocation then as twofold. It gives an overview of the main socio-economic elements of Quebec history and, at the same time, addresses important and ongoing interpretative questions. It is our modest wish that this book will serve to reinforce the maxim that "all history has to be looked at again".

* * *

A word about using the book and further reading: each chapter has a brief bibliographical note that directs the reader to important general works on the subjects and period treated in the chapter. This is supplemented by a larger and more comprehensive general bibliography at the end of the book.

On the sticky and constantly changing issue of toponymy, we have tried to strike a balance between official terminology in Quebec and current English terminology. Montreal and Quebec are unaccented, for example, and St. Lawrence is used in preference to Saint-Laurent. However, as a general rule, we have used correct French terms for places in Quebec.

The changing political reality of Quebec also poses problems of terminology. For example, in the period of New France, the French inhabitants of the St. Lawrence Valley were called "Canadiens"; in British North America they were known as "new subjects", "Canadiens", and "Lower Canadians". After Confederation, "French Canadian" was commonly used and more recently

"Québécois". Although they are neologisms, we use the terms "francophone" and "anglophone" to distinguish between the two main cultural communities of Quebec. Contemporary designations are more correct in an historical perspective and are occasionally used in the text, but they are not without ambiguity to readers outside Quebec. The English-speaking population of Quebec is heterogeneous and, here too, the terms English, Scot, Irish, and American are used to understand particular events. The term anglophone is used when members of these different English-speaking communities acted in a common fashion.

The variety of currencies and units of measurement used poses problems as well. French *livres* were commonly used until the mid-nineteenth century, overlapping with various British currencies after the Conquest. With the introduction of banking institutions in the 1820s, the dollar rose in importance and was formally adopted in 1862 when six livres equalled one dollar and £1 Halifax equalled four dollars. Throughout the text the currency used reflects that of the document. Given different measurement standards, the International (metric) System has been adopted.

Native Peoples and the Beginnings of New France to 1650

The history of early Canada has been shaped by the writings of European travellers and missionaries eager to promote settlement or missionary endeavours. From this euro-centric perspective native peoples were never more than a backdrop to the heroics surrounding the establishment of European communities in North America. In contrast to this interpretation, early Canadian history must centre on the original inhabitants who, several milleniums before the arrival of Europeans, were coping with both the harsh North American environment and the modes of evolving intertribal relations. Until the mid-seventeenth century, Europeans were a small minority on the continent who had to adjust to native independence and autonomy in their methods of conducting trade and war. It is the recent work of archeologists more than historians, that has led to a better appreciation of native history and its centrality in understanding early New France (Trigger, 1985).

The relegation of native peoples to a secondary role has been compounded by the chronological framework adopted by historians who interpret the pre-1663 period as the "Heroic Age" of French colonization. Even anthropologists studying this era from an Indian viewpoint—Bruce Trigger is an example—have been unable or unwilling to break with this traditional benchmark. Yet 1663, when the French crown assumed direct control of the colony, was essentially a political event with little significance for the colony's developing economic and social structures and with even less importance for native peoples. Indians played a decisive role in the establishment of the economic structures that enabled a French colony to take shape along the St. Lawrence. If we accept their importance, then the first major turning point of the post-contact era coincides with the demographic and economic upheaval created by the dispersal of the Huron in 1650.

Precontact Native Society

The ancestors of the native peoples were hunters who crossed the Bering Strait from Asia some 40 000 years ago and spread through North and South America. After the retreat of the glaciers more than 10 000 years ago, hunters moving into eastern Canada followed herds of caribou and other game. About 3000 years ago the climate stabilized, creating an environment conducive to population increase and the spread of habitation across Quebec. The food supply came from fish, migrating birds, and mammals such as moose, deer, and caribou. This meat diet was supplemented by wild berries and nuts. Fish, fowl, and vegetation were scarce in winter and survival depended on ideal weather conditions and heavy snows, which slowed down the prey. Population then was limited by seasonal capacity to obtain meat (Clermont, 1974).

The domestication of plants developed in tropical America about 9000 years ago. These practices spread northward and by about 1000 A.D. most peoples in southern Ontario and Quebec had adopted horticulture based on maize, beans, and squash production. In these societies, summer food surpluses fed the population during the winter, and freed population growth from limited seasonal resources. However, on the Canadian Shield, soil and climate conditions prevented the development of horticulture and although corn was obtained through trade, the population of this region remained more sparse than farther south.

By the time of European contact in the sixteenth century, the North American population was divided into complex band, tribal, cultural and linguisitic subgroups. Within the three separate language stocks—Algonquian, Iroquoian, and Inuit (Figure 1.1)—of the northeastern quarter of the continent, there were many different dialects. Nor did dialect necessarily correspond with economic and cultural delineations. For example, most Algonquians in Canada were nomadic hunters but those living along the present-day New England seaboard practised horticultural subsistence similar to the Iroquoian peoples of the lower Great Lakes.

Figure 1.1 Native people at the time of European contact: language groups and tribes. It is important not to confuse the Iroquoian-speakers with the Iroquois Confederacy made up of the Mohawk, Oneida, Onondaga, Cayuga and Seneca tribes.

The late prehistoric period was one of great cultural development in which villages became larger, warfare became more widespread, political structures were more complex and funeral rites became more elaborate, while pottery design took on distinctive regional characteristics (Trigger, 1985: 100-8). During this period most of the peoples of the Northeast adopted the behavioural patterns that were observed by the early European travellers. It must be remembered, however, that native societies were undergoing constant change, which was accelerated by the coming of Europeans.

While the exact size of the precontact population cannot be determined—even estimates for well-studied tribes such as the Huron vary by 50 percent—it is clear that North America was not a virgin land at the beginning of the fifteenth century. The Algonquian-speaking peoples in central and eastern Canada numbered some 70 000 and another 100 000 lived in New England. About 100 000 Iroquoians lived around Chesapeake Bay, the lower Great Lakes and along the upper St. Lawrence Valley. The Inuit, inhabitants of the Canadian arctic, numbered perhaps 25 000, of which 3000 lived in northern Quebec and Labrador.

Depending on local environment and resources, the subsistence patterns of these native peoples can be divided into two broad categories: the nomadic hunters of the arctic, the Canadian Shield, and the Appalachians; and the sedentary horticulturalists of the St. Lawrence lowlands.

The subsistence pattern of nomadic peoples was dictated by a sharply-defined seasonal cycle. During the winter the population divided into small bands that moved around extensive territories in search of moose, caribou, deer, and bear. When conditions impeded the capture of these larger mammals, beaver and otter were hunted. It is estimated that a nomad hunter in Quebec had to kill twenty to thirty beaver, seven moose or caribou, and a bear for his family to survive through a winter (Clermont, 1974).

Early European observers echoed Jesuit Pierre Biard's observation (1615) that "If the weather then is favourable, they live in great abundance; but if it is against them, they are greatly to be pitied and often die of starvation." Summer conditions were much easier. Individual bands congregated to form larger groups at propitious sites near lakes, rivers or the Atlantic where they lived on aquatic resources, migratory birds, fruits, nuts, and small game. "Free from anxiety about their food" (Thwaites, 1896-1900, III: 79-81), they bartered with neighbouring bands and had leisure time for social activities. Warfare was not an important part of nomadic existence; if it occurred, it was carried on during the summer months.

The technology of nomadic peoples was utilitarian. Since transportation was so important to their subsistence, their birch-bark canoes were superior to those of sedentary tribes and their moccasins, beaver robes, snowshoes, and long, narrow toboggans enabled them to travel warmly and easily through snow and forests. Other aspects of their material culture were less developed:

apart from birch-bark bowls and hunting and fishing gear, they had few utensils. Knives and arrowheads were made of stone, and needles and harpoon heads of bone and antler. Their conical lodges (Figure 1.2) with a radius of only two to three metres, were covered with bark in the summer and skins in the winter, and were easy to dismantle, transport, and reconstruct. These lodges, inhabited by as many as a dozen people, were used for sleeping and for shelter on the coldest days; most activities took place outside. A fire in the centre of the lodge served for both cooking and heating.

Figure 1.2   A Cree woman arranging firewood outside her tent. Illustrations of native peoples from the early historical period are highly stylized and often contain many inaccuracies, but more recent pictures can be helpful in reconstructing traditional life. This photograph, taken by Hudson's Bay Company trader, A. A. Chesterfield, in the Ungava District at the beginning of the twentieth century, shows a Cree caribou-skin lodge and, on the left, a toboggan. The woman and child are both clad in caribou skins and, apart from a cloth handkerchief tied around the woman's head, show little European influence.

The sedentary Iroquoian tribes lived in palisaded villages joined by networks of trails. Longhouses (Figure 1.3), the main structures in their villages, were twenty to thirty metres long, and six or seven metres wide. Constructed of wooden supports that were tied together and covered in bark, the longhouse had few interior divisions. Each contained four or five fireplaces around which several related families worked, played, ate, and slept. Raised platforms along each side provided space for sleeping in the summer, and storage in the winter. Villages had populations of about 1500 and occupied the same site for fifteen years, or until the surrounding soil or the firewood supply was exhausted.

Figure 1.3   An Iroquoian longhouse at Lanoraie. This artist's conception of an Iroquoian longhouse near Montreal is based on archeological evidence found at the site. It illustrates interior organization and important female tasks: corn production, firewood collection, pottery making, cooking, and the raising of children. The only important interior division in such structures was the storage area for grain at the end of the longhouse.

Iroquoian life also followed a seasonal pattern (Figure 1.4), although horticulture freed them from the winter survival crises of their nomadic neighbours. Iroquoian women worked in village fields growing maize, beans, squash, sunflowers, and tobacco. Men participated in farming by clearing new fields and preparing new village sites. Although meat formed only a small part of the Iroquoian diet, the men hunted beaver and Virginia deer in February and in the autumn. Fish was the major source of protein, and spawning-season fishing expeditions drew men away from their villages for several months each year. Socialization and craft production were concentrated in the winter when the community was together.

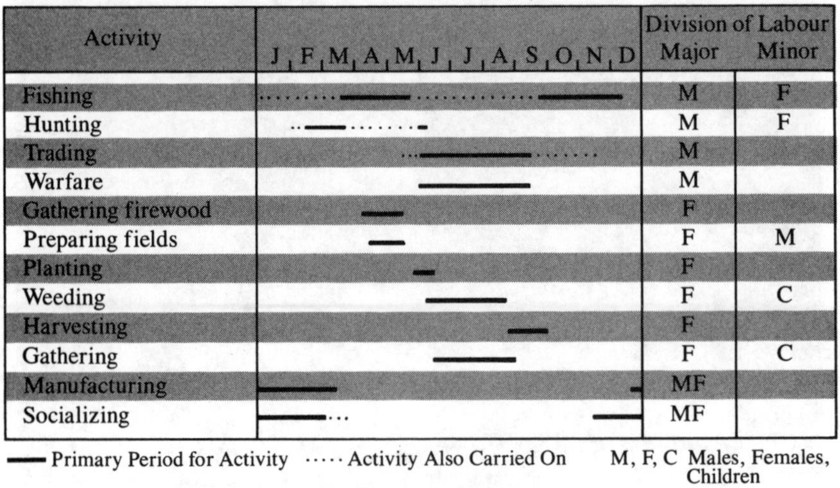

Activity	J F M A M J J A S O N D	Division of Labour Major	Minor
Fishing		M	F
Hunting		M	F
Trading		M	
Warfare		M	
Gathering firewood		F	
Preparing fields		F	M
Planting		F	
Weeding		F	C
Harvesting		F	
Gathering		F	C
Manufacturing		MF	
Socializing		MF	

—— Primary Period for Activity ····· Activity Also Carried On   M, F, C Males, Females, Children

Figure 1.4 The Huron subsistence calendar. Climate and the life cycle of the various species of fish and game caught by the Hurons determined a fairly rigid calendar in which many men left the village from the beginning of March until late November (Source: Heidenreich, 1970: Figure 12).

In addition to many of the tools and goods of the nomads, the Iroquois produced horticultural tools such as hoes, axes adapted to clearing fields, and pestles to grind corn into flour. Since sagamite—a soup made of corn flour and fish—was a staple in the Iroquoian diet, pottery cooking bowls were part of the essential Iroquoian craftwork. These people were also skilled in the production of reed baskets and mats and hemp fishing nets.

For all native peoples, the family was the basic social unit and its structure depended on subsistence patterns. Among nomads, families were patriarchal and centred around a male head who was respected for his skill as a hunter. In contrast, family life in horticultural communities centred around female members who produced crops essential for survival. This structure was reflected in the organization of their longhouses inhabited by matrilineally-related families, often a woman and her daughters or a group of sisters. All native peoples had incest taboos, and partners were chosen from outside the kinship group (the band for nomadic Algonquians; the clan for sedentary Iroquoians).

Marriage had political and social significance. In Algonquian tribes it cemented bonds between different groups sharing adjacent territories; in Iroquoian villages it reinforced the sense of community by uniting members of the different clans that made up the village. Unlike European societies, young people chose partners without parental interference. In Indian societies couples were normally monogamous although important Algonquian chiefs might have two or three wives as symbols of their power. While divorce was accepted, it rarely occurred among couples with children.

Political organization centred around the tribe. For nomads, the tribe was usually a loose association of bands that met briefly in the summer; in these circumstances unity was more cultural than political. Summer gatherings were the occasion for barter, story telling, games, and the opportunity for young people to meet and court. Political discussions generally concerned external relations, and band chiefs prepared war parties when the occasion arose. However, given that nomads ranged vast, sparsely-inhabited territories and had little contact with their neighbours, conflict situations were minimal and warfare was not an important activity.

Iroquoian society, with its components of farming, villages, and larger population, required more organization and sense of community to function. In every village each clan had a civil chief, who was responsible for order, religious ceremonies, trade, and the changing of the village site, as well as a war chief who determined war and defence strategy. These leaders were chosen by clan matrons from among suitable candidates from their own families. Chiefs from each village met occasionally in tribal or league councils to decide on matters of common interest and joint war parties. Women were not allowed to speak in village or tribal councils.

Unlike nomad society, conflict in this society was endemic because the denser population increased tensions within the tribe and at the same time added to external competition for both land and game resources. A contributing factor was the devalorization of male subsistence activities when horticulture was adopted, which led men to seek prestige through military feats. Warfare strengthened community solidarity by focusing aggression on an outside party mainly through the ritualistic torture of male prisoners. Captives were brought into the village and symbolically adopted into the family of a recently-killed tribesman before being subjected to a long ceremony during which the whole community—men, women, and children—spent hours mutilating the victim before opening the body and eating the vital organs. The prisoner was expected to show his bravery by singing his war song and by threatening his tormentors. Women and children captives were rarely tortured; they were adopted and assimilated.

Although differences in subsistence patterns influenced social organization, all Indian societies shared a sexual division of labour, similar concepts of acceptable behaviour, and the belief that the supernatural influenced daily life.

A sexual division of labour was characteristic of native societies. As well as hunting, fishing, trading, and warring, men produced spears, bows and arrows, snowshoes, and canoes. In Iroquoian tribes, men cleared land for new village sites: small trees could be chopped down with stone axes but bigger trees had to be felled by stripping their bark and burning the base.

In addition to their reproductive and childraising functions, women prepared food and hides, made clothes, collected firewood and berries, and smoked meat and fish. Other tasks depended on the main subsistence activity of the people involved. Among horticulturalists, women did all the tasks associated with farming. They also produced pottery, baskets, and mats. Whenever a band moved its camp, nomad women often carried the heaviest loads so that the men would be free to hunt en route.

Although early European observers often described native women as drudges with little control over their own lives, they were remarkably autonomous and enjoyed complete freedom to organize their tasks (Leacock, 1986). Mary Jemison, an Englishwoman adopted by the Delaware, observed that Indian women's labour was comparable to that of white women, the main difference being that "we had no master to oversee or drive us, so that we could work as leisurely as we pleased" (Axtell, 1985: 324). In contrast, explorers and missionaries described Indian men as lazy—important occupations such as hunting were considered leisure activities reserved for the nobility in Europe. The Europeans based their opinions on observations in the villages since they failed to recognize the men's contribution to horticulture and rarely followed them in their subsistence activities.

Native peoples valued individual freedom, disliked coercion and expected interpersonal relations to be characterized by politeness and respect. Social control depended on community norms such as generosity, self-sacrifice for one's family, and stoic acceptance of adversity. Social control was generally enforced by relatives, with family members responsible for their kin's transgressions. To avoid being involved in feuds with fellow tribesmen or allies, families paid reparations dependent on the seriousness of the crime, the sex, and status of the victim. In cases of murder, for example, a slain Huron chief would command greater compensation than someone of lesser importance, and the compensation for a woman (forty beaver robes on average) was greater than for a man (thirty beaver robes) (Trigger, 1976, I:60).

Chiefs governed largely through respect. Since they could not order people to act against their will there were consultations and attempts to reach consensus. Only in the most rare and dramatic forms of deviant behaviour (witchcraft, murder, and treason) did councils execute tribesmen (Trigger, 1963).

Indian society was based on communal sharing rather than private accumulation. Hospitality and helping the less fortunate were considered great virtues and those who accumulated wealth were expected to be generous by providing the less fortunate with food, clothing, and other necessities. Prestige was acquired more by donation than by accumulation.

This principle can be seen in trade relations where goods were exchanged in the form of presents, often of equal value. Trade had social as well as economic connotations and barter was usually accompanied by feasts, games, speeches, and the smoking of peace pipes. Trade in precious commodities such as copper from north of Lake Superior or wampum (beads made of polished shells and used to decorate clothing or to make armbands and necklaces) from Long Island pre-dated European contact by hundreds of years.

By the fifteenth century, trade in the Northeast increasingly centred on the exchange of agricultural surplus from sedentary tribes for meat and fur surpluses from nomads. The Huron, for example, traded corn and tobacco for pelts with their northern neighbours, the Nipissing and Ottawa. These native trading systems later formed the framework for the rapid expansion of the fur trade.

Since all native peoples believed that most aspects of nature—sun, moon, rain, and disease, for example—as well as some man-made objects such as fishing nets were animate, religion permeated daily life and the supernatural was considered responsive to human behaviour. Hunters contacted the spirit of their prey to ensure success and they disposed of inedible parts according to a strict code so that the animal's kin would not be offended. The bones of a bear, for example, were carefully buried rather than being thrown to the dogs. Gifts were made to the spirit of the rain to ensure good harvests and to the spirit of the river for safe voyages.

Dreams were an especially important medium for contacting the spirit world. In all tribes shamans, or healers and seers, interpreted dreams to learn of prospects for successful hunts or war parties and to satisfy hidden desires. Although shamans relied on a wide variety of herbal remedies for many ailments, some illness was thought to originate with spirits, in which case shamans contacted the spirit to appease or drive it from the body.

As in other cultures, myths helped to explain logically the mysteries of the universe. Native myths undoubtedly formed a coherent philosophy, but only fragments are available because missionaries recorded only stories that closely resembled biblical or western mythological traditions. The Huron creation myth of Aataentsic, for example, in which a woman fell from heaven and landed on the back of a turtle floating on the primeval sea, was considered to be a distortion of the biblical flood. Thus the assumption of a biblical umbrella makes it difficult to reconstruct native ideology and weigh its influence on behaviour.

Historian Calvin Martin argues that diseases afflicting native peoples in the early seventeenth century were blamed on animal spirits. As disease spread, the Indians came to believe that the animal world had broken its contract with the human world, which freed hunters from their obligation of killing only sufficient prey to ensure subsistence needs. This explains native people's willingness to destroy the balance in nature and to hunt animals to extinction in the fur trade (Martin, 1978). Martin's thesis is sharply contested by historians who argue that more prosaic considerations motivated Indian behaviour (Kreech, 1981). This debate draws attention to the importance of native ideology in shaping the early history of Quebec.

Native peoples believed that the soul is immortal and they gave great attention to funeral ceremony. On a person's death, the soul left the body and travelled to a land in the West. Native peoples often buried weapons, bowls, clothes, and pipes with the dead, believing that the spirits of these personal effects helped the soul face the world of the dead. In some regions of the Northeast, funeral ceremonial practice peaked in the early years after Contact.

It was in this period that the Huron Feast of the Dead took form. When the Hurons changed village sites in the early seventeenth century, they reinterred in a common grave or ossuary all who had died since the village last moved. In the reburial ceremonies, kin cleaned skeletons of any remaining tissue, wrapped the bones in new beaver robes and presented bowls, pipes, knives, tobacco, and wampum to ensure the happiness of the spirits of deceased family members in the land of the dead. Common burial sites and ceremonies reinforced tribal unity and cemented alliances with neighbouring groups at a time when solidarity was needed to face the challenges of European cultural imperialism and increased warfare. Grave offerings were also a means of redistributing wealth brought through the fur trade. This wealth threatened the egalitarian basis of Huron society (Ramsden, 1981).

With emphasis on relative egalitarianism, generosity, individual freedom, and consensus, native cultures had very different value structures than the European merchants who operated from motives of acquisitiveness. These differences were important determinants in the relations between Indians and European intruders.

The Coming of the Europeans

Despite the Viking expeditions around 1000 A.D., over the centuries North American societies had developed in isolation from other world cultures. Contact with Europe followed the voyages of John Cabot (1497) and the Corte-Real brothers (1500-02) when fishermen from western Europe rushed to exploit the cod fishery off Newfoundland's Grand Banks. By 1580 more than 400 Portuguese, Spanish, and French ships, manned by nearly 10 000 sailors, were crossing the Atlantic to Newfoundland each year. In shipping volume, the cod fishery was Europe's most important trans-Atlantic commerce, far outstripping the gold and silver trade linking Spanish America and Seville (Turgeon, 1986). This development of the Newfoundland fishery signalled the beginning of North America's integration into the world economic system of European merchant capitalism.

Fishing practice was divided into the green and dry fisheries (Figures 1.5 and 1.6). In the green fishery, the cod was cleaned and salted on board. Ships engaged in this fishery landed only briefly in Newfoundland and the continent to renew water and firewood supplies. With its huge salt requirements, the green fishery was dominated by ports in southwestern France where salt was cheap and plentiful. Cod processed this way was worth less on European markets but ships could make two trips a year.

In the dry fishery, coastal bases were established from which fishermen fished the inshore waters in small boats. The fishermen brought the cod ashore, cleaned and laid it out on drying flakes and saved the livers separately in barrels. Although the dry fishery was more labour intensive and required a two- to three-month presence in Newfoundland, it produced a higher quality and higher-priced cod. Besides its nutritional value, cod was also caught for the oil that could be extracted from the livers. This oil, along with whale oil, was the main machine lubricant and lamp fuel used at that time.

Whaling was also an important activity off the coast of Labrador and in the gulf of the St. Lawrence from the mid-sixteenth century on. Whalers required shore bases with lodgings for the crew and ovens to render oil from blubber. These bases offered native peoples both employment and the opportunity of scavenging for discarded metal wares.

The economic importance of the fishery should not be underestimated. Until the end of the French regime in 1760, France imported far more cod than fur and the fishery employed many more seamen and ships than all other French colonial trade combined. The fishery had not only a profound impact on Europe, but it also brought the native peoples of Newfoundland and the gulf of the St. Lawrence into sustained contact with the European world. From the beginning, the two groups exchanged presents, which provided the natives with metal tools and utensils in return for meat, fish, and furs. Diffused throughout the Northeast along native trade routes, European articles stimulated and reinforced trading and political alliances and prepared native populations for the fur trade.

The growth of the Newfoundland fishery was only one manifestation of the expansion of Europe, which became the dominant world economy in the period 1460 to 1620. Growth in population, in production, in the availability of bullion through the exploitation of Mexican gold and Peruvian silver stimulated the development of merchant capitalism (Davis, 1973; Wallerstein, 1974).

Figures 1.5 and 1.6   The cod fishery. These two illustrations depict the two methods practised by fishermen: the green fishery and the dry fishery. The dry fishery demanded greater organization and seasonal occupation of the shoreline, and had the greatest impact on native peoples. It provided them with opportunities to obtain European metal wares, but it also disrupted seasonal migrations, and prevented some groups from frequenting their traditional summer fishing stations and forced them to live in the interior where food was less abundant.

Chapter One

While Spain and Portugal were establishing overseas empires, French enterprise was left to private trading companies exploiting the Newfoundland fishery and the Brazil coast. The French crown did sponsor the voyages of Giovanni da Verrazano (1524), Jacques Cartier (1534, 1535-36, 1541-42) and Jean-François de la Rocque sieur de Roberval (1542-43) in an attempt to find a short route to the spice islands of southeast Asia but, apart from establishing a French claim to important parts of what is today Canada, these trips achieved little. Settlements founded by Cartier and Roberval in 1541-43 failed because of their lack of economic foundation and because of the hostility of the native population. Religious conflict in France in the second half of the sixteenth century precluded further French government involvement in North America.

The Emergence of the Fur Trade

The fishery integrated North America into a European-dominated world economic system and introduced natives to European wares. Quantities were limited, however, and direct contact between natives and Europeans was largely restricted to areas along the Atlantic seaboard.

Exchanges with the Indians took on new dimensions with the gradual development of a European market for furs, particularly beaver. The long barbs at the tip of each hair in the beaver's soft underpelt made it ideal for felt. Although the felt-making technique (the transformation of animal fur into a soft, supple, water-resistant material) had been known to European hatters since the Middle Ages, felt became a rare commodity when the European beaver became extinct. North American beaver supplies stimulated European felt production and brought the wide-brimmed hat into fashion. The fur trade became the second export staple of the Canadian economy.

Development of the fur trade in the last quarter of the sixteenth century coincided with a major demographic change in the St. Lawrence Valley. In the 1540s Cartier and Roberval had visited the important native villages of Stadacona and Hochelaga. Later in the century, for reasons that remain obscure to historians and archeologists, the St. Lawrence Iroquoians were driven from their lands or annihilated. They may have been destroyed by tribes from farther west seeking direct access to European trade, or they may have been decimated by European diseases brought by Cartier, Roberval and the French settlers. On the basis of Hochelagan pottery found in late prehistoric Huron sites, other archeologists speculate that the St. Lawrence Iroquoians were adopted by the Huron (Pendergast and Trigger, 1972). Whatever the cause, their disappearance meant that the French, unlike the British colonists farther to the south, did not have a large, well-established, sedentary local native population when they settled the St. Lawrence Valley early in the seventeenth century.

The fur trade depended on the labour of native peoples and on their centuries-old trading network. As already noted, each nomad family used annually some thirty beaver for food and for producing robes. After being worn for a year, the pelts that made up the robes shed their long guard hairs, exposing the short hairs required for the felting process. Several hundred thousand used pelts, known as *castor gras d'hiver*, would have been available annually in the St. Lawrence–Great Lakes region at the end of the sixteenth century.

By 1575 the demand for furs was rapidly increasing and European merchants were being drawn up the St. Lawrence where they tried to obtain regional monopolies. Anxious to establish its claim over the territory, the French crown gave charters with trade monopolies, but the merchants were unable to tap fully the St. Lawrence region. Until 1626, annual fur exports from Canada rarely exceeded 9000 to 12 000 pelts, and in the record year only 22 000 pelts were exported. Samuel de Champlain's establishment in 1608 of a fort and warehouse at Quebec, along with his personal contact with native chiefs, consolidated trade in the hands of one group of merchants by 1615 but did little to increase the volume that depended on Indian suppliers.

During the first half of the seventeenth century, French merchants never effectively regulated the supply of furs. They entered alliances on the natives' terms and never had the military force to impose their own objectives. Along the St. Lawrence, the fur supply depended on the Montagnais who traded the product of their own hunt and controlled access to the hunting bands of the interior. Once their requirements for European trade goods were satisfied, there was little incentive to increase the volume of trade.

Along the Ottawa River and in the Great Lakes region, the situation was more complex. The Algonquins were forced by their powerful Huron neighbours to share French trade, but this alliance created a formidable barrier blocking direct French access to other tribes. The Hurons did not hunt the beaver but used their extensive trade network with more remote tribes to exchange maize and European goods for furs. Thus, even though many natives of the Great Lakes region were becoming familiar with European technology, the French were unable to trade directly with them or increase the number of pelts.

Since trade statistics from the early seventeenth century are incomplete we have only a partial picture of exports (Figure 1.7). It is clear, however, that the trade was very unstable and it is unlikely that the monopoly holders made any net profit (Campeau, 1975; Trudel, 1979). In the best years after 1632, the value of furs shipped to France reached 300 000 livres, falling to under 50 000 livres in disastrous years. These variations underline the precarious nature of an economy dependent on native populations who did not respond to increased demand in the same way as Europeans.

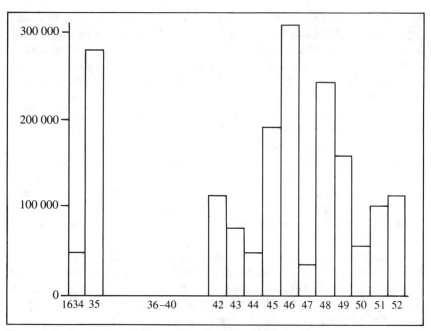

Figure 1.7 Furs exported from New France, 1634-1652.

Some of this variation was due to warfare with the tribes of the Iroquois confederacy, particularly the Mohawk. When Champlain first visited the St. Lawrence in 1603, he found the Montagnais and Algonquin warring with the Mohawk. As part of his alliance with these tribes and with the Huron Confederacy, he participated in battles against the Iroquois on Lake Champlain (1609), at the mouth of the Richelieu (1610) and south of Lake Ontario (1615).

In 1614, the establishment of a Dutch trading post at Fort Orange (Albany, New York) provided the Iroquois with an alternate source of European goods, and warfare subsided for the next twenty years. After 1640, however, when the Dutch became the source of firearms for the Mohawk, they found it easier to raid fur convoys en route to Trois-Rivières rather than hunting for pelts.

In the 1630s disease added yet another variable to this system dependent on the networks, labour, and know-how of native populations. With no immunity, natives, particularly the children and elderly, rapidly fell victim to diseases such as smallpox and influenza and whole villages were decimated. Tribes in the French alliance were particularly vulnerable since they were in constant contact with missionaries and interpreters, whereas the Dutch rarely visited the Iroquois. The Montagnais and Algonquins along the St. Lawrence suffered from measles or smallpox in 1634 and died in large numbers. Between

1636 and 1639, the Hurons were afflicted by a series of epidemics, and population declined from about 25 000 to about 10 000. Disease actually helped Jesuit missionaries increase the number of conversions because it undermined the prestige of shamans, but at the same time the epidemics were as important as warfare in reducing the supply of pelts by killing off hunters and traders.

Decimated by disease, divided by missionary propaganda, and unable to obtain firearms unless they turned their backs on traditional customs, the tribes of the French alliance fell victim to the numerically- and militarily-superior Iroquois. The Iroquoian-speaking tribes of the lower Great Lakes—the Wenro, the Huron, the Petun, the Neutral, and the Erie—were adopted by the victorious Iroquois to make up for losses suffered through disease and warfare. At the same time, Mohawk war parties raided the Algonquin and Montagnais hunters throughout the interior of Quebec, despoiling them of their pelts.

This destruction completely disrupted the French trading system and was a major turning point in Canadian history. Along the St. Lawrence Valley, native population declined so dramatically that the French were in a majority for the first time by 1650 (Figure 1.8). Without native allies to collect and transport furs to the warehouses at Trois-Rivières and Quebec, the French were forced to take over these tasks themselves. These circumstances marked the end of a commercial system entirely dependent on native labour and trading networks, and also marked the beginning of French territorial expansion by the coureur de bois supported by a preindustrial agricultural community.

The structure of the early fur trade and its economic uncertainty had retarded settlement. European nations did not recognize the native peoples' claim to their territory on the basis that they had no European-type institutions and did not live in permanent agricultural communities. Thus, when the crown granted trade monopolies, it also granted vast tracts of land and insisted that the companies settle the region. However, there was little economic need for European settlement since trade depended on native peoples trapping and transporting furs to a warehouse on the St. Lawrence. Here a few Europeans could guard the fort, prepare bales for shipment to Europe, and maintain relations with the native peoples. In this economic system there was little demand for the labour or agricultural produce of settlers. French emigrants preferred the Carribean where tobacco and, later, sugar plantations held the promise of bettering one's social and economic status. The failure of settlement policies, therefore, owes less to merchant hostility than to an economic system that depended on a native rather than a European labour force.

The formation of the Company of One Hundred Associates in 1627 changed little, although it is unfair to criticize it for failing to settle the promised 4000 immigrants within fifteen years. Through its promotion of missionary activity, the company did manage to attract a small agricultural population. Many

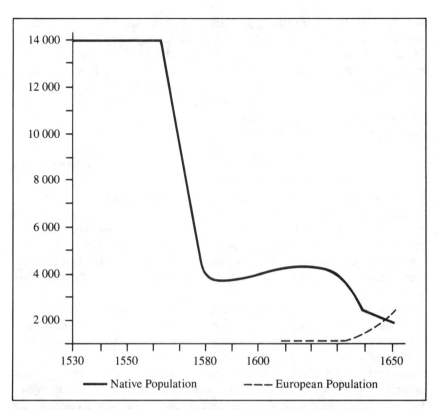

Figure 1.8 The population of the St. Lawrence Valley, 1530-1650. Population estimates for the period of early Contact are at best approximate because of the lack of data. The trends are clear, however. In the mid-sixteenth century, the St. Lawrence Valley suffered an initial depopulation as 8 000 to 10 000 St. Lawrence Iroquoians, who had lived between Lake Ontario and Quebec City during the 1540s, disappeared sometime before 1580. Although nomadic Montagnais and Algonquins moved into the area at the beginning of the seventeenth century, they were decimated by disease after 1634 and then attacked by the Iroqouis after 1641. By 1650 the Algonquins and Montagnais had started to retreat into the interior.

immigrants who settled in Canada in the period 1632-1650 came as indentured servants to the Jesuits, Ursulines, Hospital Sisters, or to the model Christian community established at Montreal in 1642 by the Société de Notre-Dame pour la conversion des sauvages. They stayed because the priests and nuns required their labour and agricultural surpluses rather than because of involvement in the fur trade.

Many people did not stay: indeed, in the period 1632-1650, 73.3 percent of all immigrants on a three-year indenture returned to France after their contract expired. After 1650, the expansion of the fur trade created a demand for European canoemen, for agricultural surpluses, and more than half (55.2 percent) of all immigrants remained in the colony—and this despite the increase in Iroquois raids. Another measure of this fundamental change is the amount of land granted to settlers. In the nineteen years before the dispersal of the Hurons, just under 6000 hectares had been ceded to settlers, but in the following five years over 15 000 hectares were granted. With these new economic conditions, the population of the colony grew from 1206 in 1650 to 2690 in 1660 (Dickinson, 1986a).

Cultural Interaction

Europeans and their trade transformed the life of native peoples. They quickly adopted such European commodities as copper kettles, metal tools and weapons, textiles, and foodstuffs such as bread and alcohol. For their part, European settlers appreciated native products such as the birch-bark canoe, snowshoes, moccasins, and toboggans. Native crops, maize and tobacco, were also adopted, although most settlers continued to prefer European grains.

Attitudes, languages, and norms of behaviour are more difficult to transfer from one culture to another than material goods. Native peoples had a world view suited to their environment and way of life, and with the importance they gave to individual freedom and tolerance, did not impose their values on others. It is very difficult to determine native attitudes to European customs since European interpretations always cloud the recorded reactions. It appears that to the native people some European behaviour was repugnant (for example, blowing one's nose into a handkerchief), whereas other practices were thought simply foolish (building large homes that could not be easily moved). The overall impression is that natives never thought themselves in any way inferior to Europeans (Jaenen, 1976a).

Europeans, in contrast, wanted complete control over both the territory and its inhabitants. Judging other cultures by European norms, they saw themselves and Christianity as superior; and they considered native peoples to be barbarians and even agents of the devil. Since they did not have European forms of government, religion, or economic organization, the Europeans dismissed the native peoples as having no culture. The French wish to civilize the native populations and to force Christianity and European culture on them is illustrated by the seventeenth century French monk Emery de La Croix: "They must be shown the road to humanity and true honour, so that they no longer live like brutes. Reason and justice must prevail, and not violence which is suitable only for beasts" (Dickason, 1984: 39).

From the arrival of the first missionary in 1615 until the end of the French regime, religious orders tried to impose Christianity on the native peoples (Figure 1.9). At first, the natives rejected the missionaries because they tried to destroy native ways of life. When European diseases ravaged the tribes, they blamed the Jesuits at first (Trigger, 1976). However, given the native belief that disease had spiritual causes, epidemics finally served the Jesuits' cause since people turned to the Jesuits when shamans failed to find cures.

Figure 1.9 "France bringing the Faith to the Savages". This painting by Recollet Brother Luc shows France, personified as the queen mother, Anne of Austria, bringing Christianity to the native people of North America. The ideology that motivates this painting is clear: France was bringing salvation to an inferior people who knelt in gratitude before one of the main financial sponsors of early missionary work. For the artist, it was not important to realistically depict Indians, their housing, or the landscape. This painting, which hangs in Quebec's Ursuline convent, was used to teach native peoples to respect their European benefactors. Religious imagery such as the picture held by the queen was an important means for missionaries to present the mysteries of Christianity.

At first, French policy aimed at the assimilation of the native populations through the teaching of French and the settling of nomadic tribes in agricultural communities. This policy was not realistic, and by 1640 the Jesuits had abandoned plans to educate young Indians in European seminaries and to settle the Montagnais on reserves. Greater acceptance of native culture, the decision to live with bands in their own environment, and company policies— the sale of firearms to converts only, for example—gave the Jesuits success with tribes like the Attikameks and the Hurons. However, only a minority of native peoples became Catholics, and many converts continued to live much as before. Conversion to Christianity meant that converts could no longer participate in the social life of their communities. As Jérôme Lalemant, superior of the Huron mission, noted in 1645:

> The greatest opposition that we meet consists in the fact that their remedies for diseases; their greatest amusements when in good health; their fishing, their hunting, and their trading; the success of their crops, of their wars, and of their councils, almost all abound in diabolical ceremonies. To be a Christian one must deprive himself not only of pastimes, and of the dearest pleasures of life, but even of the most necessary things. (Thwaites, *Jesuit Relations*, Vol. 28: 53)

Given the importance of dreams, feasts, and the family in native life, it is hardly surprising that the natives did not want to be converted. Yet, an increasing number of Hurons were baptized during the 1640s, and by the time of their dispersion a majority were Christian (Campeau, 1987).

The Europeans' conviction that they were culturally superior enabled them to adopt features of native life without losing their identity. For example, some young men liked the freedom of the woods but they did not change their basic values. The coureurs de bois might adopt native dress and transportation technology; they might even take an Indian wife, but they remained resolutely Christian, and most dreamed of re-integrating into colonial life. Native ideas and values never made a serious impression on the European population in the St. Lawrence Valley.

Warfare was the final major area of intercultural contact. Traditional histories of New France emphasize the heroism of the early settlers defending themselves from fierce warriors. The torture of prisoners and guerrilla warfare of native peoples shocked European observers. However, despite a few severe attacks, warfare directed against Europeans during this period was less endemic and bloody than is usually portrayed. Most Iroquois hostility was directed at native allies, not at the French. Indeed, Iroquois spokesmen continually asked for French neutrality.

For the half century 1608 to 1666, just over 200 settlers were killed by the Iroquois and of these a quarter died because of the strategic errors of their commanders (the case of Dollard des Ormeaux who was killed along with fifteen companions in 1660 is one of the best examples). Warfare constituted a generalized threat only between 1650-53 and 1660-61; most other years were relatively peaceful. There were important regional differences: Montreal was often threatened after its founding in 1642 but Trois-Rivières witnessed intense warfare only between 1651 and 1653. The Quebec City region, where most colonists lived, experienced Iroquois war parties only after 1650 and most deaths occurred in 1661. Nor were captives always burned at the stake; well over half were either freed or they escaped, and some chose to live with their captors (Dickinson, 1982a; Axtell, 1986).

Conclusion

The coming of the Europeans had a profound impact on native society that ran the gamut from technological advances to epidemics, alcohol abuse, and the destruction of traditional values. Through trade the native peoples would be progressively integrated into the Atlantic economy but, paradoxically, their peripheral position would condemn them to dependence on Europeans. For the white intruders the first half of the seventeenth century was a period of acclimatization to the American environment. Although they adopted elements of native material culture that were useful, the French established a colonial society with familiar institutions.

The dispersal of the sedentary tribes of southern Ontario and the dramatic decline in the nomadic populations of the interior of Quebec marked the end of that period of Canadian history dominated by native labour and trading systems. By 1650, the French dominated the St. Lawrence Valley. Economic opportunity, which had been limited by native labour, grew as French colonists began supplying foodstuffs to nomadic tribes and assuming the labour of transporting pelts to Quebec.

Bibliography

Overview
The best overview of native peoples of the Northeast can be found in Bruce Trigger, ed., *Handbook of North American Indians*, Volume 15. Those interested in prehistory should consult J.V. Wright's *Quebec Prehistory* and *Ontario Prehistory: An Eleven Thousand Year Archaeological Outline* . On the disappearance of the St. Lawrence Iroquoians, readers should consult James Pendergast and Bruce Trigger, *Cartier's Hochelaga and the Dawson Site*. A concise history of this period from an Indian point of view is provided by Bruce Trigger in *Indians and the "Heroic Age" of New France*. For a more detailed analysis of this period, readers should refer to Bruce Trigger, *Natives and Newcomers. Canada's "Heroic Age" Reconsidered*.

Individual tribes

Some of the best studies of individual tribes concern the Huron. Conrad Heidenreich's *Huronia. A History and Geography of the Huron Indians, 1600-1650* and Bruce Trigger's *The Children of Aataentsic. A History of the Huron People to 1660* give detailed accounts of these people. On the problems faced by nomads during the winter, readers can consult Norman Clermont, "L'hiver et les indiens nomades du Québec à la fin de la préhistoire". Eleanor Leacock presents an interesting assessment of Montagnais women's status in her "Montagnais Women and the Jesuit Program for Colonization".

Religion

On the importance of religion in native societies and Calvin Martin's controversial thesis, see his *Keepers of the Game: Indian-Animal Relationships and the Fur Trade* and Shepherd Kreech III, *Indians, Animals and the Fur Trade* which groups several essays on this thesis.

Early French Settlement

The most complete coverage of French activities in North America during this period can be found in Marcel Trudel's *The Beginnings of New France, 1524-1663*, which is an abridged version of his monumental four-volume *Histoire de la Nouvelle-France*. Olive Dickason's *The Myth of the Savage and the Beginnings of French Colonialism in the Americas* gives an excellent view of French attitudes toward the native peoples. John Dickinson's "Les Amérindiens et les débuts de la Nouvelle-France", evaluates the impact of native peoples on the early settlement of Canada.

Preindustrial Quebec, 1650-1815

The disappearance of Huron middlemen from New France by 1650 created new economic opportunities that started to attract French immigrants to two distinct sectors: the fur trade and agriculture. There was the work of collecting and transporting furs to Montreal and Quebec, as well as supplying foodstuffs to coureurs de bois and nomadic hunters. Growth in agriculture marked the birth of a preindustrial agricultural society that endured into the nineteenth century.

Preindustrial society had three cornerstones: the family, agriculture, and a rigid, hierarchical social structure. The family rather than the individual was at the centre of social and economic relations while legal systems defined and emphasized the rights and obligations of the family unit. The male head under French law, for example, was responsible for the actions of his wife and children and, if they were wronged, only he could initiate legal procedures.

The peasant household was the backbone of this society and the basic economic unit. Much of the capital in the preindustrial world was invested in agriculture—in land, in farm buildings, in livestock, and in farm implements (Davis, 1973: 231-33). Although most of the peasantry's production was consumed in the home or bartered within the local economy, farm households were important markets for artisanal production and the retail trade. More important, peasant surpluses supported the land-owning and clerical elite.

The state promoted a paternalistic concept of society, ostensibly protecting the weak but in reality ensuring respect for the privileges of the aristocracy. The state's principal goal was the maintenance of order. Military expenditures far surpassed civil expenditures, which were largely devoted to paying the salaries of administrative and judicial officials. Revenues, coming from imperial subsidies, seigneurial dues, land sales, and customs duties, were not sufficient to allow the state to invest heavily in public works. Fortification and road construction during the French regime used the *corvée*—the unpaid labour of the popular classes. With strong ties to the monarchy, established churches aided the state in maintaining order. Morality, as defined by Judaeo-Christian tradition, was the basis for criminal codes and the education of the popular classes. In return, the state used its power to enforce respect for religion.

Government structures remained those of the Ancien Régime. Administrators were chosen by the crown without the interference of popular assemblies. Indeed, colonists had little say over how they were governed, how government money was raised or spent, even after the creation of the first elected Assembly in 1791. Nevertheless, lack of a police force in rural areas meant that, outside of the towns, passive popular resistance to government ordinances was usually successful. Imperial governments were monarchies and believed that the aristocracy formed the natural leaders of the community. This attitude was imposed on the colony as birth and nepotism were determinant in deciding status and professional advancement in government, in the church, and in the military. Hence, government was carried out by an aristocratic elite that sought to benefit its own class.

Despite the primacy of agriculture, trade was an important force. Profits for merchant capitalists were derived by shipping commodities across time and space. In the colony the merchants exported staples—commodities such as fish, fur, wheat, and timber. They also sought to capture part of the surplus generated by the agricultural population by inciting the consumption of imported goods, thereby integrating the peasantry into the market economy.

While most merchants' capital requirements were modest, they grew during the preindustrial period. Most capital was tied up in stocks of raw materials or finished products that were in warehouses, ships, or canoes. The requirement for liquid assets was even smaller since most trade was financed by credit from industrial or agricultural producers. For large ventures, several merchants might join together to reduce risk but the duration of the partnership was often limited and, in French law, could not survive after the death of one of the members. In such partnerships each individual remained personally responsible for the debts of the association. In business dealings outside their region, merchants relied on personal contacts and good will built up by preceding generations (often with members of their extended family) for credit, information, the enforcement of contracts, and collection of debts.

Despite the formation of large trading companies to exploit colonial monopolies, such as the Company of One Hundred Associates, there is no evidence of modern capitalism in the preindustrial era. Large companies never established accounting procedures that reflected an understanding of what capital is. The main, unifying goal was the striving to gain a monopoly and activities were often decentralized. If anything, the companies reflected the desire of the state to better orient and control economic policy (De Vries, 1976: 133).

Artisans produced most goods by working in family shops with their own tools. In such a system capital requirements were small; only exceptionally large work sites such as ironworks required a significant fixed investment. Much of this production was for the agricultural community, although the aristocracy and the church encouraged luxury trades such as sculpting and silversmithing. In Europe, town guilds gave masters control over competition, prices, and quality, but in the colony market conditions were more important in regulating artisanal production. Also, European industrial expansion in the seventeenth and eighteenth centuries was fueled by cottage industries—the production of goods by members of the peasantry who had insufficient land to guarantee subsistence. In the colony, abundant land precluded the development of a large pool of rural industrial labour during the preindustrial period.

Class relations in this society were rigidly defined and enforced by the state. The popular classes—the peasantry and artisans—were expected to know their place and show suitable deference to their superiors. Upward social mobility was rare since educational institutions catered only to the bourgeoisie and the aristocracy, and family contacts were needed to enter trade and the professions.

Peasant accumulation, when it existed, was channelled into land and farm needs. In Europe, the aristocracy was the essential reference for the elite. Although most bourgeois reinvested their capital in business or in land, many aspired to accede to the nobility and invested capital in military, judicial, and administrative offices, in dowries, and in seigneurial land (De Vries, 1976: 214). The aristocracy was expected by social custom to dissipate its wealth ostentatiously by building fine homes, following fashion trends, and employing large numbers of domestic servants. These factors militated against capital investment in trade and industry. In the colonial context, the local aristocracy had fewer privileges. Its military functions implicated it in the fur trade and gave it a similar economic outlook to that of the bourgeoisie during the French regime.

Institutional and Political Development

In most societies, socio-economic conditions shape political and institutional structures. But in New France the basic administrative and clerical institutions and the law existed before the settlement of a significant European population. New France was modelled after French legal custom, which had evolved through the Middle Ages before being codified in the sixteenth century.

From its inception, New France was regulated by the Custom of Paris, a coherent body of law influenced by a religious and state ideology that valued paternal authority and responsibility. The family patrimony was protected by secret mortgages; by marriage clauses that prevented important assets from being seized by creditors; by the right to interfere in sales contracts to preserve the integrity of an estate; and by restrictions on the right to will property freely (Zoltvany, 1971). The Custom of Paris, based on a concept of property whereby all land belonged to a seigneur, encouraged an egalitarian outlook among the popular classes by enforcing strict equality among heirs of non-noble land. The provisions that reinforced the cornerstones of preindustrial society—the family, agriculture, and a hierarchical social structure—had important implications for colonial society, particularly as capitalist activity increased.

Colonial government was based on mercantilism. Colonies were founded to serve the needs of the metropolis, and economic development was closely monitored and controlled by the imperial state. Whether it was the French Ministry of Marine or the British Colonial Office, colonial policy was always judged by its potential impact on the economy of the metropolis. State and religious institutions that were formed in Europe over the centuries were imposed on the colony and administered by Europeans who often had little empathy for colonial realities.

French Colonial Administration

Under the Company of One Hundred Associates, New France was ruled by a governor who, as the European population grew, appointed court officials and a council to help him administer the colony. By 1663, when Louis XIV took over the colony, most of the essential institutions of France were in place: the sénéchaussée, a court enforcing the Custom of Paris; the seigneurial form of land tenure; and a bishop to oversee religious institutions such as schools and hospitals. Royal control merely meant that New France became a province with the same royal administrative structures as French provinces: a military governor; an intendant in charge of justice, public order, and financial administration; and a system of royal courts.

Colonial affairs, like those of French provinces, were directed from Paris. In 1663 the Ministry of Marine, headed by Jean-Baptiste Colbert, Louis XIV's principal minister, was placed in control of New France. Policy, appointments, and even pensions were decided in Versailles and the minister gave precise instructions to the governor general and the intendant. Because of the distance and the short shipping season, letters reached the colony only once a year. This infrequent communication left Versailles poorly informed about colonial problems. As a result, decisions made in France could be totally inappropriate for the colony and local officials could only delay implementation while they tried to convince the ministry to change direction.

For example, in 1696, in an attempt to curb excessive trading in beaver, the ministry ordered the abandonment of western military posts. For two decades, until the posts were reopened, the governors and intendants lobbied for reversal of this policy which imperilled the colonial economy and disrupted alliances with native peoples (Zoltvany, 1974).

The governor general was responsible for military and diplomatic affairs, including relations with the native peoples. He was assisted by lieutenant governors stationed in towns such as Montreal and Trois-Rivières, and by captains of militia in each parish. Although the captains of militia functioned primarily in a military capacity, they also reported on administrative matters such as harvests and conveyed orders on local affairs such as roads.

Given the colony's significance as a major theatre of Anglo-French imperial rivalry, the military establishment was very important to New France (Figure 2.1). From the arrival of the first royal troops—the Carignan-Salières regiments sent to quell the Iroquois in the 1660s—until the War of the Conquest a century later, the colony always had a large garrison to defend itself from the British and the Iroquois. During the eighteenth century the officer corps, recruited from local aristocrats, played an important role in the fur trade as well as in the defence of the colony. The garrison troops were made up of Troupes de la Marine sent from France. Many of these soldiers opted to settle in the colony after their tour of duty. Military pay and provisioning, important elements in the local economy (Eccles, 1971), accounted for a large part of the colonial government's annual budget.

Figure 2.1 Quebec from Pointe Levy, 1761. This view of Quebec illustrates the important strategic position occupied by the colonial capital. The citadel, on top of Cape Diamond to the left of the picture, had a commanding view of the river and was the heart of a fortification network encircling the city to the southwest. The large building on the cliff above the Lower Town is the Château Saint-Louis, the governor's residence. Ramparts lined the cliff, while shore batteries protected the port and the shipyard where the hull of an unfinished warship can be seen.

The intendant and his officials administered financial affairs, economic development, and justice in the colony. As the colony developed, the intendant delegated authority to other officials: the director of the King's domain who administered crown lands and collected customs duties; the chief road officer who was in charge of road construction and town planning; and the port captain who supervised maritime activity. The intendant's large staff worked in his "palais" in Quebec City, which doubled as the courthouse (Vachon, 1970).

Since some of the intendant's responsibilities overlapped those of the governor, conflict resulted. The governor was in charge of military matters but the intendant controlled financial affairs and had to be consulted for important action. The intendant's control over trade brought him into conflict with the governor over licences for travel in the West and over Indian policy. The intendant was responsible for justice but the governor sat on the highest colonial court, the Sovereign Council, where he claimed precedence as the king's most important representative. Competition for patronage exacerbated personality conflicts, and resultant tensions came to the public's attention as officials jostled for precedence in public ceremonies (Eccles, 1964: 77-98).

Although public offices were not purchased in New France as they were in France, administrators considered their position as property on which there should be a personal return. This concept of political morality is reflected in the correspondence of Elisabeth Bégon (daughter of a Montreal official and widow of a lieutenant governor of Trois-Rivières) with her son-in-law, the intendant's representative at New Orleans. Using the example of intendant François Bigot who was accumulating a fortune selling goods to the state at inflated prices, she encouraged her son-in-law to imitate the intendant's behaviour.

> M. de la Filière told me that Bigot should make two hundred thousand *livres* [a day labourer made about two *livres* a day] on his sales of flour to the state. [. . .] If you don't have enough wits to make some money where you are, you should be beaten since everyone knows what civil servants do and those who do not have a profitable trade are treated as idiots. You don't pay enough attention to these matters. It is all very well to do one's duty, but you should try to look after your own affairs as well.

The Judicial System of New France

As a royal province, the colony's judicial system consisted of the Sovereign Council, and subordinate royal jurisdictions at Quebec, Montreal, and Trois-Rivières. The Sovereign Council, created in 1663, was made up of the governor, the bishop, the intendant, and five councillors. For a short time, the council had important responsibilities and lawmaking powers. But by the 1670s all important regulations were drafted by the intendant before they were made public at sittings of the council, which had been reduced to an appeal court for civil decisions and criminal sentences of the royal courts. The judicial structure was completed in 1719 when an admiralty court, which heard shipping cases, was established at Quebec. Although the intendant had jurisdiction to judge any case brought before him, he rarely handled cases but referred them to the regular courts. The intendant appointed all court officials, as well as royal notaries, and ensured that they followed the Custom of Paris.

The royal courts were central to this system. They judged both civil disputes and criminal cases, as well as supervising the enforcement of regulations. Civil jurisdiction—debt recovery, disputes over property, or seigneurial dues—was by far the most frequent activity. At the Prévôté, Quebec City's royal court, this type of case made up about 98 percent of the work load. Theoretically, courts were cheap and accessible to all. However, as they were located in the three major towns while the vast majority of the population lived in the countryside, the courts were used mainly by the urban population: artisans, merchants, and members of the colonial elite.

In civil suits at the Prévôté, artisans made up over 35 percent of litigants whereas merchants and the elite made up almost 20 percent each; the peasantry, which made up about 80 percent of the total population, comprised only 18 percent of litigants. Although court costs were reduced by forbidding lawyers to practise in the colony, all cases involved some fees and often obliged litigants to be present for several sittings. For these reasons courts reinforced social segregation for the benefit of the elite (Dickinson, 1982b).

Criminal justice in New France differed significantly from today's. To open a case, the victim of a crime had to make an official statement before a judge. If the perpetrator of a crime was unknown, his capture posed a problem since there was no official police force in the colony. However, the military was often used to track down suspects such as the following:

> height, about four and a half feet (1m 45); black hair cut at the top of the ears, blue eyes, a wrinkled forehead, a wispy blond beard, a pug-nose, a dry and narrow face, ruddy complexion; he has a crooked gait with one foot on the outside and the other turned to the inside; his voice is sharp and loud and he does not speak well; age 23 to 25 years; was wearing a blue vest with copper buttons (Lachance, 1984: 135-137).

Once apprehended, a suspect was put in irons and taken to jail in Montreal, Trois-Rivières, or Quebec to await trial. The accused was not informed of charges and was not assisted by a lawyer.

When convinced that the suspect was guilty, judges could use torture to extract a confession or to learn the names of accomplices. Corporal punishment, seizure of property, exile, and capital punishment were common penalties. Although beheading, breaking on the wheel and burning at the stake were used, hanging was by far the most usual form of the death penalty. Of thirty-eight people condemned to death between 1712 and 1748, eight were women (Lachance, 1984). Imprisonment in preindustrial society was never envisaged as a punishment.

Though the royal courts dealt mainly with civil disputes and crimes, they also had some administrative functions. In the absence of municipal governments during the French regime, the intendant assumed some of the functions of today's local administrations, issuing by-laws concerning public order, health and safety, trade, and roads. Publication and enforcement of these regulations was left to the Sovereign Council and the royal courts. Most of this legislation clearly underlines the major social preoccupations of administrators in preindustrial society: hunger, fire, disease, and scandalous behaviour.

To ensure the provisioning of urban populations, stringent regulations required butchers and bakers to provide sufficient meat and bread at fixed prices and forbade retailers from buying up stocks at the biweekly markets. Regulations also provided for town planning, the inspection of weights and measures used by merchants, and set the norms for road construction and maintenance.

Given its danger and the limited means of controlling it, fire was a major concern to officials. Montreal was almost destroyed in 1734 when a slave set fire to her owner's house in revenge for being punished; forty-six homes and the Hôtel-Dieu hospital burned to the ground. Authorities regulated house construction, chimney inspection, the distribution of water buckets and axes, and the installation of ladders on roofs.

Public health was based on medical conceptions that emphasized pure air. Human and animal waste had to be removed from towns and all dwellings had to have outdoor latrines since odours from this waste were considered vectors of disease. Civil and religious authorities thought inns and taverns to be the main centres for scandalous and seditious behaviour. All proprietors had to have licenses, and had to obey strict opening hours, and serving rules. Legally native people could only purchase beer, while servants and labourers could not drink during the day without their employer's permission. Establishments had to be closed during mass and had to post royal ordinances against blasphemy (Dickinson, 1987).

Seigneurialism

Historians disagree over the significance of seigneurial tenure. Marcel Trudel described it as a social system of mutual aid established to facilitate settlement, and which protected the French Canadian nation from outside influences in the nineteenth century (Trudel, 1956). Richard Colebrook Harris, on the other hand, downplayed its importance, arguing that the pattern of settlement owed more to the physical characteristics of the land than to seigneurial activity before the Conquest, but during the British regime, seigneurs became more demanding (Harris, 1966; 1971). Research by Louise Dechêne (1971; 1974; 1981) has shown the broad implications of seigneurialism for both the peasantry and the urban population from the seventeenth century on. Allan Greer (1985) emphasizes the power of seigneurs to appropriate peasant surpluses.

Defined by the Custom of Paris, the seigneury was a form of property that regulated social and economic relations between seigneur and censitaire by imposing differing obligations on both parties. During the French regime, the most important obligations of the seigneur were to grant land to prospective settlers and to provide a grist mill. After the Conquest, lack of government supervision enabled seigneurs to withold lands and charge higher rents. For their part, peasants were obliged to pay an annual rent (the *cens et rentes*) and a levy on the sale of property (the *lods et ventes*); to clear and farm their land; and to have their grain milled at the seigneurial mill. Failure to fulfill these obligations could result in eviction.

In addition to honorific rights such as a front-row pew, the right to receive communion first, and the planting of a maypole in front of the seigneurial manor, seigneurs had even more valuable privileges. Through the corvée they could extract labour from their censitaires; they could reclaim peasant holdings by the *retrait féodal*; they had monopolies over fishing and water-power sites; and, in many cases, the right to establish a manor court. The latter was used by the seigneur to collect seigneurial dues as well as to settle local disputes—conflicts over property lines and complaints that trespassing livestock was trampling or eating the harvest. Most of the active seigneurial courts were located on lands owned by religious orders around Quebec City and constituted an important tool for seigneurial administration. The seigneurial courts also offered a useful service to local inhabitants since fees charged by these jurisdictions were much lower than those of royal courts (Dickinson, 1974b). None, however, survived the Conquest.

The Company of One Hundred Associates, and later the crown, had hoped that seigneurs would become colonization agents since it was in their interest to settle their lands. However, few seigneurs paid immigrants' passage since most had other business or government administration interests with seigneurial revenues forming but a small part of their income. Religious orders were the exception and their well-populated estates provided considerable revenue from the end of the seventeenth century. Settlement spread out progressively from the lands near the towns until, by the end of the eighteenth century, the revenue of most lay seigneuries was a significant part of their owners' income (Greer, 1985).

Seigneurialism had little influence on the geographic pattern of settlement but could influence social life (Figures 2.2 and 2.3). The physical layout of seigneurial grants was established during the regime of the One Hundred Associates and was predicated by geographic considerations. Estates were large rectangular tracts (about four kilometres by twelve kilometres) with frontage on a major river; concessions to peasants were about 150 metres wide by 1600 metres in depth. This system of land tracts facilitated surveying, road construction and maintenance, and enabled the first settlers to have access to the river. However, it militated against village formation, and made homes difficult to defend. When the first *côte* (a line of farms along the river) was full, a second côte or, as it was later known, *rang* was opened along a parallel interior road. Peasant social life centred on the côte where relatives grouped their holdings. Seigneurs, of course, could determine where and how land on their estate was to be opened for settlement and had the right to expropriate holdings for the creation of villages or the construction of mills.

Although few Canadian seigneurs descended from the old French nobility, they nevertheless constituted a Canadian aristocracy confident in their privileges and social position. Through the multiple onerous and honorific dues owed to the seigneur, the peasantry could easily identify their social superiors.

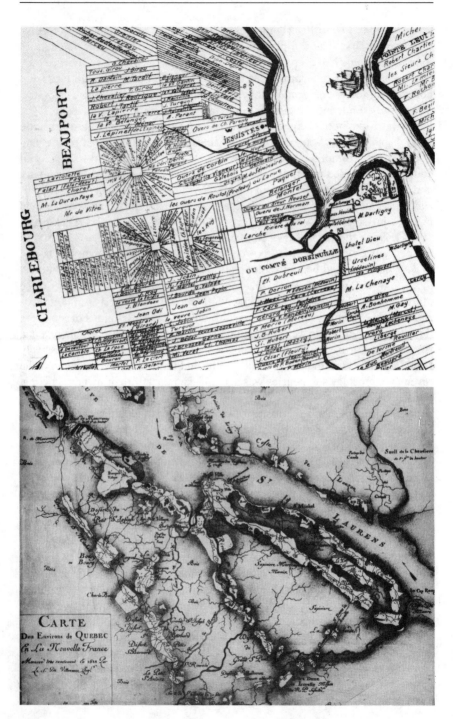

Chapter Two

Figure 2.2 and 2.3   Land distribution and settlement patterns near Quebec.
Cadastral plans, such as the one in Figure 2.2, are often used to describe
the seigneurial system and to highlight the uniformity of peasant holdings.

Figure 2.3, a 1688 map by Robert de Villeneuve, better reflects actual
settlement patterns. Clearings did not develop uniformly, but as patches in
the middle of the forest. This underlines that a sense of community was
essential in the opening up of new lands, and that settlement was not a
haphazard venture. Because of the way peasants organized their farms, the
distinctive radial villages (visible in the centre left of Figure 2.2) created by
intendant Jean Talon in the 1660s, do not stand out as oddities. The Huron
village of Lorette is in the lower right part of the map. Less than a decade
after this map was made, the encroachment of white settlers on Huron land
forced them to move their village farther north.

Religion

In seventeenth-century France the king ruled by divine right and was protector
of the church; rigorous Catholic doctrine permeated legislation. The church
enjoyed high social status. It was the first estate of the realm and protected the
prevailing social structure by preaching obedience and submission. Social
control over the popular classes was reinforced by exalting poverty. The state
also benefited by discharging responsibilities for education and health care
onto religious orders. The church, then, was a central force in the establishment of New France's institutional framework. Even before the creation of the
first parish, New France had two hospitals, two schools, and a college, all run
by the church.

To maintain the social position of the clergy, the church required large
revenues. While some financial support for the church came from collections,
donations, fees paid by the state for the care of soldiers and the poor, and royal
subsidies, the most important sources of revenue were the tithe—a levy on
agricultural production—and large land grants. To help support missions, the
One Hundred Associates gave the Jesuits huge seigneuries and by the end of
the French regime, one-quarter of all seigneurial land was held by the church
(Figure 2.4). Most of the church lands were located near Montreal, Quebec or
Trois-Rivières where population was the most dense. Over one-third of the
colonists lived on church seigneuries and they provided significant revenue for
the clergy.

During the early years, the Jesuits were active in the government of the
colony and this tradition was maintained after the arrival in 1659 of Bishop
François de Laval. Given the close ties between church and state, it was
normal for Bishop Laval to sit on the Sovereign Council. Relations between
civil and religious officials were not always harmonious, notably, concerning
the brandy trade. Laval, who considered exploitation of native people a sin,

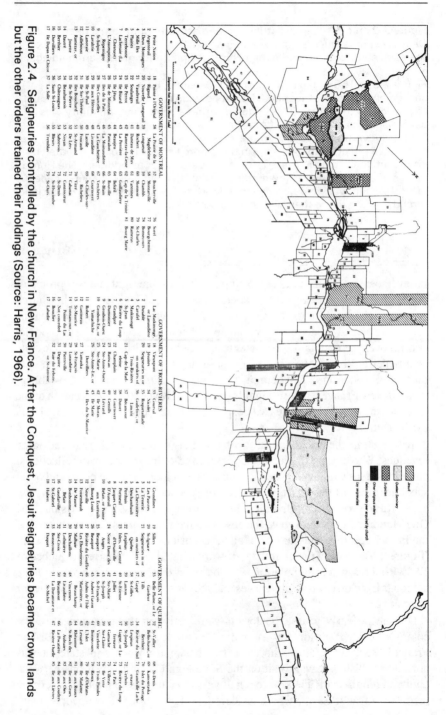

Figure 2.4 Seigneuries controlled by the church in New France. After the Conquest, Jesuit seigneuries became crown lands but the other orders retained their holdings (Source: Harris, 1966).

complained that alcoholism prevented conversions, and he threatened to excommunicate anyone who traded brandy for furs.

For their part, the governor and intendant criticized Laval for overstepping his authority. They tolerated the brandy trade because they deemed it essential for the colonial economy. Laval also disagreed with civil authorities over the tithe that the governor, responding to complaints of the local population, set at one-twentieth of the harvest in 1663 rather than at one-thirteenth as Laval proposed. In 1707 the government finally set the rate at one twenty-sixth. Despite Laval's disagreements with colonial officials, no one really questioned state control of the church, especially not Laval's successors who were mostly absentee bishops spending as much time in France as in the colony.

The social composition of the church reflected the existing social hierarchy. Bishops were all chosen from the French aristocracy, as were many Jesuits and Sulpicians. Parish priests, recruited mainly among the local bourgeoisie and trained at the Quebec seminary after 1663, had considerable local influence. Yet, the clergy was never a dominant local force since lack of numbers sometimes forced them to serve more than one parish. Apart from their religious duties, parish priests also had important civil functions. They kept the parish registers—the official record of births, deaths, and marriages—and occasionally provided the government with information on the state of the local economy. In communities without notaries, priests could draw up legal documents, such as marriage contracts and deeds.

Cloistered life was an important aspect of preindustrial society. The French church of the seventeenth century was strongly influenced by the Counter-Reformation. Within France, interior missions sought to convert the peasantry by emphasizing a rigorous morality, devotion to the Virgin Mary, and strict observance of holy days. The clergy did not escape this reforming zeal. Jesuits and Sulpicians led the drive for a better educated and more devout priesthood and, although they did not train priests in New France, it is significant that they became the dominant male religious orders.

The Jesuits' missionary work in New France has become famous, especially in Huronia where father Jean de Brébeuf and three of his companions suffered martyrdom at the hands of the Iroquois in 1648 and 1649. The Jesuit college at Quebec City, founded in 1635, was the first post-secondary educational institution in America north of Mexico. Jesuits also served the state as explorers (Charles Albanel who crossed Quebec from Tadoussac to James Bay and Jacques Marquette who helped discover the Mississippi are good examples), and helped maintain alliances with the native peoples by distributing gifts at their missions in the interior. With eight seigneuries around Quebec, Trois-Rivières and on the south shore of the St. Lawrence opposite Montreal, the Jesuits were the largest landowners in the colony. After the Conquest, the order was dismantled, its college closed, and their lands were taken over by the British crown.

The Sulpicians were involved in the founding of Montreal in 1642 and became the seigneurs of the Island in 1663. With two other seigneuries nearby, they were the dominant male religious order in the Montreal region. Important landowners, parish priests, and missionaries, the Sulpicians opened a classical college—the Collège de Montreal—at the end of the eighteenth century.

Female religious communities were active in health care and education. The first nuns, the Ursulines, arrived in the colony in 1639 to teach native girls. Abandoning this mission, they established schools for daughters of the colonial elite at Quebec, Trois-Rivières, and New Orleans where catechism, reading and writing, needlework, and good manners were taught. The Ursulines were accompanied by the Hospitalières de la Miséricorde-de-Jésus, who established a hospital for native converts; however, the Indians did not trust French medicine, so the hospital served mainly the European population.

The religious zeal that animated the first immigrants to Montreal led to the founding of new orders. Jeanne Mance founded Montreal's famous Hôtel-Dieu hospital in 1642 to take care of both Europeans and native peoples. Sixteen years later, the Congrégation de Notre-Dame was established by Marguerite Bourgeois. Aiming at making colonists' daughters devout Christian wives and mothers, this order established many elementary schools throughout the colony from Montreal to Louisbourg. Later, general hospitals were established in both Montreal and Quebec to care for the poor and the aged. These institutions, useful as social control measures, ensured that poverty was less visible and that the poor would be cared for within the confines of a segregated, regimented community.

Although deep religious conviction motivated some candidates, religious life also fitted into the family strategies of the elite in preindustrial society by reducing the number of offspring that had to be provided for by the estate. Convent entrance fees were significant, but they were inferior to marriage dowries. The female orders rapidly became Canadianized and by the eighteenth century a majority of nuns had been born in the colony. Many daughters of the Canadian nobility—about 20 percent of all adult women in this class were nuns—joined the nursing orders and the Ursulines (Gadoury, 1988). The Congrégation de Notre-Dame admitted seventeen nobles but also accepted girls from a broader social spectrum.

Sons of the colonial elite had fewer options. Apart from the Recollets who acted mainly as military chaplains, male religious orders recruited new members almost exclusively in France. Only three Canadians entered the Jesuit order and none became Sulpicians before the 1770s. The reasons remain unclear. There seems to have been an anti-colonial bias on the part of the clergy but the Canadian aristocracy's preference for military careers was also partly responsible. The secular clergy was more open but less attractive to the elite since high positions were taken by Frenchmen until after the Conquest; in 1776 Jean-François Hubert became the first Canadian to be consecrated bishop.

Imperial Rivalry and the Conquest

Throughout the seventeenth and eighteenth centuries, France and Britain competed for supremacy in Europe, India, the West Indies, and North America. Although France had four times Britain's population and ten times its army, its navy was less than half the size of Britain's. In a conflict involving colonies scattered around the world, naval supremacy proved determinant.

During the seventeenth century neither empire was dominant and territories such as Acadia changed hands regularly. Acadia, which included present day Nova Scotia, Prince Edward Island, New Brunswick, and Maine, was claimed by both France and England. The French, English, and Scots all unsuccessfully tried to found settlements there in the first third of the seventeenth century. In 1632 Acadia was in the hands of France and the Company of One Hundred Associates established a small base at Port-Royal on the Annapolis Basin. New Englanders conquered the territory in 1654 but were forced to give it up again in 1670. English expeditions ravaged French settlements in 1690, 1696, and 1704 before finally conquering the colony in 1710. Thereafter, England controlled most of Nova Scotia and western Maine, while France controlled Cape Breton and Prince Edward Island (Figure 2.5). Eastern Maine and New Brunswick was a disputed territory controlled by the Abenakis allied with France.

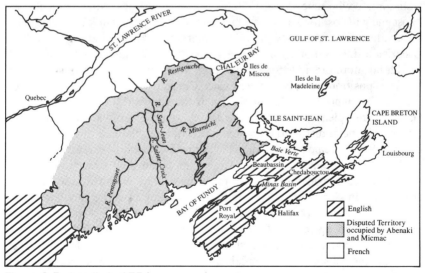

Figure 2.5 Acadia in 1754.

The War of the Spanish Succession (1702-13) marked an important change. France lost the war both in America and in Europe and had to cede its claims over vast territories in the Treaty of Utrecht in 1713. On the Atlantic coast, France gave up claims to peninsular Nova Scotia and Newfoundland, retaining only fishing rights to the "French shore" along the northern coast of the island. In the North, the French had to recognize British control over the Hudson Bay drainage basin where fur traders from both countries had been competing since 1670. Finally, France had to recognize British control over the Iroquois and all their lands, so British American traders based in New York had access to the Great Lakes region.

This treaty determined the future of imperial relations in North America. France strengthened its determination to block British expansion on the continent by building forts to link Montreal and Louisiana and by reinforcing its Indian alliances. The fortifications at Quebec, Montreal, and at stone forts along possible invasion routes such as at Chambly on the Richelieu River were built or improved. The fortress of Louisbourg on Cape Breton Island was also erected as a naval base to protect the fishing fleet and the Gulf of St. Lawrence.

The French and British colonies in the Americas were strikingly different. New France's small population was concentrated along the St. Lawrence but its territory extended from the Gulf of St. Lawrence to the Gulf of Mexico. Its export economy was based on the fur trade, and the large garrison needed to stop English expansion reinforced the autocratic nature of its government.

In mercantilist terms, the colony produced little benefit for its metropolis and this burden was recognized by Governor Roland-Michel Barrin de La Galissonière who reported in 1750 that the French North American colonies "cost and will cost for a long time far more than they bring in." However, they were valuable because they provided a market for French industry and their fisheries trained sailors. They were also a source of manpower, "a form of wealth far more precious for a great king" than any colonial produce. Their strategic position was also evident since Canada was "the strongest barrier that can be opposed to the ambitions of the English" (Groulx, 1970). La Galissonière's pleas to strengthen the colony went unheard, however, since the crown's financial difficulties and the protection of the more profitable sugar colonies were foremost in the minds of metropolitan administrators.

The thirteen colonies had a much larger population, a more varied economy, and produced considerable wealth for Britain. The New England colonies specialized in fishing, the slave trade, shipbuilding, and the carrying trade; the middle colonies (New York, Pennsylvania, New Jersey, and Delaware) produced large agricultural surpluses; the southern slave colonies grew tobacco and cotton for the British market. British industries found a huge market in the colonies, and colonial trade was important for the prosperity of the British merchant navy.

Although imperial rivalry set the stage for conflict, war was precipitated by a local event. By the 1750s British American settlers were encroaching on the rich Ohio valley, a French fur trading area. The Seven Years War began in July 1754, with an attack by British soldiers led by George Washington on a French reconnaissance party near the site of present-day Pittsburgh. Within months the two empires were at war in North America, on the oceans, and in Europe.

The Acadian deportation was one dramatic result of the early war years. Although conquered in 1710 by the British, Acadia attracted few English settlers and for two generations the Acadians had retained their lands and traditions. When war broke out in 1754, Nova Scotia's governor, Charles Lawrence, ordered the Acadians to swear allegiance to the British crown.

Hoping to maintain their traditional neutrality, the Acadians refused to take an oath that implied taking up arms against the French. Lawrence ordered their deportation, citing supposed Acadian support for Micmac raids against British colonists and an Acadian presence at the French forts Beauséjour and Gaspereau. However, demands by New Englanders for land were an equally important consideration. Although some Acadians escaped to Quebec or France, more than 10 000 were herded onto ships and dispersed among the thirteen colonies. Family separation, loss of property, and the Acadian legend of Evangeline were the result. Some Acadians made their way back up the Atlantic seaboard to what became New Brunswick, while others sought refuge in Louisiana (Griffiths, 1973).

Despite initial French victories, British naval superiority and Prime Minister William Pitt's determination to ensure British commercial superiority led to the conquest of France's North American colonies. Pitt, freed from European obligations by his new alliance with Frederick II of Prussia, sent 20 000 regular troops to reinforce the 22 000 colonial troops and militia already in North America. France, in contrast, was hindered by both manpower and strategy. It had only 7000 regular troops in the colony, and the defensive strategy of General Louis-Joseph Marquis de Montcalm allowed the British to close in on the St. Lawrence, especially after the fall of Louisbourg in 1758. In the summer of 1759, a British fleet with 18 000 men sailed up the St. Lawrence and laid siege to Quebec.

Initial attacks on French positions were unsuccessful. By pillaging the countryside around Quebec City, the British commander, General James Wolfe, hoped to force Montcalm out of his defensive position and into a pitched battle. While reducing much of the city and especially the port area to rubble through a summer of bombardment (Figure 2.6), Wolfe ordered General Robert Monckton to ravage the countryside.

> I shall burn all the houses from the village of Saint-Joachim to the Montmorency River, and I would have you burn every house and hut, between the Chaudière and the River Etchemins; Churches must be spared. The houses, barns etc. from your camp down to the Church of Beaumont may be consumed at the same time.

Short History of Quebec

Figure 2.6   The Bishop's palace after the bombardment of Quebec. During
the French regime, important religious buildings—the cathedral, the Jesuit
College, the Seminary, the Ursuline convent, the Hôtel Dieu hospital—
symbolized the power of the church in preindustrial society. During the
1759 bombardment the Lower Town near the port was almost completely
demolished. The Bishop's palace, overlooking the Lower Town, suffered
extensive damage as did many of the houses on the street leading down to
the port, as can be clearly seen here.

In September the Kamouraska region met the same fate: "Upon the whole,"
reported Major George Scott, "we marched fifty two Miles (83 km), and in
that distance, burnt nine hundred and ninety eight good buildings, two sloops,
two schooners, Ten Shallops and several Batteaus and small craft, took fifteen
prisoners (six of them women and five of them children), killed five of the
enemy". At Beaupré, American Rangers scalped the local priest and thirty
militia, and burned the villages of Sainte-Anne and Château-Richer.

In a last attempt to draw out Montcalm before winter set in, Wolfe and 4500
elite troops scaled the cliffs at Anse-au-Foulon on September 9 and drew up on
the Plains of Abraham. French troops were stationed primarily at Beauport to
the east of the city while another force, led by Colonel Louis-Antoine de
Bougainville, was located behind the British army at Cap Rouge. Instead of
waiting for Bougainville to come up behind Wolfe, Montcalm brought his
troops from Beauport, left the fortifications, and hurried out to meet the
British in the open field. Tired from their long march and lacking strong
leadership, the French were defeated in twenty minutes.

In the spring of 1760, the French won a battle at Sainte-Foy, but the arrival of the English fleet forced the French to retreat to Montreal. British forces moved in on Montreal by three of its river systems—up-river from Quebec City, down the Richelieu, and down the St. Lawrence from Lake Ontario. To avoid further bloodshed, the besieged French army surrendered in September. Thus, unlike Quebec, Montreal was spared the agony of a long siege.

While Canada's fate awaited the outcome of the war in Europe, the colony was subject to military rule. The articles of capitulation of Montreal (September 1760) guaranteed the preservation of the "entire peaceable property and possession of the goods, [lands], merchandizes, furs and even their ships." The rights of Catholics were not guaranteed, however, and the death of Bishop Henri-Marie Dubreuil de Pontbriand posed a problem by leaving Catholics without a bishop to confirm children or ordain new priests. Native peoples were also in an uncertain position since the British refused French requests to protect their native allies, their lands, and their missionaries.

The articles of capitulation gave all inhabitants of the colony the right to return to France. However, only a few hundred people—mostly important bureaucrats with careers closely linked to the French empire and some merchants representing French companies—left the colony. Most merchants, along with the artisans and peasants, remained tied to their shops and to their lands in the colony. Members of the clergy also opted for Canada. While the Jesuits could no longer return to France because the order had been banned in 1764, the Sulpicians transferred ownership of property from the mother house in Paris to Canadian members.

The colony had been devastated by six years of war. With the area around Quebec City in ruins, the military authorities assisted in rebuilding and in getting fields back into production and tried to minimize British intrusion on daily life. At Quebec, General James Murray ordered his troops to respect Catholic processions, visited the Lorette mission and let the Huron live on their lands. Most important, he ordered inventories of the harvests and organized the shipment of foodstuffs to stave off starvation.

The British administration faced problems with native peoples. In 1763, western tribes under the Ottawa chief, Pontiac, attacked British traders throughout the Great Lakes region and captured all British forts except Detroit. During the war years the Indians had received few trade goods and had complained of the prices British traders charged, of the poor quality of their goods, and of the lack of presents traditionally given to confirm alliances. Fears that the British would take their lands increased with British refusal to recognize native land claims in the St. Lawrence Valley. The different tribes, however, were not sufficiently united and, with the official disappearance of the French after the treaty of Paris in 1763, the alliance fell apart; peace was finally signed in 1766.

The Debate about the Effects of the Conquest

The Conquest has traditionally been seen as a major watershed in Canadian history. For French Canadian nationalists it is at the root of over two centuries of national oppression. For English Canadians it marks the beginning of a distinct bi-ethnic North American society developing within the framework of British institutions. Although the Conquest's political impact must not be underestimated, its socio-economic impact was not dramatic.

The Conquest introduced greater ethnic diversity to Quebec but changed little in the colony's economy or class structure. Peasants continued to pay their tithes and seigneurial dues. Since seigneurs could no longer rely on military positions, they administered their lands with greater care to extract more revenue from the peasantry. Fur traders continued to ship European trade goods to natives in the West while local merchants functioned as before. Most Roman Catholic institutions maintained their position although their financial and juridical bases were less assured. The change in metropolis did modify trading patterns and brought about a change in the business climate by increasing competition, but these changes were not sufficient to destroy the colonial mercantile community (Igartua, 1974).

Because of the Conquest, the French, who had been the dominant power, became a conquered people. While generations of English Canadians have been taught to perceive the Conquest as what American historian Francis Parkman described as: "a happier calamity never befell a people than the conquest of Canada by British arms", it is seen as a major catastrophe by French-Canadian nationalists. The French regime became a golden age; the period after the Conquest a long struggle for survival.

During the 1950s, the Conquest took on new significance as neo-nationalist historians such as Maurice Séguin and Guy Frégault interpreted it as the root of the social and economic inferiority of modern Quebec. In interrupting the normal process of development, the Conquest had prevented the colony from becoming an independent state.

> As long as French Canada remained alone, as long as the reasons for its
> birth and for its growth as a people [continued], the mother country
> sustained it, protecting it from a military point of view, colonizing it with
> her sons, her institutions, her capital resources. As long as these conditions
> existed it was in a position to become a normal nation (Séguin, 1968).

In this interpretation the Conquest also meant the loss of a dynamic class, the bourgeoisie. The failure of modern French Canadians to dominate Quebec's economy was attributed to the exodus, or "decapitation" of the colonial elite in 1760. Because the embryonic bourgeoisie of New France was destroyed, French Canada was forced to turn inward and to idealize rural life as the best means to preserve its nationality (Séguin, 1970).

In 1760 Canada was completely crushed. The colony which passed to
Britain three years later was an economic ruin. It was also a political ruin.
Finally, in 1763 the country was ruined socially. During the years 1760-1763
Canada was not merely conquered and ceded to England; it was defeated.
Defeat means disintegration... The Canadians, eliminated from politics,
from commerce and from industry, turned back to the soil. If they came to
boast that they were "children of the soil", it was because defeat had affected
not only their material civilization but also their ideas. They had higher
pretensions when their community was more complete (Frégault, 1964).

This interpretation was widely accepted during the "Quiet Revolution" of the
1960s, and helped shape nationalist outlook toward English Canada. The Parti
Québécois government used it to support its 1980 proposal for sovereignty-
association:

Sooner or later [New France] would have rid itself of the colonial yoke and
acquired its independence, as was the case in 1776 for the United States of
America. But in 1763 the hazards of war placed it under British control.
Deprived of their leaders, many of whom had to go back to France, subject
to new masters who spoke another language, kept out of the civil service by
the Royal Proclamation of 1763, our ancestors, lacking influence and
capital, and ruled by British law, saw the entire commercial and industrial
structure they had built pass gradually into the hands of English merchants
(Government of Quebec, *Québec-Canada: A New Deal*, 1980).

Although satisfying to many Québécois, this interpretation is reductionist
and does not account for important differences in the social and economic
structures of preindustrial and modern Quebec. Another current interpretation denies that New France had a viable business community and insists that
the colony's Ancien Régime mentality condemned it to a conservative outlook
that contrasted sharply with the progressive business mentality of the Anglo-
Saxon merchants who arrived after the Conquest (Creighton, 1956; Ouellet,
1980). This interpretation is equally unsatisfactory.

Like all colonies, New France had social classes. Administrators and
military officers were closely tied by patronage to the empire but at the same
time they developed roots in the colony through their extensive land holdings.
At the Conquest this group had to decide whether to remain in Canada and
retain their seigneuries or to pursue their careers in the French empire. Most
of the important administrators left but most military officers remained.

Merchants faced the same choice. The import-export trade, the most
profitable sector of New France's economy, was dominated by agents of
metropolitan trading companies and these merchants opted to return to
France. Most merchants, however, were completely integrated into colonial
society. For example, the Montreal fur traders, as well as the rural merchants,
had few direct links with France and chose to continue in familiar business
surroundings. The Conquest forced them to find new suppliers and sources of

credit but they did have a base of clients and superior knowledge of local business conditions (Igartua, 1974).

The Conquest modified the composition of the administrative elite. Between 1763 and the Quebec Act of 1774, Catholics could not hold office in the colony. This meant that the francophone seigneurial elite had to give up their army commissions and turn to revenues from their seigneuries. Although after 1774 British administrators named a significant number of the seigneurial elite to official positions, most patronage went to anglophones. Government positions were an important form of work for professionals in preindustrial society and, with the creation of an Assembly in 1791, patronage became hotly disputed as francophones sought their fair share (Paquet et Wallot, 1973).

The influx of anglophone traders after the Conquest, and especially after the American Revolution, changed business practices in Quebec. The most powerful merchants, with strong ties to British firms and sources of credit, were able to drive many of the smaller merchants, both francophone and anglophone, out of business. By the 1790s a new commercial elite had emerged centred around the North West Company, which was almost exclusively anglophone. The emergence of the timber trade after 1800 created new opportunities but entrepreneurs in this sector were usually recent immigrants with close family ties to important British or American merchants. As the importance of capital and technological innovation increased, access to these and a better knowledge of the imperial or United States markets favoured British or American immigrants over native-born Canadians, regardless of ethnicity. Francophone merchants continued to be important in local trade and as large landholders in the growing urban centres but they were no longer at the apex of the commercial capitalist hierarchy.

Integration into the British empire brought greater prosperity to the colony and more commercialization of agricultural production. Linkage between the wider imperial world and local economies was ensured by a growing francophone bourgeoisie made up of local merchants, notaries, and other professionals. As population and trade grew, revenues for notaries and merchants increased dramatically through land transactions and the sale of imported goods. At the same time, the wealth of the local clergy increased through the tithe and through fees for baptisms, marriages, and burials. By the beginning of the nineteenth century this bourgeoisie and the clergy fought for domination of the political and social life of the countryside.

Within the popular classes there was greater diversity by the beginning of the nineteenth century than had been evident in the early years of settlement. Artisans continued to be independent producers, but were joined in the towns by an increasing number of day labourers. Farmers with large holdings in the rich Montreal plain benefited from greater integration into the Atlantic economy, but more and more farmers with small holdings and those in outlying regions were forced to seek employment outside agriculture.

Constitutional Change under British Rule, 1763-1791

The Treaty of Paris in 1763 finalized the Conquest and gave Britain a new colony, the Province of Quebec, inhabited by French Catholics who knew nothing of British traditions. In October 1763 the Royal Proclamation established the province's territorial and administrative structures. Elaborated by the Grenville ministry, which was attempting to reorganize imperial administration and strengthen central control over taxation, commerce, and politics, the proclamation showed little understanding of the realities of Quebec. It attempted to transform the colony into one with both British institutions and a British population; it promoted an elected assembly, British laws, and British immigration. At the same time, it separated Montreal from its natural fur trade hinterland by creating a vast Indian reserve in the interior of the continent (Tousignant, 1979).

Despite his instructions to establish English law and the Anglican Church and to use English schools as vehicles of assimilation, Governor James Murray understood that, with the exception of the institution of British criminal law, such a policy was unworkable. Of the 70 000 French Canadians, 85 percent were rural inhabitants isolated from contact with the British and their institutions. Most of the few hundred British merchants who had come to the colony lived in Quebec City and Montreal and there was little immediate prospect of substantial British immigration.

Murray's dilemma was made more difficult by the Test Act, an English law in force in Great Britain since 1673, which prohibited Catholics from holding public office. By extension, French Canadians could not hold government positions nor sit in an assembly in the colony. Given this situation, Murray never held elections for an assembly, preferring to rule through a council sympathetic to the French Canadians. He also helped the Catholic Church maintain its position in the colony by allowing female and male religious orders (the Jesuits were an important exception) to function normally, and by authorizing Jean-Olivier Briand to go to France to be consecrated as Bishop.

Murray's sensible reaction to political reality enraged British merchants who demanded and finally obtained his recall. They were angry with his refusal to call an assembly, with his empathy with the francophone seigneurs, with his toleration of Catholics, and with the failure of his bureaucrats to support merchant goals for a great commercial empire. They accused his administration of being "vexatious, oppressive and unconstitutional" and demanded "the blessings of British Liberty". For his part, Murray had no use for the British merchants who were trying to have him recalled.

> ...nothing will satisfy the licentious fanatics trading here [i.e., the British merchants] but the expulsion of the Canadians who are perhaps the bravest

and the best race upon the globe, a race, who could they be indulged with a few privileges which the law of England deny to Roman Catholics at home, would soon get the better of every national antipathy to their conqueror and become the most faithful and most useful set of men in this American empire.

Murray's successor, Sir Guy Carleton, also shared the social class of the Canadian elite and viewed the clerical and seigneurial aristocracy as the natural leaders of French Canada. It was therefore natural for him to follow Murray's policies.

By the 1770s it was clear that the Royal Proclamation was not realistic since, failing strong British immigration, the colony retained its French Catholic character. The administration of justice, Indian lands, and the impracticality of instituting representative institutions remained pressing problems. Growing unrest in the thirteen colonies convinced the ministry that concessions were in order to ensure the loyalty of the French Canadians. Concessions to the new subjects, however, were intended to reinforce, not weaken, control by London and, moreover, were viewed by one of their principal artisans, Lord Wedderburn, as "essentially a temporary" measure (Tousignant, 1979).

The Quebec Act of 1774 recognized the right of Catholics to exercise their religion and allowed the clergy to collect the tithe. Although the crown still had the right to nominate the bishop, the clergy was in no immediate danger; the Test Act was replaced by an oath of loyalty that allowed Catholics to hold office. Seigneurial tenure was confirmed. The act made a Legislative Council appointed by the crown the governing body; no assembly was planned. A dual judicial system was adopted: English criminal law was retained but French law was normally used in civil cases. The boundaries of the colony were also changed to give the colony control over a large part of the Indian territories in the West (Figure 2.7).

With their social position recognized, the clergy and the seigneurs expressed satisfaction with the Quebec Act. Even though the boundary modifications gave anglophone merchants control over the western fur trade, they were unhappy because there was no assembly. The act changed little for the rest of the population.

The Quebec Act also had an impact on the thirteen colonies where it was considered one of the "intolerable acts" passed by the British government. To many colonial Americans, the autocratic nature of the administration envisaged for Quebec was symptomatic of the thrust for greater centralized power inherent in much British legislation. The new boundaries of the province alienated New York merchants because Albany was cut off from the fur trade. The boundaries also offended many in Pennsylvania and Virginia by preventing settlement in the Ohio Valley, while the act upset Puritan New England because the Catholic church had been protected.

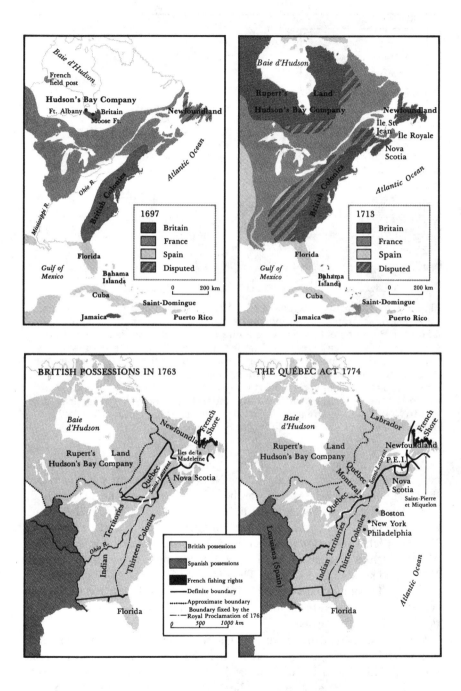

BRITISH POSSESSIONS IN 1763

THE QUÉBEC ACT 1774

1697
Britain
France
Spain
Disputed

0   200 km

1713
Britain
France
Spain
Disputed

0   200 km

British possessions
Spanish possessions
French fishing rights
Definite boundary
Approximate boundary
Boundary fixed by the
Royal Proclamation of 1763

0   500   1000 km

Short History of Quebec

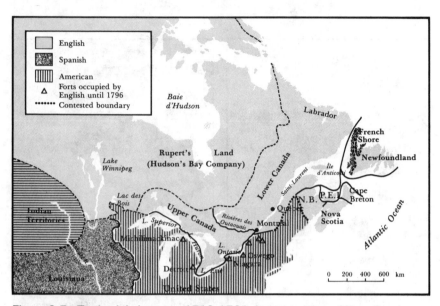

Figure 2.7 Territorial changes, 1713-1791. Incorporation of New France into the British empire had important effects on the colony's boundaries. In 1763 the Province of Quebec was limited to the St. Lawrence Valley from Gaspé to the Ottawa River. The Quebec Act gave it back the Magdalen Islands, Labrador, and an extensive territory around the Great Lakes. In the aftermath of the American Revolution, Quebec's boundaries were again reduced to the area east of the Ottawa River. In 1911 Quebec obtained control of the Ungava district from the federal government. Labrador was lost to Newfoundland by a decision of the British Privy Council in 1927, a decision that the Quebec government has never recognized.

As unrest in the thirteen colonies continued to grow, the continental congress sent delegations to Quebec and Nova Scotia in an attempt to convince the inhabitants to rebel. Apart from the anglophone merchants of Montreal, these American missions met with little success. In 1775 the rebels took up arms and two American armies invaded Quebec to drive the British out. General Richard Montgomery marched down the Richelieu and captured Montreal without a fight while Benedict Arnold, coming down the Chaudière Valley, laid siege to Quebec City. The two American armies joined forces at Quebec in December but were held off by Carleton until the arrival of British reinforcements in the spring forced the Americans to withdraw and removed the threat of another invasion.

French Canadian attitudes to the Americans were ambiguous. The seigneurs and the clergy urged support for the British with Bishop Briand ordering Catholics to be loyal to the king. The popular classes, however, remained neutral. Peasants sold supplies to the Americans for cash but refused when paper was offered. Over 500 militia took up arms to defend Quebec in 1775 but none volunteered to join the British army in attacking the American colonies later in the war.

The granting of independence to the American colonies by the Treaty of Versailles in 1783 had important consequences for the remaining British colonies, which we can now call British North America.

With the creation of the United States, Quebec lost its territory south of the Great Lakes although Canadian merchants continued to trade in the area until the end of the century. Britain, however, kept the richest fur trading areas in the Northwest and many traders moved north from Albany to Montreal. Most important, peace saw the arrival of Loyalists who would challenge the predominantly French nature of Quebec and would force the British to seek a new constitutional solution.

The Quebec Act, which had reinforced French Canadian religious, seigneurial, and judicial structures was unsatisfactory to both the anglophone merchants of Montreal and the Loyalist immigrants. While members of the seigneurial elite told the governor that an assembly would be "useless", the emerging bourgeoisie made up of merchants, notaries, and lawyers joined their anglophone compatriots in petitioning him to have the Quebec Act repealed and to grant an elected assembly. Regardless of the wishes of the colonists, however, legislation was passed in Britain where society was still based on landed property, and the spirit of the "old colonial system" prevailed (Tousignant, 1973).

The Constitutional Act of 1791 amended the Quebec Act, establishing a political structure that maintained strong imperial control to fulfill the traditional mercantile needs of the empire. Fearful of democratic excesses, which they saw as factors in the American Revolution, British authorities maintained strong executive power exercised through the governor, the executive council, and the legislative council. These councils served to cement the crown's alliance with its traditional allies in what had come to be known as the Château Clique, which included the upper clergy, seigneurs, bureaucrats and important merchants.

At the same time, certain limited democratic institutions were permitted and the colonies were encouraged to assume a larger share of their administrative and defense costs. To this end, a legislative assembly, the first popularly-elected assembly in Quebec's history, was created. The franchise gave the vote to almost all rural property-holders and tenants (Ouellet, 1980: 25), and, although it was less generous in towns, it still enfranchised many artisans. The voter also had to be twenty-one, a British subject by birth, naturalization or conquest, and could not have been convicted of treason. Although women who held property had the vote—at least until 1834 when they were disqualified by the Assembly—only widows and unmarried women benefited since property was in the name of the male family head.

Not only did the act fail to meet the political expectations of the anglophone merchants, the division of Quebec into Upper and Lower Canada separated them from the 10 000 Loyalists settled around Lake Ontario. The act also made fundamental changes in the property and religious structures of Lower Canada. It left intact important parts of the Quebec Act guaranteeing institutions with strong French, Catholic, and Ancien Régime connotations such as the seigneurial system. At the same time, the act also introduced British elements giving state support to the Anglican Church and to education by establishing clergy and crown reserves. These reserves were made up of one-seventh of the unceded public lands that were now divided into townships where grants were made in freehold tenure. This change in tenure meant that property was held outright by individuals in these areas, without the restrictions of the seigneurial system.

The duality created by these provisions further complicated the contradictions within the legal system, which remained a mixture of British and French traditions. Lower Canada would continue to use French civil law while English common law would be applied to Upper Canada. It was not clear, however, if anglophone settlers in areas of Lower Canada (for example, in the Eastern Townships where freehold tenure prevailed) could use English common law when they made contracts, wills or business deals among themselves. And, of course, the anglophone merchants in the colony's major towns continued to be subject to French commercial law.

The Emergence of French Canadian Nationalism

By institutionalizing political debate, the Constitutional Act channelled a political confrontation that was inflamed by deepening social and ethnic conflict in Lower Canada. The first session of the Assembly opened in 1792 with "a determined spirit of party amongst the French members" who voted as a block to have French recognized as an official language of the House. Anglophone members quickly sided with the governor while the francophone bourgeoisie used its new position to challenge the leadership of the seigneurial elite and the autocratic nature of government.

During the 1790s, authorities were particularly nervous about the effects of the French Revolution on French Canadians. The Revolution broke out in 1789 and, in the early years, smashed the privileges of the crown, the church, and the aristocracy; members of the colonial elite feared that the Assembly might spread such ideas. Toussaint Pothier, for example, described the elected members of the Assembly as members of the lower class who had lost "their sense of subordination", and the clerical elite strongly supported British institutions in sermons praising monarchic institutions. These fears were largely unfounded, however, as membership in the British empire started to pay economic dividends. Demand for Canadian grain was high and, after the imposition of Napoleon's continental blockade in 1806, Canadian timber products became a major element of imperial trade. With general prosperity in the colony, neither peasants nor the francophone bourgeoisie was eager to sever links with England.

Prosperity did not, however, stop conflict from developing between the francophone bourgeoisie and the anglophone aristocracy. Attempts by government authorities such as Herman Ryland and Jonathan Sewell, as well as efforts by Anglican Bishop Jacob Mountain, to bring the Catholic Church under government control and to institute a public anglophone education system met with sharp resistance. Ethnic conflict peaked in the period 1805-1811 with taxation bills, battles for control of the civil list, and projects to ban government cronies from sitting in the Assembly.

Although historians often interpreted this conflict as one between a vibrant anglophone bourgeoisie and a retrograde francophone professional class (Creighton, 1956; Ouellet, 1981), more important issues were at stake. The Gaol Bill of 1805, by which a tax on wine and tea was levied to build new jails at Montreal and Quebec, is an excellent example. The anglophone merchants sought to protect the old colonial system: "The taxing of trade will lessen bonds to the Mother country and the metropolitan centre's control over trade and commerce [. . .] as it may hereafter be applied to discourage the Importation of British Manufactures in order to encourage such as are local". The francophone bourgeoisie, on the other hand, sought to establish the Assembly's prerogatives in matters of local taxation.

Ethnic conflict was made more visible by the publication of party newspapers, the *Quebec Mercury* by the anglophone elite, and *Le Canadien* by the francophone reformers. The *Mercury* bitterly attacked all that was French.

> This province is already too much a french province for an english colony. To *unfrenchify* it, as much as possible . . . should be a primary object, particularly in these times . . .
> A french system is an arbitrary system, because it is a military one, it becomes therefore the interest, not of englishmen only, but of the universe, to raise mounds against the progress of french power. To oppose it is a duty. To assist it . . . is criminal. To a certain extent the french language is at present unavoidable in this province; but its cultivation, beyond what may be necessary, so as to perpetuate it, in an english colony, can admit of no defence, particularly in the present times.

Le Canadien defended francophone rights:

> You say that the [French] Canadians use their privileges too freely for a conquered people, and you threaten them with the loss of those privileges. How dare you reproach them for enjoying the privileges which the British Parliament has granted them? . . . You ask absurdly whether the [French] Canadians have the right to exercise these privileges in their own language. In what other tongue could they exercise them? Did not the parliament of Great Britain know what their language was?

Short History of Quebec

Beyond the ethnic confrontation lay more fundamental constitutional issues. The Reform party, or parti canadien, closely followed constitutional development in both Britain and other colonies such as Jamaica, and demanded that the Assembly be given increased powers that resembled those of the British House of Commons. Members of the parti canadien remained loyal to British parliamentary institutions and sought to use them to attain their goals; republicanism, whether of the French or American variety, was frowned upon. Debate centred around the civil list (financial provision for the civil service) and the control of government patronage, which had favoured members of the Château Clique, as reformers demanded that the Assembly have complete control over appointments. Autocratic governors, of course, resisted this attack on their privileges and were supported by the anglophone bureaucrats who benefited from this patronage (Paquet et Wallot, 1973). As the parti canadien's constitutional demands became more articulate, an exasperated Governor James Craig seized the presses of Le Canadien in 1810 and jailed twenty of its owners and distributors for "treasonous practices".

This ethnic and constitutional conflict was more than a struggle between different concepts of government. In preindustrial society, civil expenditures focused on the general administration, justice, and the army; capital expenditures on public works to modernize the economy were not yet important. The civil list, therefore, was a key element of power and its control was essential if the Assembly was to have real power in the colony.

Despite these conflicts, French Canada remained loyal to Britain when the War of 1812 broke out with the United States. French agents tried unsuccessfully to arouse French Canadians to join the Americans. The parti canadien did not support the Americans, while Le Canadien opposed French interference in Canadian affairs and described Napoleon as "the lawless leader of France". The Assembly voted funds for the British military and raised 6000 militia to defend Canada. The first French-Canadian regiment of regular soldiers, the Voltigeurs led by Charles-Michel de Salaberry, actively defended the colony at the Battle of Châteauguay in 1813.

The church also called for loyalty to Britain, with Bishop Joseph-Octave Plessis reminding francophones of the religious freedom and "good government" that they enjoyed under British rule. This unflinching loyalty to the crown by successive bishops did much to ingratiate the church with colonial governors. In 1818 Mgr. Plessis was officially recognized by the British government as Catholic bishop of Quebec and was nominated to the legislative council. The creation of auxiliary bishoprics in the Maritimes, Montreal, Upper Canada, and in the Red River colony by 1821 placed the Catholic church on an even firmer footing.

Conclusion

British attempts to find a constitutional solution to the problems of governing a French Catholic population led to the guaranteeing of basic institutions of the French regime such as seigneurial tenure and French civil law. And despite the creation of an Assembly in 1791, the ideology of colonial government had not changed. The Colonial Office continued to direct policy through a governor much as the Ministry of Marine had done in New France. Political power and patronage in the colony were vested in the hands of a small elite that continued to favour class and family connections. Although the seigneurial elite found it more difficult to pursue careers in the army, its revenues from lands enabled it to maintain an aristocratic way of life.

The other main factor in the institutional framework of the French regime, the Roman Catholic Church, faced many difficulties. The threat of domination by an Anglican king was ever present. Some religious orders, notably the Jesuits and Recollets, had disappeared from Canada by the beginning of the nineteenth century but most were preserved. Indeed, the French Revolution helped to reinforce communities such as the Sulpicians who welcomed emigré priests fleeing revolutionary France. Although the loss of royal subsidies had been a hard blow, the rapidly growing Catholic population, and the prosperity of rural regions at the end of the eighteenth century ensured a solid financial base through the tithe and donations. Thus the church was consolidating both its financial and political positions by the beginning of the 1820s.

Bibliography

History of New France
On the general history of New France, readers should consult William John Eccles' works and notably *Canada Under Louis XIV* and *The Canadian Frontier*. Marcel Trudel's *An Initiation to New France* is succinct and useful. The best summary of the administrative structures can be found in André Vachon's introduction to the *Dictionary of Canadian Biography*, Volume II. Civil judicial administration is treated by John A. Dickinson in *Justice et justiciables. La procédure civile à la Prévôté de Québec, 1667-1759* and criminal administration by André Lachance in *La justice criminelle du roi au Canada au XVIIIe siècle. Tribunaux et officiers* and *Crimes et criminels en Nouvelle-France*.

Seigneurialism
The traditional view of the seigneurial system can be found in Marcel Trudel's *The Seigneurial Regime*. A geographer's perspective on this question is given by Richard Colebrook Harris, *The Seigneurial System in Early Canada*. The best recent studies of seigneurial tenure are Louise Dechêne's "L'évolution du

régime seigneurial au Canada. Le cas de Montréal aux XVIIe et XVIIIe siècles", and Allan Greer's *Peasant, Lord and Merchant. Rural Society in Three Quebec Parishes, 1740-1840.*

The Church in New France

The church in New France has been examined by Cornelius Jaenen in *The Role of the Church in New France*. On the problems faced by the clergy in its quest for official recognition, the reader should consult Lucien Lemieux, *L'é-tablissement de la première province ecclésiastique au Canada, 1783-1844.* Conflict between the church and the *parti canadien* has been outlined by Richard Chabot in his *Le curé de campagne et la contestation locale au Québec de 1791 aux troubles de 1837-38.*

The Conquest

Two collections are available that give summaries of the debate over the Conquest: Cameron Nish's *The French Canadians, 1759-1766: Conquered? Half-Conquered? Liberated?* and Dale Miquelon's *Society and Conquest. The Debate on the Bourgeoisie and Social Change in French Canada, 1700-1850.* The best single article that points out the weaknesses in the arguments put forward is Serge Gagnon's "Pour une conscience historique de la révolution québécoise".

British Administration

On British Administration, the two most useful surveys are Hilda Neatby's *Quebec in the Revolutionary Age, 1760-1791* and Fernand Ouellet's *Lower Canada, 1791-1840: Social Change and Nationalism.* Pierre Tousignant gives an insightful analysis of "The integration of the Province of Quebec into the British empire" in the introduction to Volume IV of the *Dictionary of Canadian Biography.* Also useful on the conditions under which the Constitutional Act was adopted is his "Problématique pour une nouvelle approche de la constitution de 1791". Gilles Paquet and Jean-Pierre Wallot, *Patronage et pouvoir dans le Bas-Canada (1794-1812)* is useful for an understanding of political conflict at the turn of the nineteenth century.

Preindustrial Society and Economy

Evolving within a colonial framework, preindustrial Quebec's society and economy were partially shaped by transatlantic metropolitan centres. Yet much of its development was due to local factors beyond a central administration's control. Although its basic social, economic, and administrative structures remained constant from 1650 to 1815, preindustrial Quebec was not a static society. It underwent rapid demographic growth within a context of an expanding agricultural frontier and merchant capitalist exploitation of staple products. Quebec was fashioned by the institutions and cultural traditions of two European peoples, but its peasant economy, its staple-based export economy, and its social reproduction strategies based on abundant land made it quite different from either of the European mother countries.

Demography

Since the fur trade required little European labour before 1650, French settlement in Canada grew slowly, reaching a population of about 1200 by mid-century. Because of financial problems resulting from the capture of its first two fleets by English pirates, the Company of One Hundred Associates defaulted on its commitment to bring out 4000 settlers by 1642. It tried to pass on the costs of settlement by granting seigneuries with the provision that seigneurs recruit colonists; few did. Most settlers before 1650 were sponsored by missionaries who had a variety of motives: eagerness to lessen their reliance upon native peoples; a need for adequate supplies of local foodstuffs; or, in the case of Montreal, a wish to create a model Christian community.

The dispersion of the Huron by 1650 had two important effects: it provided work for the French as middlemen in the fur trade and agricultural markets both for the local French population and for the nomadic tribes in the French alliance. In the decade 1663-72 the European population reached 7000 with the French crown paying the passage of several thousand immigrants and forcing the disbanded soldiers of the Carignan-Salières regiment to settle in the colony. Of these immigrants 800 were young girls (*les filles du roi*), mostly from Parisian orphanages. The crown provided a dowry as soon as they married and, given the shortage of nubile European women in these early years, few were unmarried after a month or two.

By the 1670s, however, immigration slowed when work opportunities declined and government sponsorship disappeared. With population growth largely dependent on natural increase, the government attempted to encourage large families through fines for bachelors and bonuses for families with ten or more living children, providing none had entered religious life. These policies were largely ineffectual, however. Despite the filles du roi, the imbalance between male and female immigrants was such (the sex ratio in 1681 remained about three adult men for every two women) that many men remained unmarried.

Since a farm required female as well as male labour, many men who were unable to farm found work in the fur trade and lived with native women in the West. Their descendants were assimilated into their mothers' culture and these people later became known as Métis. Without contraception, married women had children at regular intervals (about every second year) throughout their childbearing years. The size of families was regulated by the age of women at marriage, by social attitudes placing value on a numerous progeny, and by infant mortality—one fifth of the children died before their first birthday. The state could do little to modify these situations. Except during the war years (1744-48 and 1754-60) when it declined, the annual birth rate remained stable at about fifty-five births per 1000 population (compared to a Canadian birth rate in the 1980s of about eighteen per 1000). Families averaged seven children, well below the requirement for a government bonus. Indeed, demographer Hubert Charbonneau has estimated that less than 2 percent of families could have met the requirements (Charbonneau, 1975: 222-3). Despite women's average age of twenty-two at marriage and men's average age of twenty-seven, religious strictures against premarital sex were shared by society, and premarital conceptions and illegitimate children were very rare (Bates, 1986; Paquette et Bates, 1986).

During the French regime most immigrants came from western France, particularly Normandy and the La Rochelle area, or Paris. Although the vast majority of settlers were French, there was some diversity. For example, Pedro Dasilva was among the Portuguese immigrants who founded families in Quebec in the seventeenth century. During the intercolonial wars of the second half of Louis XIV's reign (1689-1713), more than 1000 captured New England settlers were taken to Montreal and Quebec where many—mostly orphaned children—were adopted by Canadian families (Axtell, 1985). Other American colonists, such as Quebec merchant William Strouds, came to New France to escape legal difficulties.

By 1650 almost all of the original native inhabitants of the St. Lawrence Valley had been killed by disease or warfare with the few survivors distancing themselves from white settlements. Between 1650 and 1760 new Indian populations were settled along the St. Lawrence in villages that the missionaries established for their Christian converts. Usually isolated from French settlements, these formed the basis for present-day reserves. The first such village, established at Sillery near Quebec City in 1637 to assimilate Montagnais and Algonquins, had not been a success. Huron refugees occupied several locations near Quebec City after 1650 before moving to a permanent village at Lorette in 1697.

In the 1660s, the Jesuits established a village for Iroquois Christians at Sault-Saint Louis, the present site of Kahnawake. In the same period, the Sulpicians started a mixed Iroquois and Algonquin village on the outskirts of Montreal. Ostensibly to isolate its inhabitants from the brandy trade, the

Sulpicians moved this village twice, finally locating it at Oka on the Lake of Two Mountains. These changes in village site benefited the Sulpicians because they enlarged their seigneurial domain by using native labour to clear land. Some of this land was later sold to European settlers (Tremblay, 1981: 84-88, 111-15). Other villages were established at Bécancour and Saint-François for Abenaki refugees who had fled the English colonists in Maine. Life in these communities was patterned after that in traditional Iroquois villages, with women tilling the soil and men participating in the fur trade and in war parties against New England.

Three-quarters of the colony's European population was rural, spreading out along the St. Lawrence before occupying lowlands along rivers such as the Richelieu and the Chaudière. However, most settlers lived near Quebec and Montreal; elsewhere the population was spread thinly in a ribbon along the rivers. Quebec, with a population of some 8000 in 1760, was the only city; Montreal, with only half the population of Quebec, remained a frontier community while Trois-Rivières, whose population never exceeded 800 during the French period, was little more than a large market and an administrative and service town. Although the small villages of Beauport, Boucherville,

Table 3.1 Population Change in Quebec's Catholic Population, 1711-1815

Period	Average Population	Birth Rate	Marriage Rate	Death Rate
1711-15	19 800	55.9	9.5	27.8
1716-20	22 900	57.8	10.3	21.5
1721-25	27 200	52.6	9.4	20.3
1726-30	31 600	54.2	10.2	26.1
1731-35	36 200	58.1	9.9	30.4
1736-40	42 300	54.7	8.9	21.2
1741-45	49 100	51.2	8.7	25.1
1746-50	55 000	50.9	10.3	33.1
1751-55	61 200	54.5	10.1	29.5
1756-60	67 200	51.4	10.0	37.9
1761-65	74 400	56.8	11.6	29.3
1766-70	86 200	56.8	8.3	27.3
1771-75	98 100	55.7	9.2	27.2
1776-80	110 400	52.8	8.1	30.3
1781-85	125 700	51.6	8.1	27.7
1786-90	141 900	50.6	8.2	25.7
1791-95	160 300	52.5	9.2	25.9
1796-00	183 700	51.9	8.3	24.6
1801-05	208 900	52.6	8.8	27.8
1806-10	238 600	50.4	8.3	25.2
1811-15	269 300	50.1	9.1	26.9

(Charbonneau, 1973: 43)

Charlesbourg, Laprairie, Pointe-aux-Trembles, Terrebonne, Varennes, and Verchères acted as service centres for the surrounding rural population, one could hardly speak of an urban network.

The Conquest did not alter the basic characteristics of the Canadian population. Marriage, birth, and death rates remained relatively constant and, despite immigration being cut off from France, a healthy rate of natural increase insured the predominance of a French Catholic peasantry in the new British colony. Settlement continued to spread out in the seigneuries of the St. Lawrence and Richelieu Valleys. Only at the beginning of the nineteenth century as new generations had increasing difficulty finding new seigneurial land, did overpopulation in the St. Lawrence lowlands become a problem.

Before the American Revolution, British immigration was largely limited to a small number of merchants, artisans, bureaucrats, and soldiers, most of whom settled in the towns. More than the Conquest, it was the American Revolution that brought significant demographic change when the Loyalists quickly constituted a sizeable anglophone minority (Figure 3.1). Although the Americans portrayed the Loyalists as an elite of Anglican clergy, bureaucrats, and merchants living off government favours, most of them were of humbler

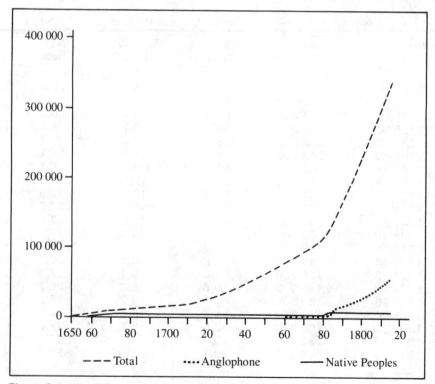

Figure 3.1 The Population of Quebec, 1650-1815.

origin: recent immigrants from Britain, members of religious and ethnic minorities, Indians from the Iroquois confederacy, and farmers.

By 1780 refugees were going overland to Quebec from New York and Pennsylvania. Although several hundred remained in the more settled areas, especially Montreal and Sorel (then known as William Henry), 6000 Loyalists settled west of the seigneurial lands along the upper St. Lawrence and Lake Ontario. Colonists were granted 100 acres in freehold tenure plus fifty acres for each member of their families, with some officers receiving special grants up to 5000 acres.

As can be seen by John Stuart's writing in 1783, a sense of community was already developing in towns like Kingston.

> I have 200 acres within half a mile of the garrison, a beautiful situation and tolerable good land. The town increases fast; there are already above 50 houses built in it and some of them very elegant. It is now the port of transport from Canada to Niagara, having a good harbor. The number of souls to the westward of us is more than 5000 and we gain daily new recruits from the States—we are poor, happy people, industrious beyond example. Our gracious King gives us land gratis and furnishes provision and clothing, farming utensils etc. The greatest inconvenience I feel here is there being no school for my boys. If I succeed in erecting an Academy, I shall die here contented.

Establishment of the Loyalists meant, effectively, the birth of English Canada. From a small merchant and military population of some 500 in the 1760s, the anglophone population of Lower Canada grew to 50 000 by 1815. From 1785 to 1815 most immigrants were New Englanders who settled in freehold lands in the Eastern Townships. By 1815 15 000 anglophone settlers had moved to this area, most around Missisquoi Bay and Stanstead.

The division of Quebec into Upper and Lower Canada in 1791 separated Lower Canada's anglophone population from the British and American immigrants who settled west of the Ottawa River. Although anglophones constituted a majority in the Eastern Townships and significant minorities in Montreal and Quebec, their numbers were insignificant elsewhere in Lower Canada. In areas where they had no contact with a sizeable nearby anglophone community many were assimilated by their francophone neighbours.

For their part, native peoples remained distinct minorities occupying lands set aside for them during the French regime, or they lived in new communities established for them in regions such as the Gaspé. Most of these people—Huron, Iroquois, Algonquin, and Micmac—had the same work experiences as whites. They were canoemen, forest workers, river drivers or timber rafters, and fishermen. Only in northern Quebec where the Hudson's Bay Company forbade settlement until the 1840s did the Cree, Montagnais, Naskapi, and Inuit continue to follow traditional subsistence patterns, little affected by European society.

Staples in the Preindustrial Economy

The staple theory, since its origins in the 1930s with the works of University of Toronto economist Harold Innis, has dominated Canadian political economy (Innis, 1956; Easterbrook and Watkins, 1967: 49-73). Innis emphasized Canada's dependency on foreign trade and maintained that trade in staple commodities such as cod, beaver, wheat, and timber constituted the motor of Canada's economic and social development.

During the French regime fish and furs were the main staples, but by 1800 these products were being overtaken by exports of wheat and timber. However, while exports of these staples did dominate trade with metropolitan centres throughout the preindustrial period, the staple theory has underestimated the importance of local markets and the dynamics of the peasant economy.

Despite the emphasis placed on fur in our historiography, the fishery was the first North American staple and it remained the most valuable North American export to France throughout the French colonial period (Brière, 1986; Turgeon, 1981). Although the French fishery, centred on the Newfoundland coast and on Cape Breton Island, was dominated by ships from Saint-Malo and Granville exploiting the rich Mediterranean market through forwarders at Marseille, colonial merchants also became active in this trade. Early in the eighteenth century, Quebec City entrepreneurs such as Denis Riverin and Pierre Haimard set up fishing bases in the Gaspé while Marie-Anne Barbel developed sealing operations along the Labrador coast. These Quebec merchants, supplying the local market's demand for fish for the fast days of Fridays and Lent, also exported some of their catch to the French West Indian possessions. Sealing operations provided exports of train oil and pelts for the metropolitan market.

Although France retained lucrative fishing rights along the "French shore" of Newfoundland after the Conquest, the Gulf of St. Lawrence fisheries, and especially those in the Gaspé came under the dominance of Channel Island families like the Robins. By 1800 the Robins were exporting some £16 000 of cod annually. The fishery also encouraged the creation of a local shipbuilding industry, not only for schooners and shallops used by the fishermen, but also for larger ships and brigs that were later sold in Europe. Population growth in this area started with the arrival of Acadian refugees in the 1750s and was bolstered by the arrival of some Loyalist families in the 1780s.

Despite significant local production, the 5000 settlers in this region at the turn of the century remained dependent on the great merchants of the fishery. Instead of paying fishermen in cash, merchants used the truck system—paying for the catch by extending credit to buy equipment, clothes, and food at their stores. The truck system resulted in a growing indebtedness of the fishermen, and thereby reinforced the dependence of the fishing population, while increasing merchant profits in the local retail trade (Lee, 1984).

Despite the greater economic importance of the fishery, it was the fur trade that had drawn Europeans to the St. Lawrence Valley and eventually led to settlement. As we have seen, the destruction of the Huron forced the French to seek out new suppliers. In 1653 Médard Chouart, sieur des Groseilliers, the first coureur de bois, set out to encourage western tribes to bring their furs directly to Montreal. His success showed that French agents in the interior could guarantee the supply of pelts. This led the French crown to send agents (often members of religious orders) such as Charles Albanel, Jacques Marquette, François Dollier de Casson, and René de Bréhant de Galinée to find new trade routes and start missions in the Great Lakes and Hudson Bay drainage systems.

Although native peoples did all the work of trapping and preparing pelts, native canoemen, especially the Ottawa who had provided much of the labour to transport fur from 1653 to 1670, were increasingly replaced by coureurs de bois who sought complete control of trade in the interior.

The period 1670-1681 was one of anarchy in the fur trade. Metropolitan officials tried unsuccessfully to stem the proliferation of coureurs de bois by outlawing them since they were seen as a drain on the colony because they did not farm. Local officials, on the other hand, particularly governor Louis de Buade de Frontenac and his associate Robert Cavelier de La Salle, continued to encourage the expansion of the fur trade in the hope of personal gain. Apart from men like Frontenac and La Salle, only the Compagnie des Indes occidentales, which had the monopoly over fur exports, profited during this period.

Although the coureurs de bois were independent traders, fierce competition (authorities estimated that 500 men were trading in the west in 1680) cut heavily into their profit margins and hardly made worthwhile the threat of prosecution, the danger of Iroquois attack, and the physical hardship of paddling and portaging. The coureurs de bois were, however, an essential link in the staple trade. They contacted tribes, exchanged European metalwares, textiles, and brandy for furs, and transported pelts to Montreal. Merchants who supplied trade goods to the coureurs de bois fared little better. Competition and the difficulty of recovering debts from outlawed coureurs de bois eliminated many after a couple of years and only Jacques Leber and Charles LeMoyne managed to accumulate significant capital (Dechêne, 1974).

To put an end to this disorder, the monopoly company, the government, and the most important merchants joined forces in the 1680s and important structural changes resulted. After 1681 the company dealt only with established traders, while the government started issuing special permits called congés to trade in the West. The establishment of army posts at strategic portages enabled the government to effectively police the trade. It had also become evident that only important Montreal merchants who had enough capital to maintain large stocks of trade goods and extend credit could survive. By the 1690s the coureurs de bois who had acted as independent traders had been replaced by employees called voyageurs. Although some voyageurs maintained their independence and shared in the profits, the vast majority were wage labourers who contracted with a merchant to transport goods and furs to and from posts in the West.

New France's expansion across almost half the continent renewed conflict with the English and their Iroquois allies. When French trading in the Mississippi cut off the Iroquois' main supply of furs, they started attacking French traders in the West. The attacks began in 1681 and by 1689 the Iroquois were ravaging settlements near Montreal. Until peace was concluded in 1701, the Iroquois continued to disrupt both the fur trade and settlement in the Montreal region.

Rapid expansion of the trade also brought an oversupply of beaver. In good years before 1650, about 30 000 pelts were exported; the volume rose to about 50 000 pelts by 1670, and to over 100 000 pelts by the 1680s. As the number of poorer quality pelts from the Mississippi Valley increased, French markets became flooded. Prices fell and expansion was temporarily halted. Indian alliances, however, vital to New France's economy and to limiting British expansion, could be maintained only through trade, and colonial officials fought successfully with the French ministry to maintain a limited number of posts in the West.

After 1717, markets for beaver improved and expansion of the fur trade was renewed. Army officers such as Pierre Gaultier, sieur de la Vérendrye, and his sons extended the fur trade across the prairies and integrated scores of tribes into the French alliance. However, this period of expansion was slower than that of the seventeenth century. Rational exploitation of the trade to insure stability of supply and profitability was ensured by granting army officers monopolies over specific territories. These officers formed partnerships with important merchants and hired men to transport goods to the West (Allaire, 1987). The types of pelts became more varied as exports of deer, marten, bear, moose, seal, and lynx skins supplemented the beaver trade. The value of exports was fairly stable after 1720 at just over 1 000 000 livres, or about twice the value of fur exports in the early 1690s.

After the Conquest the fur trade continued to dominate exports. In the 1760s and 1770s Montreal traders pushed ever farther into the West, culminating in Alexander Mackenzie's voyage along the Mackenzie River to the Arctic Ocean in 1789 and his crossing the Rockies to the Pacific in 1793. The basic structure of the fur trade remained unchanged until the 1780s and francophone merchants continued to play an important role. However, they and the smaller anglophone merchants were gradually eliminated by the large influx of Albany traders after the Quebec Act and by the fierce competition that ensued. With growing distances, the increased capital and credit required were available only to the most important anglophone merchants such as Robert Ellice, John Forsyth, and John Richardson, who benefited from trading partnerships with English companies. These traders formed the North West Company and dominated the trade out of Montreal by the end of the 1780s.

With the lengthening distances, work for voyageurs also changed. Some, called "winterers" who transported goods in the shipping season from posts such as Fort Chipewyan on Lake Athabaska to Great Lakes transfer depots like Grand Portage or Fort William, stayed in the West permanently. However, most of the transport workers remained seasonal (known as "pork-eaters" because of lard, their staple food) and paddled the large canoes from Lachine to the Great Lakes depots. The Montreal region continued to be the main source of voyageurs, many of whom were urban dwellers. Others came from rural parishes such as Laprairie and Sorel.

Seasonal labour in the fur trade fitted into a rural family economy that relied on outside cash to provide subsistence in poorer areas and to enable sons to buy farms in richer ones. In the sandy region of Sorel, for example, inadequate farm surpluses forced families to obtain cash by having a male member in the fur trade. In the 1790s one-third of the adult males in Sorel served as voyageurs, a fact that has led Allan Greer to describe them as a semi-proletariat (Greer, 1985).

The labour of native trappers and francophone voyageurs enabled the great Montreal merchants like Simon McTavish, William McGillivray, and Joseph Frobisher to make fortunes. In the 1780s the North West Company shipped more than 100 000 beaver, about 50 000 muskrat, and tens of thousands of other types of pelts to England for local hat and clothing production, or for re-export to France and the Baltic. Profits can be gauged from the example of 1791 when the North West Company spent about £16 000 and sold its furs in London for £88 000.

In the years after its formation, the North West Company competed vigorously with the Hudson's Bay Company. While the Hudson's Bay Company had an enormous geographic advantage, the Nor'Westers were experienced and tough traders who maintained good contacts with the native trappers.

For its part, the Hudson's Bay Company followed construction of its first inland post at Fort Cumberland on the Saskatchewan River in 1770 with dozens of posts across the West. In 1812 it threatened the North West Company's trade routes and food supply by permitting Lord Selkirk to establish a Scottish settlement at the junction of the Red and Assiniboine Rivers. The Nor'Westers burned settlers' buildings and tried to starve the Scots by cutting off the pemican supply and, in the Seven Oaks Massacre of 1816, twenty settlers were killed. Competition between the two companies was ruinous, however, and in 1821 the Montreal company was merged into the Hudson's Bay Company.

Although the export of agricultural staples had long been a goal of colonial administrations, it was hindered by the small population and the isolation from large markets. In the eighteenth century, New France exported wheat and peas to the fortress of Louisbourg and to French sugar colonies in the West Indies, but the export of foodstuffs never became a staple during the French regime. With the Conquest, the change of metropolis integrated Quebec into the larger trading network of the British empire.

During the American Revolution, Quebec foodstuffs were in demand to supply British forces. In the 1780s, wheat became an important export commodity with a culmination in 1802 when record exports of a million bushels were shipped from the port of Quebec to growing markets throughout the empire (Ouellet, 1981). However, the situation changed dramatically in the second decade of the nineteenth century with bad harvests, rural overpopulation, and cheaper Upper Canadian wheat combining to turn Lower Canada into a net importer of wheat.

At the beginning of the nineteenth century, timber became an important export commodity. When the Napoleonic wars closed its access to Baltic timber, Britain turned to British North America's white pine and oak forests for construction materials. Tariffs and the war exigencies of the British navy drove up prices; by 1810 lumber and timber products made up 75 percent of the value of exports from the port of Quebec. Timber was exported to the British markets in several forms with square timber being the least-processed. Barrel staves, deals (7.5-centimetre planks of pine, oak, or elm), smaller planks, and potash made from ashes were also exported.

Figure 3.2 Timber rafts passing Oka on the Lake of Two Mountains. Every year hundreds of rafts floated down the Ottawa, Richelieu, and St. Lawrence Rivers to Quebec City, providing employment for raftsmen and river pilots.

The trade in square timber and deals created new forms of work in the lumber shanties, along the rivers, and on the timber beaches and shipyards of Quebec City. Lumberjacks felled and squared the timber, and teamsters hauled it to small rivers. Then drivers floated it to the Ottawa or St. Lawrence where raftsmen and river pilots rafted the timber to Quebec (Figure 3.2). Finally, it was measured and marked by cullers. Apart from providing seasonal employment for farmers in frontier regions, these activities brought a great increase in employment opportunities outside of agriculture and signaled significant change to the rural economy of Quebec.

The Structure of Preindustrial Commerce

In the preindustrial period, merchant capitalists profited from both international and local trade. Their activities ranged from Robert Dugard's (Miquelon, 1978) work of trading within Normandy, with Holland, with Quebec, and with Martinique, to supplying the needs of the local community, which is what rural merchant François-Augustin Bailly de Messein did (Michel, 1979).

Imperial policy was largely dictated by mercantilism in which monopoly was emphasized and colonies were seen as suppliers of natural products and markets for goods produced in the metropolis. In France, Louis XIV's principal minister, Jean-Baptiste Colbert, issued numerous regulations to improve and standardize the quality of French products. He also used tariffs and privileges to protect metropolitan industry. Colonial commerce was encouraged but the production of goods that might compete with metropolitan commodities was discouraged. Mercantilism's main goal was to assert centralized state authority over the economy and it was accompanied by detailed control, meticulous inspection, and reliance on privilege (De Vries, 1976).

Merchants were an important element in the colonial system, often occupying important positions in government. During the French regime there was a degree of specialization, with Quebec merchants handling the import-export business and Montreal traders specializing in the fur trade. At the top of the hierarchy were import-export merchants, usually the agents of French trading houses.

For example, François Havy and Jean Lefevre, representing the Dugard Company of Rouen from 1732 until the 1750s, imported French textiles, wines, brandy, and hardware, and wholesaled these commodities to merchants such as Montreal fur trader Pierre Guy, or retailed them in their Quebec City store. They also exported agricultural produce to Louisbourg and the West Indies, built ships to be sold in France, and invested in sealing expeditions along the Labrador coast. At the height of their success, Havy and Lefevre controlled about one-third of Canadian trade. Like other important import-export merchants of their time, they remained tied to France and returned after the Conquest (Miquelon, 1978).

Alexis Lemoine Monière (1680-1754) is representative of a Montreal merchant-outfitter in the fur trade, and his career emphasizes the importance of matrimonial alliances in the commercial capitalist environment of the preindustrial period. The son of a small trader in Trois-Rivières, he moved to Montreal and first worked as a voyageur before financing his own trips in 1712. Three years later he married Marie-Louise Zemballe, established a store in Montreal, and began financing the fur trade expeditions of his brothers-in-law and other traders.

His second marriage in 1725 to Marie-Josephte Couagne, daughter of one of the wealthiest Montreal merchants, helped him consolidate his position with the military and merchant elite. Although the fur trade dominated Monière's business, his Montreal store also served the local inhabitants, particularly retired voyageurs, and military officers. Like many successful merchants, Monière invested some of his capital in land; his son married into the same social class and carried on the family business even after the Conquest.

Although Quebec remained the most important port during the preindustrial period, developments in the fur and wheat trades increasingly enabled the Montreal directors of the North West Company to deal directly with English suppliers. This trend continued after the turn of the nineteenth century as Montreal expanded to service the rapidly growing population of Upper Canada.

Simon McTavish (1750-1804) was a dominant merchant capitalist in the North West Company who left an estate of £125 000. Born in Scotland, McTavish emigrated to New York and traded at Detroit and Michilimackinac before moving his operations to Montreal at the end of the American Revolution. With capital accumulated in the fur trade, McTavish imitated other rich anglophone merchants in buying a seigneury. His seigneury of Terrebonne represented more than status and a secure investment for his merchant capital. Besides the seigneurial gristmill, McTavish opened a biscuit bakery, a sawmill, and a barrel factory to supply fur traders in the West. Known as the "Marquis" because of his elegant style, McTavish built a Montreal mansion and, when forty-three, married an eighteen-year-old French-Canadian, Marie-Marguerite Chaboillez. After her husband's death, she retired to England with his fur trade capital.

While the colony's small population confined trade to urban centres throughout much of the seventeenth century, traders also moved into the countryside as the rural population grew. Rural merchants, such as Joseph Cartier at Saint-Hyacinthe, sold imported textiles, hardware, and alcohol (Table 3.2), buying wheat and other agricultural produce in return. Over a thirty-eight-month period from 26 October, 1794, to 30 December, 1797, he sold over 55 000 livres of goods to 317 different clients. Since there was little currency in circulation, credit was an essential part of this trade, and rural merchants became important lenders and mortgage-holders in their communities. Cartier's experience is a useful example: at the end of the period discussed above, only six clients owed nothing whereas the other 311 had accumulated 38 000 livres in debts. A bad harvest in 1796 undoubtedly accounts for the magnitude of the debt, but peasant indebtedness was nonetheless a dominant feature of rural trade.

Table 3.2 General Store Sales by Joseph Cartier, 1794-97

Merchandise	Percent of sales
Textiles	35
Clothing	10
Alcoholic beverages	21
Foodstuffs (seed, spices, sugar)	8
Hardware	10
Kitchenware	5
Farm implements and tools	5
Diverse goods (leather, wood, tobacco, etc.)	6

(Desrosiers, 1984)

Some of these merchants, for example, François-Augustin Bailly de Messein (1709-1771) and Samuel Jacobs (d. 1786), built up thriving businesses and left considerable fortunes. Bailly, the son of a Quebec City army officer, moved to Varennes in 1731. Within a decade he became the most important retailer in the region with a clientele spread over adjoining parishes. As an older man, Bailly entered semi-retirement but continued to administer his extensive land holdings and to lend money to peasants (Michel, 1979).

Although Samuel Jacobs' career followed a similar pattern, his wealth was due as much to lucrative government contracts during the American Revolution as to local trade. Jacobs arrived in the colony with Wolfe's army in 1759 and, after unsuccessful attempts to establish a distillery and potash works at Quebec, he settled at Saint-Denis in 1770. He became the dominant merchant in the Richelieu Valley with his chain of stores selling cloth, hardware, and rum and buying wheat in return.

The American Revolution provided Jacobs with a key opportunity to expand since he was named assistant commissary-general with responsibility for laying in provisions for the large number of British troops in the region. He left an estate of almost £20 000 made up mainly of accounts receivable, merchandise, and real estate in the Saint-Denis area (Greer, 1985).

Merchants in preindustrial society had difficulty investing their capital and, as the extensive real estate holdings of Bailly and Jacobs illustrate, land appeared to guarantee the best and safest return on capital. Near cities, merchants like Henri Hiché and William Grant, John Mure and George Pozer opened subdivisions on which artisans and labourers could build houses in return for a perpetual rent (Dechêne, 1981). Seigneuries also offered interesting investment opportunities and wealthy merchants were attracted to the status of seigneur; by 1791 32 percent of the seigneuries in Quebec were totally or partially owned by anglophones, and about the same percentage had been acquired by members of the francophone bourgeoisie (Harris, 1987: Plate 51).

Artisans

While merchants lived by exchanging goods across time and space, artisans lived by producing goods, generally using craft methods. In preindustrial society artisans worked alone or with a limited number of journeymen and apprentices and controlled their own work, tools, and shop (Figure 3.3). Since there were no guilds or corporations to control standards and access into trades, Canadian artisans had greater liberty than their European counterparts and market forces were determinant in the evolution of trades. Butchers and bakers, whose numbers, production, and prices were regulated by the state, were notable exceptions. Although some crafts such as the leather and metal trades, were relatively prosperous, seasonal unemployment was a recurrent problem especially since many crafts were dependent on commerce. Coopers and carters, for example, worked mainly during the shipping season. Seasonal unemployment was heightened by the winter shutdown of the construction and shipbuilding industries.

Figure 3.3 A shoemaker's shop. This illustration from Denis Diderot's famous eighteenth-century *Encyclopédie* shows the scale of production in an artisan's shop. As the master measures a client's foot, two apprentices are making shoes. Different wooden forms, used to find the right size, are to be seen on the back wall underlining the fact that all shoes and boots were made to measure.

Since the immigration of artisans did not keep pace with population growth, expansion of a trade depended on the apprenticeship system by which boys (and for specific trades such as dressmaking, girls) were apprenticed to masters for three to seven years. Apprentices provided cheap labour, but in return they learned a trade, were incorporated into the master's household, and received a modest payment at the end of their apprenticeship. In the Canadian context, apprenticeship proved a rational means of adjusting the supply of labour to the needs of the marketplace (Hardy et Ruddel, 1977). As in other preindustrial societies, the apprenticeship system was also an important mechanism of social reproduction.

Throughout the preindustrial period, shops remained mostly small family enterprises where a master and his wife worked alone or with one apprentice. Personal relationships dominated the workplace and there was little division of labour since journeymen and more experienced apprentices could produce a finished product.

Some shops in the more prosperous trades were larger, employing several journeymen and apprentices. Already in 1744, Richard Corbin's Quebec City forge had four employees and cooper Louis Paquet had three assistants. The tendency to larger shops employing over five workers, and a greater division of labour, increased at the beginning of the nineteenth century with the growth in the local market. Whereas master craftsmen produced goods on order, merchant artisans began producing standardized items for sale in rural retail outlets (Bluteau, et al., 1980).

The relatively small population of the colony gave little opportunity for development of a vigorous rural artisanry. Although some artisans such as carpenters, millers, and blacksmiths were established in most rural communities, these craftsmen were usually dependent on farming to supplement their trade. Unlike preindustrial Europe, rural industry in New France was slow to develop and only the Saint-Maurice ironworks offered part-time industrial labour to neighbouring peasants (Figure 3.4). Established just north of Trois-Rivières in 1739, the ironworks offered employment to peasants in extracting ore, making charcoal, and as carters, enabling them to supplement their farming income. Because of the close links between agriculture and industry and the emergence of a rural proletariat, Roch Samson has interpreted the ironworks as an example of proto-industrial activity (Samson, 1985).

Some production went beyond the scale of the artisan's shop. From the 1660s on, colonial officials encouraged local mining, shipbuilding, and pitch and tar production to reduce France's dependence on foreign sources of these products. Apart from the Saint-Maurice ironworks, the naval shipyard at Quebec, which built several men-of-war for the French government, was the most important industrial site of the French regime; it employed almost 200 workers (Mathieu, 1971). As well, private shipbuilders with yards employing between fifteen and thirty labourers built oceangoing and coasting vessels.

Shipbuilding continued to grow in the British regime and, with the timber trade, became a leading sector of the economy in the early nineteenth century.

Figure 3.4 Les Forges du Saint-Maurice. Canada's first industrial establishment, the ironworks produced bar iron and stoves for more than a century before being forced to close in 1883. When the works first opened in 1741, there were only a dozen permanent employees, but over 150 part-time workers.

The Peasant Economy

The vast majority of the population was engaged in agriculture for home or local consumption. Although Canada was barely self-sufficient in essential foodstuffs half a century after its establishment, by the eighteenth century an expanding agricultural population was producing regular surpluses for export to other colonies or to western trading posts. Agriculture was always risky and subject to climatic vagaries. A cold, damp summer did not allow time for grain to mature in the short growing season (120 frost-free days in the region around Montreal and about five days fewer near Quebec City) of the St. Lawrence Valley. Late spring or early autumn frosts such as those in 1815 and 1816, were disastrous. Parasites, such as the Hessian fly that started decimating Lower Canadian wheat in 1809, were another danger. As long as land was plentiful and the initial fertility was not exhausted, there were few regional variations in Quebec agriculture. However, as settlement progressed in the mid-eighteenth century in the rich Montreal plain with its better soil and climate, regional variations became more pronounced.

Getting land into agricultural production was arduous. Settlers in the St. Lawrence lowlands were granted land in seigneurial tenure. It normally took a family two years to clear a hectare of hardwood forest and to build a log cabin, and five years to clear three hectares, the minimum for self-sufficiency.

During this period, the family consumed locally-produced foodstuffs some-times bought at the market but more often supplied by relatives. Since families were large and peasant family strategies aimed at keeping the farm intact by leaving it to a single heir, most members of each new generation were consumers while they were clearing land. Thus, much of the colony's produc-tion was geared to meeting these and other local needs such as payment of the tithe and seigneurial dues, leaving only a small part of each harvest for sale in the towns or for export.

Rural families were never completely self-sufficient and bought cloth, clothing, alcohol, tea and coffee, salt, tools, home furnishings and kitchen-ware. Christian Dessureault's study of Saint-Hyacinthe (1986) reveals that by the early nineteenth century even the poorest peasant households bought items such as copper pots and pans, iron tools, and clothing. The average peasant family owned an iron stove, a major investment that often accounted for a third of its total moveable assets, as well as a wide variety of consumer goods. The richest families had an abundance of copper, pewter, and iron kitchenware and some acquired china and silverware as well.

By the end of the eighteenth century, the custom by which elderly parents donated their farm to one of their children in return for a *pension alimentaire* provides further evidence about consumption patterns. Annual supplies of tobacco, lamp oil, salt, pepper, rum, wine, and tea appeared on a list Joseph Blanchard promised to his parents in 1791:

30 minots flour	200 onions
91 kilos of pork	5 kilos of candles or 3 pots of
1 fatted sheep	lamp oil
2 minots peas	14 kilos tobacco
1 minot salt	4.5 kilos butter
450 grams pepper	25 steres of firewood
100 heads of cabbage	1.5 kilos wool
3 pots rum	a milk cow, six hens and a rooster
3 pots wine	4 shirts of homespun and a complete
11 kilos maple sugar	suit of work clothes
450 grams tea	Sheets and shoes as needed

Blanchard also promised to purchase a set of Sunday clothes from a merchant every three years (Greer, 1985: 35).

Wheat was the main crop in Canada, accounting for about two-thirds of all grain produced. Whereas newly developed land was sown almost exclusively in wheat to capitalize on its commercial value, equal amounts of wheat, oats, peas and/or beans would be planted on well-developed farms of about ten hectares. Peas and wheat were the main cash crops with some hemp, flax, and maize being marketed. Farm gardens and small orchards produced carrots, cabbages, onions, salad vegetables, squash, strawberries, apples, pears, and other fruits for family consumption with surpluses being sold in areas with access to an urban market (Figure 3.5).

Figure 3.5 Château-Richer c. 1785. This watercolour by Thomas Davies is one of the best illustrations of a settled rural landscape. The garden in front of the white-washed stone house produced vegetables for home consumption as well as for the nearby urban market in Quebec. The weirs in the river were used to catch eel that was smoked and sold to urban residents.

Emphasis on wheat rather than fodder crops, together with limited markets for meat, contributed to keep herds small. Since livestock had to be sheltered and fed over winter, most farmers slaughtered all but the animals needed for traction and breeding. Although this strategy provided a winter meat supply, it resulted in insufficient manure to fertilize all fields and led to declining yields as the soil lost its initial fertility.

During the seventeenth and early eighteenth centuries agricultural growth was steady and closely tied to demographic expansion. The opening of new export markets in the second quarter of the century and after the beginning of the American Revolution acted as a stimulus for agricultural production, and the amount of new land cleared vastly surpassed population growth. At the beginning of the nineteenth century, the growth of towns and the introduction of new crops such as potatoes, which were consumed by anglophone immigrants and used as animal fodder, created greater local demand. This expansion continued until the second decade of the nineteenth century when climatic disasters and the Hessian fly contributed to undermine the wheat basis of Quebec's agricultural economy.

Table 3.3 Agricultural Production

	1695	1734	1784
Population	12 786	37 716	113 012
Lands cultivated (hectares)	9 610	55 768	536 721
Land in pasture (hectares)	1 230	6 037	(not given)
Domestic animals			
Horses	580	5 056	30 146
Cattle	9 181	33 179	98 951
Sheep	918	19 815	84 696
Swine	5 333	23 646	70 465

(Census of Canada, 1871, Vol. 4)

With social reproduction of peasant families as the main goal of the peasant economy, the devolution of land was the central problem. The Custom of Paris, by its stipulation of equal inheritance for all children of a marriage, complicated this situation since it implied the parceling out of family holdings.

Peasant families had various solutions for this social, economic, and legal dilemma. Some peasant families tried to acquire large holdings to offset the effects of inheritance. In areas where land was plentiful, farmers sought additional concessions to ensure viable farms for their children when they married. Another common family strategy was that the heir of the family farm, quite often the youngest child, paid an indemnity to his or her siblings (Michel, 1986; Paquet et Wallot, 1986). The result of these strategies was that peasant landholdings rarely remained divided in small parcels.

As settlement became more dense and families could no longer obtain new land in the same community, more prosperous farmers bought established farms from poorer neighbours who used the capital to start new farms in another parish. Over time, those who could not maintain viable farms increasingly turned to wage labour to supplement their incomes; thus the peasantry, which had been fairly egalitarian during the seventeenth century, by the early nineteenth century had become quite hierarchical.

Another important element in this structuring of rural society was the unequal possession of draught animals. The more prosperous peasants had at least one team of oxen whereas poorer ones had to rent this important means of production from their neighbours (Dechêne, 1974; Michel, 1986; Dessureault, 1986). By the beginning of the nineteenth century, land in the seigneurial zone was at a premium while expansion to freehold areas was impeded by poor communications and the existence of large clergy and royal reserves. Subdivision of plots became more common, leading to the emergence of villages inhabited by the growing class of day labourers (Courville, 1984).

Foreign observers were critical of peasant farming methods at the turn of the nineteenth century. These criticisms have been reiterated by Fernand Ouellet who argues that an agricultural crisis beginning in 1802 was caused by the conservative mentality of Quebec farmers (Ouellet, 1981). However, English agronomists who visited Canada failed to understand the particularities of colonial agriculture and the rationale behind peasant strategies. For example, English observers disapproved of the Canadian plough, but it was probably the kind best suited to the heavy soils of the St. Lawrence Valley. Canadian emphasis on cereal crops reduced manure production, and instead of spreading a limited amount across their land, farmers concentrated this fertilizer in the garden or on the more demanding crops such as potatoes.

The expansion of settlement onto marginal lands was an important phenomenon at the beginning of the nineteenth century. Here, work in the forest was as important as agriculture. Census statistics for the province as a whole do not account for these factors and give a misleading image of agricultural production. The opening of new regions also increased local food demand as the new settlers looked to more established areas to feed them, thereby lessening the amount of surplus available for export (Dechêne, 1986).

The absence of reliable statistical series on agricultural production—aggregates for the colony found in the infrequent census reports are often misleading (Courville, 1984)—complicates attempts to make overall assessments of Quebec agriculture during the preindustrial period. Although traditional historiography has stressed the self-sufficient nature of the peasantry and its failure to capitalize on market opportunities (Maurice Séguin, 1970; Ouellet, 1980), recent research has demonstrated that significant capital accumulation took place in the richer agricultural regions (Dessureault, 1986; Paquet et Wallot, 1986). Rather than a generalized crisis affecting all of Quebec's agriculture, the problems of the early nineteenth century reflect growing regional diversity. Farmers in the Montreal plain and near Quebec City, able to maintain viable holdings, were prosperous, but those in remoter regions as well as the growing rural proletariat suffered.

Daily Life

Rural life was bound to the seasons: from May to October the farm population ploughed, planted, mowed, weeded, and harvested; in the winter the people threshed the grain, marketed the surplus, and cleared new land. Farming necessitated a well-defined division of labour among family members. Men, with the help of their adolescent sons, performed the heaviest, outdoor physical labour: ploughing, cutting wood, removing stumps, ditching. Women mothered the children, cooked, cleaned, made everyday clothing, and worked in the garden and orchard and took care of livestock. Young children helped their mothers and thus provided an important source of labour in the peasant family. All family members from an early age participated in the harvesting.

Rural homes were normally built of squared logs, and in 1731 ninety-three percent of rural housing on Montreal Island was still of wood. Houses were small (about six metres by eight metres) and, with only one or two rooms, afforded little privacy. Toward the end of the French regime, stone houses became more widespread in the countryside, especially in the older parishes near Quebec and on the prosperous south shore of the St. Lawrence near Montreal. In more-recently settled areas wood dominated throughout the preindustrial era. When seventy-year-old German settler Johannes Monk decided he was too old to farm in 1810, his lease with Peter Buss of Sorel described his Missisquoi property in the townships as including "dwelling log house, old but in middling good repair, a framed barn (also in good repair)". Most farms would have a barn and a stable, while some areas had more specialized buildings such as sties, coops, sugar shacks, and icehouses.

During the seventeenth century, home interiors were austere and often smoky with the main furnishings consisting of a large curtained bed for the parents, a chest, a table with benches, cooking utensils, and straw mattresses for the children. In the summer, houses were infested by mosquitoes and flies; in the winter, family activity centred around an open fireplace. Living conditions improved in the eighteenth century as rural prosperity permitted the purchase of more elaborate furniture and imported textiles. With the beginning of iron production at les forges du Saint-Maurice in the 1740s, stoves became widespread and this had dramatic effects on heating and cooking.

Urban housing and living conditions varied sharply depending on class (Figure 3.6). Merchants, administrators, and the clergy lived in large stone houses, some of which were quite luxurious. Wall tapestries reduced the cold and dampness; expensive silverware graced dining tables, and parlours were furnished with several comfortable chairs. Parents had private bedrooms, and most children had beds, even if they had to share their rooms. Artisans' homes, on the other hand, approximated the size and appearance of those of the average peasant and, in addition, often contained their shops. Quebec City fire regulations, dictating that houses be built of stone, added to artisans' housing costs. In Montreal wood structures prevailed until after the Conquest; this apparently allowed artisans to spend more on furniture and clothes (Hardy, 1987).

With urban development at the turn of the nineteenth century, wooden buildings in the suburbs provided low-cost housing for the popular classes while the core areas increasingly became the preserve of the elite. Although some transient merchants, artisans, and day labourers were tenants (one third of Montreal's households rented their accomodation in 1741) most urban families owned their own homes (Massicotte, 1987: 52).

Figure 3.6 Montreal's rue Notre-Dame in 1785. This sketch illustrates one of Montreal's most important thoroughfares. For more than a century after its founding, Montreal's neighbourhoods were not segregated by class. By the end of the nineteenth century this was beginning to change. Although Notre-Dame street included some popular class housing, especially at its eastern end, most residents were merchants, officials, professionals, or important master artisans by 1785.

Merchants lived above their stores and warehouses and their businesses usually involved the labour of several family members. Freed from domestic chores by servants, wives might help their husbands keep books or operate the store; widows sometimes took over their husbands' businesses. Marie-Anne Barbel became one of the colony's most successful merchants after her husband, Louis Fornel, died in 1745. She expanded the business by establishing a pottery and, in 1748, obtained a monopoly over all trade on the North Shore from Charlevoix to Labrador.

Towns were dirty and unsanitary. Court records show that inhabitants permitted cattle and pigs to forage freely, that "speeding" horses were a threat, as were chamber pots that were emptied from upper-floor windows.

When ships arrived from Europe, Quebec City was filled with sailors anxious to celebrate. Paradoxically, while the garrisons served to enforce the public peace, soldiers were often the cause of criminal activity; André Lachance indicates that in the eighteenth century over 20 percent of criminals were members of the military.

Bread was the staple food in both France and Canada. An adult male consumed about 500 grams of bread a day. Bakers were closely supervised and had to supply loaves at fixed weights and prices. Meat, especially pork, was important in the peasant diet; families normally slaughtered pigs in the autumn and ate the smoked and salted pork through the winter while calves were sold to urban butchers. During Lent, cod and smoked eel became staples. When the fresh vegetables and fruit of summer were exhausted, families began using their supply of onions, cabbages, carrots, pickles, and various beans stored in a root cellar.

Although some beer was brewed in the colony, most men drank French wine and brandy while women usually drank water. With integration into the British empire, tea became a common drink and rum replaced wine and brandy among the popular classes. English preferences gave a new importance to beer and breweries, such as John Molson's (1786), developed by using local agricultural produce.

Education and Culture

While most of the elite and many artisans could read and write, the popular classes were largely illiterate. Allan Greer has estimated that fewer than 10 percent of peasants could sign their marriage act during the second half of the eighteenth century (Greer, 1978). Since there were no printing presses in New France, there were no newspapers, and books were imported from France. In the absence of public libraries, some religious colleges loaned their books to graduates.

After the Conquest, printing presses were imported and the first newspaper, the *Quebec Gazette*, started publication in 1764. Newspapers like the *Gazette* were published once or twice a week by printers who worked alone or with a journeyman or an apprentice, on hand-operated, wooden, flat-bed presses that printed about sixty copies an hour. Initially sales were low—the first issue of the *Quebec Gazette* sold 143 copies—and publishers relied on government advertising to survive.

By the beginning of the nineteenth century, however, newspapers such as the *Montreal Herald* were selling about 1000 copies of each issue. Montreal's first newspaper was the bilingual *Montreal Gazette*, established in 1778 by Fleury Mesplet, a Lyonnais printer who came to Montreal to encourage Canadian support for American independence. Suspended in 1779, the *Gazette* began publishing again in 1785. By 1822 it had become an English newspaper closely identified with anglophone merchants. The Quebec tradition of political journalism really started after 1805 when papers with clear political affiliations started publication. The *Quebec Mercury* represented the anglophone merchants and *Le Canadien* represented francophone reformers.

Education in preindustrial Quebec society was dominated by the established churches. During the French regime, the Jesuit College at Quebec provided males in the colonial elite with a post-secondary education comparable to that in a provincial French town. The Quebec Seminary ran the most important elementary school, the Petit Séminaire, and trained Canadian priests in its theological college. From its base in Montreal, the Congrégation de Notre-Dame dominated female education with elementary schools in the largest towns. After the Conquest, the disappearance of the Jesuit College was a serious blow to post-secondary education, which started to recover only at the beginning of the nineteenth century with the creation of a province-wide system of classical colleges with programs that emphasized literature, rhetoric, and philosophy.

One of the earliest of these classical colleges was the Collège de Montreal established by the Sulpicians using their French mother house as a model. After 1803, this elite boys' school with pleasant grounds on the western extremity of the city had 120 resident students who lived in fine large dormitories that featured indoor toilets. Each student paid substantial fees and provided his own bedding and silverware. Pupils rose at 5:30 a.m. and, after mass and breakfast, were in class by 8:00; the Sunday regime featured a procession by the student body to the parish church.

Despite the classical nature of these schools, scientific education was not completely absent. The Jesuits played an early and important role in teaching hydrography, and many missionaries showed considerable interest in American flora and fauna as well as ethnology. The leading scientific figures in New France's history were governor La Galissonière who amazed Swedish naturalist Pehr Kalm with the breadth of his scientific knowledge, and doctor Michel Sarrazin whose botanical observations and experiments received recognition from the French Academy of Sciences.

Professionals, such as notaries and lawyers, normally attended classical colleges and then entered into apprenticeship as a clerk to be trained in the profession. Family partnership or the transfer of a practice between father and son, the intimacy of pew, parish and school, and intermarriage cemented the bourgeoisie. The necessity of financing studies in a classical college, finding a professional willing to train a clerk, and having social contacts to establish a practice ensured that boys from the popular classes did not often enter the professions.

Since the Church opposed most theatre, opera, dancing, and much of the Enlightenment's literary production, culture was underdeveloped in the colony. Molière's controversial play *Le Tartuffe*, which poked fun at religious bigotry, was banned by the bishop in 1694 and in 1753 Bishop Pontbriand incited Catholics to shun impious books in circulation. Occasional plays were staged by college students but lay theatre, apart from performances by military officers, did not develop until the establishment of the Molson

Theatre in 1825. Through religious confraternities (for example, the Congrégation de la Sainte-Famille and the Congrégation des hommes) and by their
example, priests tried to control the morality of the francophone elite and
encourage the popular classes to opt for pious entertainment. Musical production was centred on religious ceremonies and the surviving scores produced in
this period all relate to church music.

Despite clerical censure, dancing was a favourite pastime of the colonial
elite in both the French and British regimes. French fashions featuring
"scandalous" low-cut dresses were imported for the winter social season of
balls and dinners given by leading members of the colonial administration.
When governor La Galissonière and intendant François Bigot visited Montreal during the pre-lenten carnival in 1749, members of the local elite outdid
each other. Madame Bégon describes dances lasting until six-thirty in the
morning and sermons threatening to withhold Easter communion from those
who dared participate.

Little is known of popular culture, although in the countryside fiddlers and
storytellers maintained the oral and folklore traditions of their French ancestors and added original elements of their own. Feast days—in addition to
Sundays there were thirty-seven of them before 1744 and twenty thereafter—
provided opportunities for processions and socializing. Few artisans or
peasants owned books, and pious literature, especially the lives of saints, was
dominant in private libraries of all social classes (Drolet, 1965; Dickinson,
1974). The advent of newspapers provided some cultural content but local
literary production did not become important until the mid-nineteenth
century.

Religiosity is difficult to measure. Since Protestants were not allowed in
New France, all inhabitants were officially Catholics and this monopoly gave
the church a strong influence over colonial cultural life. In the eighteenth
century some Protestant merchants, such as François Havy, came to the
colony but they could not marry or hold religious services. One must be wary
of generalizations based on Bishop de Saint-Vallier's criticism of the transgressions of the faithful and on letters from a couple of overbearing priests
underlining the deviant practices of their parishioners (Jaenen, 1976). The
standards set by a rigourous clergy could not have been met by even the most
pious population.

In all preindustrial societies, religion was a central feature of popular
culture. Pilgrimages, religious clauses in wills, low rates of illegitimacy, the
small number of children conceived out of wedlock, and participation in
religious confraternities (Cliche, 1978; Bates, 1986; Paquette et Bates, 1986;
Caulier, 1986) underlined the importance of religion (Figure 3.7). However,
evidence points to a sharp decline in religious fervor late in the eighteenth
century; for example, membership in religious confraternities suffered a long
period of decline from the 1760s until the 1820s. With the banning of the

Jesuits and the Recollets, the number of faithful per priest jumped from 350 in 1759 to 1075 in 1805 when almost a hundred parishes lacked a resident curate. Uncertainty over the right to collect tithes before 1774 encouraged evasion (Wallot, 1971). Although the influx of a few émigré priests during the French Revolution helped improve theological training, many priests were of marginal quality.

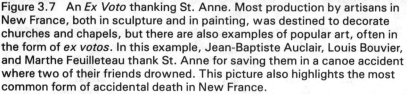

Figure 3.7   An *Ex Voto* thanking St. Anne. Most production by artisans in New France, both in sculpture and in painting, was destined to decorate churches and chapels, but there are also examples of popular art, often in the form of *ex votos*. In this example, Jean-Baptiste Auclair, Louis Bouvier, and Marthe Feuilleteau thank St. Anne for saving them in a canoe accident where two of their friends drowned. This picture also highlights the most common form of accidental death in New France.

Protestant religious practice centred on the established churches—the Church of England and the Kirk of Scotland—in urban centres. Much of the popular religion of the Eastern Townships, however, was brought by non-conformist American circuit riders using Vermont as a base. One such missionary made his rounds following a line of marked trees between settlements; he supported himself by farming in the summer and shoemaking in the winter (Smith, 1975: 81). Despite the official declaration of war in 1812, a border-area Methodist minister organized what he called a "love feast" with parishoners on both sides of the border holding hands during a service (Smith, 1975: 54). The construction of small Protestant churches throughout the region is testimony to the importance of non-conformist religion in pioneer life.

Criminal Activity in New France

The analysis of criminal activity provides unique insights into social relations. Court records from the French regime are fairly complete and have been used as the bases for several excellent studies. Those of the British period, in contrast, have received almost no archival treatment and are still largely unexploited.

New France is often depicted as a harmonious and peaceful society in which religion and strict morality dominated. However, criminal activity, particularly in the form of physical violence, did exist in the colony. André Lachance counted eighty-two cases of serious crimes like murder, dueling, and infanticide (suicide is included in Lachance's list since it was considered murder) during the period 1712-59. Brawls in taverns and barracks and among neighbours were commonplace and account for half the activity of criminal courts. In one case, two Quebec shoemakers, Louis Rousseau and Joseph Dugas, argued over a game of billiards. Dugas accused Rousseau of cheating and after exchanging insults, the two men attacked each other. Rousseau bit off two of Dugas' fingers and Dugas bit off part of Rousseau's cheek.

After physical violence, theft was the most prevalent crime. Although the poor occasionally stole food to feed themselves the most prevalent form of property crime was night-time break-and-entry into homes or stores.

Table 3.4 Criminal Activity in New France

	1650-99		1712-59	
Type of Crime	Number	Percentage	Number	Percentage
Crimes against the church	19	3.9	12	1.2
Crimes against the state	32	6.5	149	15.0
Murders	43	8.8	82	8.2
Assaults	141	28.7	357	36.0
Insults	54	11.0	83	8.4
Thefts	83	16.9	204	20.4
Sexual offences	105	21.4	55	5.5
Others	14	2.8	53	5.3

(Lachance, 1984)

Crimes against the state took two major forms: assault on judicial officials and forgery. For example, when bailiffs François Clesse and Pierre Courtin came to seize Joseph Ménard's property in 1737 as part of a judgment for debt, the two officials were threatened with an axe. Forgers were active in the colony; many were soldiers who made or altered card money.

Social protest was discouraged by denying people the right to congregate to discuss public issues except under the supervision of judicial officials. Occasionally, popular unrest took the form of mobs. In 1714, for example, the habitants (some armed with muskets) of the parish of Saint-Augustin twenty kilometres southwest of Quebec marched on the colonial capital to protest their poverty and the cost of imported goods. When troops barred their entrance to Quebec, they dispersed.

Crimes against the church such as blasphemy and witchcraft were the exception, but given the church's strict moral code, there were a significant number of sexual offences. Seduction was the most common form but other offences such as rape, adultery, and bigamy did occur. There are recorded cases of couples charged for co-habiting before marriage.

Women in Preindustrial Quebec

In preindustrial societies, collective rights and responsibilities, particularly those of the family, took precedence over individual rights. As we have seen, marriage normally involved a strategy of helping all children to obtain land. Parental permission to marry was required for minors (the age of majority in New France was twenty-five), and even when they were of majority age marriage that did not fit family strategy was frowned upon. The role of women must be seen from their vantage point as members of the wider family. While they often had considerable freedom in deciding their work, they were always subject to the imperatives of family life.

French law was based on a paternal and authoritarian ideology in which women were subordinate to their fathers and husbands. As minors, women were under paternal control and could not marry or enter into any other contract without permission. In marriage the male head exercised legal powers over the family, and his wife and children were to respect his authority. He was to provide for his family and was permitted to punish them physically; battered wives had to prove that their lives were in danger before being granted separation.

Although men managed their wives' estates, property that women brought into marriage or that they inherited could not be mortgaged or alienated without their permission. Occasionally, a married woman would file for a separation of estates on grounds that her husband was mismanaging her affairs or because of alcoholism and beatings. Divorce, of course, was prohibited by the church and couples were always considered married even though they lived apart (Savoie, 1987). Only adult women outside marriage, usually spinsters or widows, had any legal autonomy.

Despite these restrictions, some women used their legal rights to manage properties, to decide inheritances or to run businesses. For example, Marie-Anne Barbel, mentioned above, and Marie-Charlotte Denys de la Ronde, widow of the lieutenant governor of Montreal, Claude de Ramezay, became important businesswomen. When her husband died in 1724, Denys took over her husband's business, notably a Chambly sawmill that produced planks for the local market and for export. She and her unmarried daughter, Louise de Ramezay, were important landowners and also became involved in other industrial activities including a brickyard, a tile factory, and a tannery.

Women often helped in their husband's business and it was not unusual for a man to give his wife full legal powers to administer his affairs during an absence, or to represent him in court. Female religious communities, while under the bishop's authority, did have a certain amount of autonomy and offered women an avenue to exercise certain power.

This legal dependence was accentuated by the lack of employment opportunities for women in the colony. Women could not hold any official position and were barred from the professions. Clerical work, such as that of the scribes who worked in the intendant's offices, was a male occupation. Young girls were employed as domestic servants but married women were expected to work in the home. Widows from the popular classes often had to take in boarders, wash clothes, or, in some cases, become domestic servants in order to survive. As the notarial contract between Catherine Thibault and Pierre Couraud illustrates, destitute widows often hired their children out as servants.

> Catherine Thibault, widow of Nicolas Benoist, habitant of Rivière-des-Prairies, now living at the sieur de L'Espérance's house in Longue-Pointe, who has the care of four young girls and is without any financial means, has decided to place them in the domestic service of honest families to ensure their survival. To achieve this end, she promises to send her twelve year old daughter, Marie-Joseph Benoist, to serve Pierre Courraud de Lacoste for six years. Mister Lacoste promises to feed and clothe her, to bring her up in the Catholic religion. Marie-Joseph Benoist promises to serve her master faithfully and loyally and to look after his interests in all things. At the expiration of the contract, Mister Lacoste will give her a new set of clothes fitting her social condition, which will consist of a new coat, a new skirt, a pair of stockings, a pair of shoes, and six new shirts, along with all the other clothes that she might have.

Other widows tried to operate a small business such as a tavern; of twenty-three people fined for operating a tavern without a licence in Quebec in 1751, six were widows.

Conclusion

Preindustrial Quebec's social system was based on a farming population with reasonable access to new land. The peasant household was the basic unit of production, and although part of its surplus supported a seigneurial and clerical establishment, it was able to ensure its social reproduction. Through rural merchants, the peasant economy was linked to the larger market economy. Much of the colony's trade was based on the export of staple commodities for European markets.

Quebec remained a rural, preindustrial society across its first two centuries. Quebec City and Montreal were the only real urban centres and both had modest populations around 10 000 by the beginning of the nineteenth century. Montreal, for example, at the end of the Napoleonic Wars was a city without large public buildings: few were over two stories and its most important church, the original Notre Dame, was small, unimpressive and squarely blocked a main thoroughfare. Its visible elite from the garrison, merchant houses, seminary, and royal bureaucracy lived cheek-by-jowl with the artisans and day labourers, their taverns and boarding houses within the confines of the stone fortifications.

The city's grain, firewood, and vegetables came largely from the island of Montreal; some of the city's flour was ground at Pointe Sainte-Anne whose seigneurial mill was in sight of the port. Except in winter when foreign trade was stopped by ice, timber, fur and wheat staples passed through the city. However, aside from the port, counting houses and warehouses, much of the city's flavour, its smells and sounds were part of daily life: carters, hay, market odours, woodsmoke, human and animal waste, stagnant and dead water, hawkers, anvils, soldiers tramping, and church bells. Wood remained the most important fuel and building material; the horse, the human, wind and water produced the city's energy.

Away from Montreal and Quebec City, regions developed with little interference from central political or judicial authority. In the Richelieu Valley, peasants, as they had for the past century, produced wheat, peas, and oats primarily for family consumption with surpluses going to pay the seigneur, the church, and the local merchant. Remote areas like the Gaspé had no land connections to Quebec City and remained in the orbit of Jersey and London.

Women had essential roles in the provision of shelter, food, drink, clothes, and in agricultural work and transportation in these preindustrial, locally-defined economies. Dressmaking was the most important female artisan trade while the wives of shopkeepers, butchers, and artisans supervised apprentices, books, stocks, and sales. Girls from the popular classes worked as domestics in bourgeois homes while widows retained their husband's shops and trades or found work in the mongering, victualing, hawking, peddling, millinery, tavernkeeping, ferryboat, boarding house, or innkeeping professions.

Bibliography

Preindustrial Quebec
Among the better general introductions to preindustrial Quebec are R.C. Harris and John Warkentin, *Canada before Confederation*. Along with works

cited in the previous chapter, readers should consult Marcel Trudel, *The Beginnings of New France* and Dale Miquelon, *New France, 1701-1744*. André Lachance's *La vie urbaine en Nouvelle-France* gives an excellent overview of urban life. The first volume of the *Historical Atlas of Canada* is also essential.

The Programme de recherches en démographie historique of the Université de Montréal has played a leading role in demographic studies in Canada. Along with Jacques Henripin's pioneering *La population canadienne au début du XVIIIe siècle*, Hubert Charbonneau's *Vie et mort de nos ancêtres* is the best introduction to this science in the context of New France.

The Staple Theory

The importance of staples has been long debated. Work on the fisheries has regained vigour with the studies of François Brière ("Pêche et politique à Terre-Neuve au XVIIIe siècle: la France véritable gagnante du traité d'U-trecht", "Le commerce triangulaire entre les ports Terre-Neuviers français, les pêcheries d'Amérique du Nord et Marseille au 18e siècle: nouvelles perspectives"), and Laurier Turgeon ("Pour une histoire de la pêche: le marché de la morue à Marseille au XVIIIe siècle", "Pour redécouvrir notre 16e siècle: les pêches à Terre-Neuve d'après les archives notariales de Bordeaux"). The fur trade has received more attention. Harold Innis, *The Fur Trade in Canada*, is essential and is complemented by a recent debate between William John Eccles, "A Belated Review of Harold Adams Innis's *The Fur Trade in Canada*", and Hugh M. Grant, "One Step Forward, Two Steps Back: Innis, Eccles and the Canadian Fur Trade". W.T. Easterbrook and M.H. Watkins, *Approaches to Canadian Economic History*, is also useful.

Commerce

Preindustrial commercial enterprises have not drawn as much interest as their later counterparts, but Dale Miquelon's *Dugard of Rouen* is an excellent case study of colonial commerce in the eighteenth century. Equally important is James Pritchard's article on shipping, "The pattern of French Colonial Shipping to Canada before 1760". Jacques Mathieu's *Le commerce entre la Nouvelle-France et les Antilles au XVIIIe siècle* analyses inter-colonial trade. The fur trade has been treated by José Igartua, *The Merchants and Négociants of Montréal, 1750-1775: A Study in Socio-Economic History*, and Gratien Allaire, *Les engagés de la fourrure, 1701-1745: une étude de leur motivation*. Lately, much attention has been paid to rural merchants, notably by Louis Michel, "Un marchand rural en Nouvelle-France: François-Augustin Bailly de Messein, 1709-1771".

Industrial Production

The best English language study of preindustrial Quebec artisans is Peter Moogk's *The Craftsmen of New France*. Jean-Pierre Hardy and Thierry Ruddel's *Les apprentis artisans à Québec, 1660-1815* includes changes wrought by the introduction of British practice after the Conquest. Large enterprises have been covered by Jacques Mathieu's *La construction navale royale à Québec, 1739-1759* and by Cameron Nish's *François-Etienne Cugnet. Entrepreneur et entreprises en Nouvelle-France.*

Peasant Society

Peasant society has been best treated by Louise Dechêne in her *Habitants et marchands de Montréal au XVIIe siècle* and her "Observations sur l'agriculture du Bas-Canada au début du XIXe siècle" is brilliant. Fernand Ouellet has had an important impact on the study of this period through his *Economic and Social History of Quebec.* Along with Allan Greer's book cited in the previous chapter, readers should refer to Christian Dessureault's *Les fondements de la hierarchie sociale au sein de la paysannerie: le cas de Saint-Hyacinthe, 1760-1815.*

Religion

Cornelius Jaenen's overview of religion in New France cited in the previous chapter and Jean-Pierre Wallot's "La religion catholique et les Canadiens au début du XIXe siècle" should be tempered by Marie-Aimé Cliche, *La religion populaire dans le gouvernement de Québec sous le Régime français d'après la pratique des actes surérogatoires*, and Brigitte Caulier, *Les confréries de dévotion à Montréal du 17e au 19e siècles*, which are less impressionistic.

Women

Women's history has not yet fully embraced the preindustrial period. The attempt to reconstruct a woman's view of history in the Collectif Clio's *Histoire des femmes au Québec* is not very successful for the preindustrial period. More provocative is Jan Noel, "New France: Les femmes favorisées". Lilianne Plamondon, "A Businesswoman in New France: Marie-Anne Barbel, the Widow Fornel," gives an example of a businesswoman's career.

Economy and
Society
in Transition,
1816-1885

At the beginning of the nineteenth century, Lower Canada was predominantly preindustrial. Its agricultural and artisanal production was based largely on the family and goods were consumed locally. Montreal, which was to become the pivot of industrial capitalist society in Quebec later in the nineteenth century, was still a preindustrial city (Figure 4.1).

During the nineteenth century Quebec went through the transition to industrial capitalism. Industrial production progressively replaced artisanal forms; market-oriented agriculture increased; and capital became increasingly important in determining social relations. In 1816 small-scale artisanal activities using muscle power dominated. By the 1890s the share of manufacturing in the Gross National Product was almost as high as it was in the 1980s (Pomfret, 1981: 123).

In Quebec, the value of manufactured goods rose from $600 000 in 1851 to $15 000 000 in 1861 and to $104 660 000 in 1881. In that year, the Grand Trunk Railway had 2904 employees, and some 14 000 people in Montreal were directly dependent on the railway (Hamelin et Roby, 1971: 267). Productivity per worker increased dramatically, and an increasing percentage of industrial production was for home consumption: the growing importance of meat packing, sugar refining, and the factory production of butter, cheese, bread, cigars, and textiles emphasize that family self-sufficiency in certain types of clothing and food was declining.

The transition to industrial capitalism, much more than the use of steam or new technology, brought fundamental change to traditional work and social relations. For those who were able to accumulate capital, the period was one of growing wealth, power, and social privilege. To defend their power, those with authority were able to use the growing civil powers of the state, changing police and judicial powers, ethnic divisions, and the ideological and institutional influence of the church.

For pioneers, peasants, wage labourers, and widows, survival was often a daily struggle of finding work and making ends meet. Amidst ethnic conflicts, epidemics, and strikes, resistance to the fundamental changes in work and social relations can be discerned. This opposition took various forms. Sometimes it was organized into riots, strikes, and political manifestations. Sometimes resisting authority meant individual actions of arson, aggression, or simply refusing to attend church or to pay tithes, taxes or seigneurial dues. None of these acts were particularly new but represented, instead, an ongoing process of social struggle.

In the area of work, we can see the effect of the transition on the work site, on the work process, on the gender and age of the labour force, on certain artisanal skills, and on the ownership of tools. In the financial sector, the transition brought to the fore new banking and insurance institutions for which the accumulation and investment of capital were more important than the traditional exchange functions of banks.

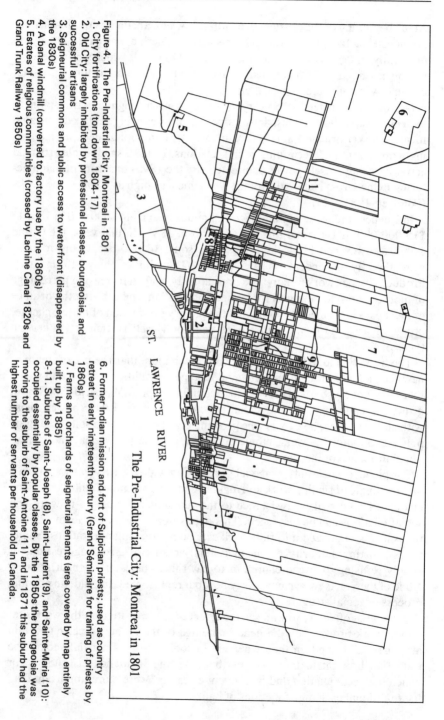

Figure 4.1 The Pre-Industrial City: Montreal in 1801

1. City fortifications (torn down 1804-17)
2. Old City: largely inhabited by professional classes, bourgeoisie, and successful artisans
3. Seigneurial commons and public access to waterfront (disappeared by the 1830s)
4. A banal windmill (converted to factory use by the 1860s)
5. Estates of religious communities (crossed by Lachine Canal 1820s and Grand Trunk Railway 1850s)
6. Former Indian mission and fort of Sulpician priests; used as country retreat in early nineteenth century (Grand Séminaire for training of priests by 1860s)
7. Farms and orchards of seigneurial tenants (area covered by map entirely built up by 1885)
8-11. Suburbs of Saint-Joseph (8), Saint-Laurent (9), and Sainte-Marie (10): occupied essentially by popular classes. By the 1850s the bourgeoisie was moving to the suburb of Saint-Antoine (11) and in 1871 this suburb had the highest number of servants per household in Canada.

ST. LAWRENCE RIVER

The Pre-Industrial City: Montreal in 1801

Quebec's institutional structure—its state bureaucracy and social system, its land and mortgage system, its land law and civil code—took new forms during the transition. Growing public subsidies for roads, canals, and railways; the formation of a federal state in 1867; and implementation of the National Policy a decade later were clear indications that, by the end of this transition period, Quebec was an integral part of a larger Canadian state.

The transition was also characterized by significant changes in social relations. The rebellions of 1837-38, the sacking of the parliament in Montreal in 1849, the religious riots of the 1850s, and the strikes and development of unions in the 1850s and 1860s were manifestations of conflict inherent in the transition. The re-alignment of the elite in the 1840s, the developing strength of the Catholic clergy, and the subordination of seigneurs and many merchants emphasized the importance of the emerging alliance among Quebec's religious, political, and industrial capitalist leadership. At another level of the social scale, women in the popular classes, landless peasants, children, immigrants, and the urban unskilled formed distinct elements in a growing Quebec proletariat.

During the nineteenth century, bourgeois democracy was established in Lower Canada. Ancien Régime institutions such as the established churches, authoritarian government, the seigneurial landholding system, and the preindustrial legal system, gave way to elected officials, parliamentary institutions, new bureaucracies, and a new civil code and judicial jurisdictions. The whole was legitimized by an ideology that emphasized the individual, freedom of property and contract, and the competitive qualities of capitalism.

The transition was not an even process. Some rural regions remained peripheral to the market circuits. Other regions were characterized by urbanization, higher production, and specialization for specific markets. Industrial production, as opposed to artisans' work, was introduced at different times in various trades. At large construction sites, shipyards, foundries, breweries and distilleries, industrial production occurred early in the century, while the artisanal mode remained strong much later in other sectors. In leather, for example, different modes of production co-existed—artisanal production, the putting-out system, and factory production. And, as we shall see, steam power, even at the end of the century, was less important than power generated by watermills.

The years 1816 and 1885 serve as useful parameters for the transition period. The end of the Napoleonic wars marked both the beginning of renewed official interest in the colony and of heavy immigration from the British Isles. The year 1816 was dramatic in rural life: the worst harvest in memory underlined the problems of Lower Canadian agriculture. Heavy immigration from the British Isles heralded a new demographic pattern. It also coincided with developing pressure by industrial producers for the reform of seigneurial and legal structures.

At the other end of the period, the metropolitan dominance of Montreal is evident. The 1880s were the decade of the Royal Commission on the Relations of Labour and Capital, Quebec's first factory laws, and ongoing strength of the Knights of Labour. The 1880s also coincided with Montreal's solidifying position as corporate headquarters for the country's major transportation, financial and industrial enterprises. The execution of Riel in 1885 and the growing significance of the National Policy emphasized to Quebec the political, ideological, and industrial implications of the federal state established in 1867.

In preindustrial Canada, merchants, seigneurs, the upper clergy, and colonial administrators formed the elite. During the transition, they were superseded and, in some cases, co-opted by industrial capitalists. Industrial producers objected to the seigneurial system and to impediments to freedom of property and labour. They also pushed for a strong centralized state, abundant labour and cheap food, new canal and rail facilities, and protection for their capital and manufactured goods.

Demography

Despite nineteenth-century British immigration, Quebec remained overwhelmingly francophone as the province's overall population quadrupled from 340 000 in 1815 to 1 359 027 in 1881 (Figure 4.2). Urbanization was a major demographic factor. Dramatic increases in the size of Montreal and in the number of small urban centres contributed to reduce the relative importance of the rural population. Montreal's population rose from some 9000 in 1815 to over 50 000 at mid-century. Serge Courville has charted the early nineteenth-century growth of villages in the seigneurial zone. In 1831, 208 villages, concentrated in the Montreal region, represented 44 108 of the rural population of 392 485, while Montreal, Trois-Rivières, and Quebec had a total

Table 4.1 The Population of Lower Canada, 1815-1881

Year	Total Population	Urban Population	Urban Percentage	Emigration (previous decade)
1815	340 000	c 30 000		
1822	427 000			
1831	553 134	56 668	11.1	
1844	697 000			
1851	890 261			35 000
1861	1 111 566			70 000
1871	1 191 516	271 851	22.8	100 000
1881	1 359 027	378 512	27.8	120 000

(Bernier et Boily, 1986; Lavoie, 1972)

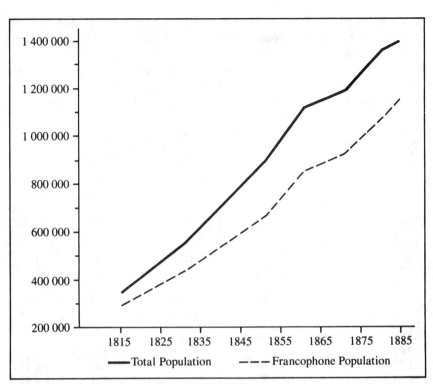

Figure 4.2   Quebec Population, 1815-1885

population of 56 668 (Courville, 1984). The percentage of the Quebec population that was urban rose from 11.2 percent in 1831 to 27.8 percent in 1881.

The growth of Quebec's francophone population was due to natural increase. With stable birth and death rates, the French Catholic population rose from 288 000 in 1815 to 929 817 in 1871. The number of births per Catholic marriage (including anglophone Catholics) was 7.1 in 1816 to 1820 and 6.7 in 1876 to 1880. The significance of these rates must not be exaggerated, for they are comparable with the United States and other parts of Canada. In 1871, for example, the Quebec birth rate was lower than that of Ontario. It was only after this period that Ontario's birth rate began dropping faster than Quebec's. Nor did the death rate change significantly over the period. The annual number of deaths per 1000 Catholic inhabitants was 24.5 in 1816 to 1820 and 24.3 in 1876 to 1880 (Charbonneau, 1973).

The size and heterogeneity of the anglophone population increased rapidly. In chapter three it was clear that immigration from the United States was the dominant factor in the growth of the anglophone population before the Napoleonic Wars. American settlement was concentrated in Montreal and along the border from the counties of Huntingdon, Missisquoi, and Beauharnois into the Eastern Townships. After the Napoleonic Wars, agricultural depression and industrial crises in the British Isles brought new immigrants. Between 1815 and 1851, almost 800 000 British and Irish immigrants were recorded at the port of Quebec. Although most of these were en route to Upper Canada and the United States, some 50 000 did settle in Lower Canada.

Table 4.2 Arrivals at the port of Quebec, 1829-1851

From	England	Ireland	Scotland	Total
1829	3 500	9 600	2 600	15 700
1830	6 700	18 300	2 400	27 400
1831	10 300	34 100	5 300	49 700
1832	17 400	28 200	5 500	51 100
1833	5 100	12 000	4 100	21 200
1834	6 700	19 200	4 500	30 400
1835	3 000	7 100	2 100	12 200
1836	12 100	12 500	2 200	26 800
1837	5 500	14 500	1 500	21 500
1838	700	1 400	500	2 600
1839	1 500	5 100	400	7 000
1840	4 500	16 200	1 100	21 800
1841	5 900	18 300	3 500	27 700
1842	12 100	25 500	6 000	43 600
1843	6 400	9 700	5 000	21 100
1844	7 600	9 900	2 200	19 700
1845	8 800	14 200	2 100	25 100
1846	9 100	21 000	1 600	31 700
1847	31 000	54 310	3 700	89 010
1848	6 000	16 500	3 000	25 500
1849	8 900	23 100	4 900	36 900
1850	9 800	17 900	2 800	30 500
1851	9 600	22 381	7 000	38 981
Total	192 200	410 991	74 000	677 191

(Ouellet, 1981)

This immigration raised the percentage of anglophones in the total population from 15 percent in 1815 to a high of 24.3 percent in 1861; thereafter, anglophones began a slow decline as a percentage of the Quebec population. With concentrations in the Gaspé, the Eastern Townships, the Ottawa Valley, and the urban centres, in 1871 anglophones represented over 38 percent of the population of the island of Montreal and 20 percent of the Quebec population. Of the province's population, 5.9 percent was English in origin, 4.2 percent Scottish, and 10.4 percent Irish. Only a handful of these anglophone immigrants were gentry or, as was the case with Hugh Allan and William Price, the offspring of prominent British merchant families.

Most immigrants arrived in the unhealthy and overcrowded holds of timber ships deadheading back to Canadian ports. Wily shipowners and captains managed to cram as many as eighty or ninety people in spaces about eight metres square. James Hunt, an Irish immigrant on the brigantine *William*, which brought ninety-seven adults and forty-four children from Dublin to Quebec City in 1823, testified that he embarked with his pregnant wife and two relatives:

> that neither he or his family had a berth excepting his wife, who was nearly starved with cold (sic), and was permitted for three nights to sleep in the cabin; that during the first ten nights, they were obliged to sleep between the berths; and at other times in the long boat upon deck. For the last three weeks of the passage, he says they lay in the hold on some ropes, where the child he had with him died, and where his wife was delivered of another.

Infectious diseases like typhus, measles, and cholera were often carried on immigrant ships. Thousands died at sea or at the quarantine station at Grosse Ile near Quebec City. Epidemics spread to the general populace. Of Lower Canadian cholera epidemics in 1832, 1834, 1845, 1851, 1854, and 1867, the worst, the Asian cholera of 1832, was introduced from the immigrant ship, the *Voyageur*. There were 2723 cholera-related deaths in Quebec City in 1832, 2547 in Montreal, and an undetermined number in the countryside (Dechêne et Robert, 1979; Bilson, 1980: 179).

While Don Akenson has emphasized those Irish who became rural inhabitants, it is clear that signficant numbers became the rough labour of industrial society (Akenson, 1984). About 5 percent of Irish immigrants stayed in Quebec; 15 percent went to Upper Canada where most settled in rural areas; and the rest emigrated to the United States. The Irish who did stay in the ports of Montreal and Quebec City became an important source of wage labour. A significant factor in Lower Canadian ethnic politics was the fact that by 1831 over 40 percent of the day labourers in Montreal were anglophones.

Anglophones took on growing economic importance. As contractors, bankers, and industrial producers, they were often favoured in competition for British government, military or institutional contracts. Anglophone merchants dominated the Lower Canadian banking system as well as Canadian circuits in international finance. Foreign capital in Quebec was predominantly British, but American capital became increasingly important by the 1880s. In the transportation and manufacturing sectors, many of the engineers, entrepreneurs, patent-holders, and importers of technology were American and British.

The growing anglophone presence in certain regions contributed to the development of Quebec nationalism, particularly in the years before 1837-38. Francophone professionals in Montreal, merchants and peasants in the Richelieu Valley, and forest and river labourers in the Ottawa Valley were rankled by the expansion of anglophone communities and by the growing separateness and vociferousness of anglophones. Their power in local economies added to this hostility. The case of Stephen Tucker in the seigneury of Petite-Nation is an example. This seigneury was overwhelmingly francophone and Catholic, but ninety-six of the 145 debt contracts signed before a local notary during 1837-45 recognized debts owing to Tucker, an anglophone general merchant and sawmill operator. In the mid-1840s Tucker, who was rumoured to have offered $40 to Catholics who would convert to the Baptist Church, owned forty-four properties. Most of these were repossessed from debtors among the francophone peasantry (Baribeau, 1983: 136).

Nor were francophones happy with the privileges and settlement policies of monopolistic land companies like the British American Land Company. Privately, the upper clergy accused the British of swamping Lower Canada with its landless and cholera-ridden proletariat.

Emigration had a major impact on the demographic changes in industrializing Quebec. With travel facilitated by railway networks, much of the surplus rural population sought work in the industrial centres of Quebec or New England. Bruno Ramirez has argued that emigration became a more attractive family strategy than colonization. Families sent out members to specific New England towns that had parish links to their community. Emigrants from the Berthier area near Montreal favoured Rhode Island mill towns while Rimouski emigrants preferred southern Massachusetts industrial communities like Fall River.

In contrast to this family and community unity in emigration to the United States, colonization strategies within Lower Canada differed greatly. While the Lac Saint-Jean area was settled by organized colonization societies, settlement along the Ottawa Valley was characterized by a greater diversity among its francophone settlers. From 1815-54, of 151 francophones in Petite-Nation whose origins can be traced, twenty-six had already lived for a period in Upper Canada, eleven were from urban centres, and the remaining 124 were from fifty-three different Lower Canadian rural localities (Baribeau, 1980: 39).

In comparison to settlers, industrial workers earned immediate cash and, thanks to railways, often had easier access to their home communities. Another factor important to family economic strategies was that women and children were valuable wage workers in mill towns while seasonal forest labour in colonization areas was essentially male. Between 1840 and 1880 some 325 000 Quebecers, overwhelmingly francophone, emigrated to the United States.

The overcrowding, migration, and new forms of work inherent in the transition had profound effects on family life and social relations. The number of illegitimate births in Quebec City increased sharply, especially in the 1860s (Figure 4.3). Postponed marriages and illegitimacy are also suggested by

statistics on the number of newborn babies abandoned at Montreal's Grey
Nuns Foundling Hospital, even if it is not clear how many of these were
abandoned by married women or by rural women who came to Montreal to
have their babies.

Table 4.3 Children Abandoned at the Grey Nuns Foundling Hospital in
Montreal, 1820-40

Year	Abandoned	Number Placed in Families	Number Who Died
1820	64	6	55
1825	98	3	88
1830	108	9	98
1835	131	13	108
1840	152	8	135

(Gossage, 1983)

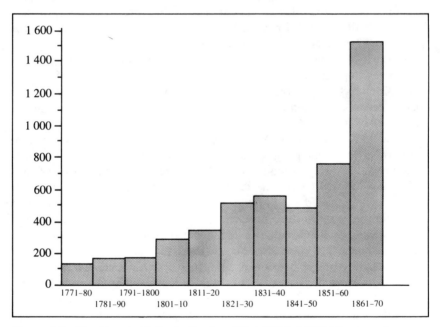

Figure 4.3   Illegitimate Births in Quebec City, 1771-1870 (*Census of
Canada*, 1871, V: 359).

By 1871 the native population represented only 6988 of Quebec's total
population of 1 191 516. Although their status, number, and influence were
increasingly marginal to white society in Quebec, their work experience in
industrializing society was often parallel to that of white workers. Like other

forest workers in the Ottawa Valley, the Mohawks, established at Kahnawake since the l670s, combined garden-farming with work in the fur and timber trade. Esteemed across Canada as canoemen, transport workers and packers in the fur trade, Kahnawake men were later highly-skilled river drivers and timber rafters. On the Lake of Two Mountains Reserve, the Seminary of Montreal had 200 homes occupied by Mohawks and Algonquins who lived as tenant farmers or forest workers.

Urbanization

From the perspective of the staples trades, Montreal's future was not bright in the first decades of the nineteenth century. The city was losing the fur trade and its political influence in the West to the Hudson's Bay Company while the square-timber trade of the St. Lawrence was concentrated in Quebec City. The fact that Montreal grew steadily across the period of the transition forces us to look beyond a staple interpretation of Canadian history.

Growth was mainly due to the city's expanding industries that provided work for both the skilled and unskilled. In 1881 Montreal and its suburbs produced 52 percent of the value of Quebec's manufactured goods while Quebec City accounted for only 9.3 percent (Hamelin et Roby, 1971: 298). Montreal's population grew from 10 000 in 1816, to 57 715 in 1851, and 140 747 in 1881. Its metropolitan dominance was enhanced by developing waterpower, canal and rail facilities, and its concentration of both financial and industrial capital.

In the 1840s and 1850s, Montreal's political elite used expanding local institutions like municipal government, the Board of Trade, and the Harbour Commission to foster a transcontinental dimension to their bailiwick. Politicians such as George-Etienne Cartier, who had clear links to industrial capitalists, obtained the improvement of the ship channel downstream from Montreal to deep water and of upriver routes such as the Lachine Canal to American and Upper Canadian hinterlands. Construction of the Grand Trunk Railway and the building of the Victoria Bridge at Montreal gave the city the province's only bridge over the St. Lawrence, and accentuated Montreal's dominance of railway networks. In 1885 Montreal was the terminus for international and continental railway systems such as the Grand Trunk, Canadian Pacific, Vermont Central, and Delaware and Hudson. Railways stimulated industrial production. The Montreal area accounted for 40 percent of Canadian production in the food and beverage sector and the same percentage in the production of transport equipment.

Quebec City fared badly in the transition to industrial capitalism because it was dependent on shipbuilding and the square-timber trade, both of which declined in the second half of the century (Figure 4.4). Quebec City's economic health was further threatened by Britain's abolition of Baltic timber duties, by rising American demand for sawn lumber that was shipped on north-south canals and railways, and by the Reciprocity Treaty of 1854, which permitted the free entry of lumber into the United States. As a result, Quebec City's population grew only slowly and its ocean port declined. Even before 1867 its political and administrative functions were in decline and in 1871 the British garrison was removed.

Figure 4.4 The Anse-au-Foulon timber cove and shipyard. During the first half of the nineteenth century, Quebec City lived by the timber trade. Large rafts coming from the Ottawa were beached at Sillery before the square timber was loaded on board ships or used in shipbuilding. After the 1860s, exports and the building of wooden ships declined dramatically: from an average of over 18 million board feet of square timber in 1862-66, exports declined to just over 7 million board feet in 1882-86.

A major seaport without a bridge over the St. Lawrence, the city was isolated from canal and rail networks. As early as 1844, a Maine newspaper, the *Eastern Angus*, predicted Quebec City's death knell as a commercial or industrial city.

> Quebec has for many years ceased to be a place of any considerable business . . .
> and though a place of great attractions for its military fortifications and
> historical incidents, its junctive position in the midst of a mountainous
> region, renders it comparatively forbidding as a place of residence, and with
> the exception of its lumber trade, its business is still on the decrease. Nine
> tenths at least of all the travel to, and from Quebec is by the way of Montreal.

Short History of Quebec

A number of Quebec towns became regional industrial and service centres: Trois-Rivières had a population of 7570 in 1871, Sherbrooke 4432, Hull 3800, Saint-Hyacinthe 3746, and Saint-Jean 3022. In 1850, Quebec had fourteen towns with a population of 1000 to 5000, compared to thirty-three towns in Ontario; in 1870 the figure had risen to twenty-two in Quebec and sixty-nine in Ontario.

Table 4.4 Number of Towns in Quebec and Ontario, 1850-70

	Quebec		Ontario	
	1850	1870	1850	1870
Town Size				
25 000 +	2	2	1	2
5000-25 000	0	3	4	10
1000-5000	14	22	33	69

(McCallum, 1980: 55)

Trois-Rivières illustrates a preindustrial service town changing into an industrial city. In 1852 when it was given diocesan status, Trois-Rivières had a population of only 5000. In that year George Baptist built his sawmill in the Saint-Maurice Valley and the government began constructing sluices and booms to prevent logs from being smashed by the falls and rapids of the Saint-Maurice. This development of its hinterland gave the town new regional importance. In 1865 the 182 oceangoing ships that docked in Trois-Rivières loaded over 20 000 000 board feet of lumber for export to British, American, and Latin American markets. In 1878 a railway was built up the Saint-Maurice River and by 1881 Trois-Rivières had rail connections to Montreal and Quebec City. The population of Trois-Rivières grew from 4900 to 8600 during the period from 1851 to 1881, and in 1871 the city had 1018 people working in manufacturing. Industrialization accelerated in the 1880s with the opening of a biscuit factory, woodworking shops, ironworks, and shoe manufacturing.

Table 4.5 Industrial Activities in Trois-Rivières, 1871

Sector	Number of Manufacturers	Number of Employees
1. Food, drink and tobacco	14	25
2. Leather	24	193
3. Textiles, hats, clothing	30	206
4. Wood, furniture	25	454
5. Metal	21	91
6. Other	10	49
	124	1018

(Hardy et Séguin, 1984: 182)

Transportation

Transportation was a central factor in Quebec's transition to industrial capitalism. In 1809, brewer John Molson launched Canada's first steam vessel, the *Accomodation*, and it transformed shipping between Montreal and Quebec City. The paddle-steamer *Royal William* was constructed in 1831 at Quebec City. Powered by a 200-horsepower engine built in Montreal, it was the first merchant vessel to cross the Atlantic largely under steam. Steamships and railways brought new dimensions of industrial production, capital, company organization, and labour concentrations. However, the transportation revolution in the St. Lawrence Valley contrasted sharply with transportation conditions in more remote regions, and, as late as 1885, much of the province was served by only rough roads and sailshipping.

As a major port for ocean vessels, Montreal tried to protect the St. Lawrence system as well as its Upper Canadian and American midwest trade against New England and middle Atlantic competitors. Completion of the 605-kilometre Erie Canal in 1825 was a particular threat, but by the late 1840s Montreal's access to the interior had been improved along the Richelieu, Ottawa, and St. Lawrence River axis. The Lachine Canal, originally completed in the 1820s, was rebuilt in the 1840s with new locks and turning basins, and the Beauharnois, Cornwall, and Welland canals were constructed. These developments permitted ships to run from Montreal to Lake Ontario and beyond.

Coastal and inland trading along the St. Lawrence and Atlantic were also dependent on transportation networks. Although anglophone merchants dominated the trade to Upper Canada, raft towing and trade downstream from Montreal was dominated in the early period by francophones. The Richelieu Company was established in the 1840s by local merchants such as Jacques-Félix Sincennes of Sorel. Trading to important riverfront agricultural, service and sawmill communities such as Saint-Césaire, Beloeil, Saint-Denis, and Saint-Jean, as well as shipping lumber to American markets via the Richelieu/Lake Champlain system, made the company flourish. After 1853, declining trade on the Richelieu, construction of the Grand Trunk Railway, and the increasing dominance of integrated steamship systems led to the transfer of company control to Montreal and its incorporation into a larger steamboat and rail network.

Even during the heyday of canal construction, attention was shifting to rail transportation. Steam engines rolling on iron rails permitted freight to move on a year-round basis. At the same time, new engineering techniques opened regions inaccessible by water routes. Railways attracted the attention of both merchant and industrial capital, permitting access to new markets and resources and extending their owners' political, financial, and industrial influence.

The first major inter-provincial and international railways were proposed in the 1840s, and in 1846 railways were chartered to join Montreal and the ice-free port of Portland, Maine. When completed in 1860, the Grand Trunk Railway extended from Sarnia, Ontario, through Montreal and the Eastern Townships to Portland. The Grand Trunk continued to expand its network on the south shore of the St. Lawrence, and by 1860 had extended its line to Rivière-du-Loup. In 1876 the Intercolonial linked Montreal to the Maritimes via the Matapedia Valley and New Brunswick's north shore.

Construction of the Grand Trunk Railway was much more than an isolated engineering and entrepreneurial feat. Its significance for the Montreal economy can be seen from its influence on independent carters. The hauling of goods and people was an essential ingredient in the urban economy and carting was an important nineteenth-century occupation. The transformation of carting shows changes both in the labour process and in power relations in industrializing Montreal. As independent commodity producers who traditionally competed among themselves, the carters faced a new scale and form of competition from the centralized industrial capital that accompanied canal and rail transportation. In 1861 some 70 percent of Montreal's 1188 carters were still independent operators owning their own horses and carts. A minority had become wage labourers and drove for employers with large stables and fleets.

Figure 4.5 Victoria Bridge. Plans for the Victoria Bridge were drawn up by Robert Stephenson, the bridge engineer and son of the inventor of the steam locomotive. Work began in 1854 with the crucial centre span being erected in the winter of 1858-59. Scaffolds were built on the ice, and work continued around the clock to assemble the bridge before spring breakup. Opening of the bridge in December 1859 gave Montreal access to the ice-free port of Portland, Maine.

The opening of the Lachine Canal in the 1820s had already deprived carters of the important Montreal-Lachine route. By mid-century, access to railway stations was the central issue to assure survival of the independent Montreal carter. At first, the Grand Trunk Railway stimulated local carters who hauled goods from the port to the railway depot in Pointe Saint-Charles, or across the St. Lawrence ice, until completion of the Victoria Bridge in 1859 (Figure 4.5). However, with the rationalization of Grand Trunk operations, an exclusive contract was awarded in 1863 to John Shedden. His cartage company had already expanded rapidly in Upper Canada through a monopoly to serve certain Grand Trunk stations. The Montreal contract that gave Shedden rate privileges in delivering and picking up goods at the Grand Trunk's Montreal depots and station had an immediate effect. When Shedden hired twenty-four carters and built a stable for sixty-four horses, independent carters protested that the contract jeopardized their livelihood.

In September 1864 the carters went on strike, accusing the Grand Trunk of violating its charter by instituting a monopoly. Although the carters were well-organized and could paralyze transportation in Montreal, they did not rally significant political support from merchants or municipal authorities. When they ended their strike a few days later, their cause was effectively lost while the power of the Grand Trunk and its forms of business were reinforced (Heap, 1977).

Construction of the Grand Trunk and its heavy subsidization by the Canadian government greatly disadvantaged other communities, particularly in the Quebec City and Trois-Rivières regions along the North Shore of the St. Lawrence. Although Quebec had 1235 km of railway in 1871, almost none served the North Shore. A rail trip from Quebec City to Montreal in 1854 took twenty-one hours and entailed crossing the St. Lawrence by ferry at Lévis and (until completion of the Victoria Bridge in 1859) again at Montreal.

Lack of capital, fierce hostility from the Grand Trunk, and the weakness of Quebec City and the North Shore economy hindered construction of the North Shore railways. In addition, the combination of the province's weak position in the federal state created by Confederation and the strong alliance between the central government and the Grand Trunk, meant that this railway project dragged on for thirty years and brought Quebec close to bankruptcy. The North Shore railways were finally completed in the 1880s.

As was clear from the Grand Trunk's effect on Montreal carters, railways were not just a means of transportation. Historians Tom Traves and Paul Craven describe the Grand Trunk as Quebec's first large-scale vertically- and horizontally-integrated industrial corporation (Craven and Traves, 1983). They point out that even before its completion, the Grand Trunk was rebuilding its line and repairing track, communicating by telegraph and operating grain elevators and steamships. It also had complex management, accounting, and engineering structures.

Railways represented a heavy investment of capital. The Grand Trunk's shops in Montreal were built on farm land located south-west of the city between the Lachine Canal and the St. Lawrence River. The forty-one hectare site was bought from four religious communities at prices ranging from £700 to £1500 a hectare and, with canal-side industries, stimulated the growth of Pointe Saint-Charles and other working-class communities that spread along the Lachine Canal (Hoskins, 1987).

The Grand Trunk's 1854 plans show 1000-metre-long foundations for its Pointe Saint-Charles shops that included blacksmith, foundry, warehousing, and locomotive-erecting facilities. As part of its organization, independent contractors were systematically eliminated. In addition to manufacturing its own cars, locomotives and rails, the Grand Trunk added ancillary shops such as a sawmill, a planing mill, and a paint and varnish shop to its Pointe Saint-Charles facility. The shops were illuminated by 700 gas lights and steam-heated by burning sawdust from the sawmill. By 1871, 750 employees worked in the Pointe Saint-Charles shops. Although many of these were skilled workers, the steam hammers, huge drilling machines, and daily work reports emphasize the factory production and management organization that characterized the Grand Trunk.

Industrial Producers

Well before the transportation revolution, industrial production occurred in brewing, shipbuilding, and milling in Montreal. As early as 1831 the Ogilvies had a steam mill in Montreal. Brewer John Molson and mason John Redpath illustrate the transition from artisanal to industrial production.

The decline of self-sufficiency and the growth of urban food consumerism offered urban producers expanding markets. By the 1850s, Montreal breweries had annual sales of £750 000 (Pomfret, 1981: 122). As early as 1785 John Molson, Sr. owned a Montreal brewery and early in the nineteenth century, he and his three sons began using their capital to branch into steamshipping, foundries, steamship construction, whiskey distilling, saw-milling, land speculation, warehousing, banking, and railways. The Molsons are an indication of the important relationship between industry, the accumulation of capital, and its investment in landed property. By mid-century the Molsons were by far Montreal's largest lay land-proprietor; the property of just two Molsons was evaluated at £43 296.

Redpath also illustrates the transition from artisanship to industrial capitalism. Scottish-born, he became an important Montreal stonemason in the 1820s and 1830s and accumulated capital through large building projects. He constructed canals, churches and other public institutions: large projects like Notre Dame Church and the Rideau Canal represented a scale of contracts that facilitated new business and work practices. In an eighteen-month period

(1826-27), Redpath submitted fourteen tenders for contracts that included the Montreal Water Company, the British and Canadian School, a house for the Molsons, a store for merchants Forsyth and Richardson, and the lock-keeper's house on the Lachine Canal. With the capital that he accumulated, Redpath built Canada's first sugar refinery (Figure 4.6).

Figure 4.6 The Redpath Sugar Refinery. The seven-story Redpath sugar refinery was built in 1854 and represented an investment of £40 000. Within a year it had 100 employees and was refining 3000 barrels a month of refined sugar from West Indian cane. The illustration emphasizes the importance of the Lachine Canal and gives a sense of the distance of this emerging canal-side suburb from Montreal. Also of note are the presence of carters and both sail and steamshipping.

Ownership of much of the capital and of the means of production was in the hands of Quebec anglophones. A cultural interpretation of this phenomenon poses difficulties and Everett Hughes' image of French Canada's family structure and its "closed rural system" must be rejected as an explanation for the francophone elite's inability to dominate industrialization and the accumulation of capital in Quebec (Rioux and Martin, 1964: 85). Indeed, there is ample evidence of francophone participation in railway and industrial development.

Urban professionals such as George-Etienne Cartier adapted effectively to the changing conditions of nineteenth-century capitalism. Cartier's ethnic origins did not restrict his geographic mobility and he thrived in the masculine, extrafamilial, and inter-ethnic world of Montreal business and politics. As a lawyer, his corporate clients included the government of France, the Seminary of Montreal, the Grand Trunk Railway, and various mining, railway, and insurance companies. He supplemented his law and political income with property investments that returned substantial rents. By the 1860s he was investing his surplus capital in bank and, to a lesser extent, industrial stocks.

Nor did the traditional elite, the clergy and seigneurs, oppose industrial capitalism. To take one example, the Seminary of Montreal was one of the two largest Canadian investors in the Grand Trunk Railway, while in Quebec City the local clergy invested in regional railways. Calling the railway to Quebec City "a work of patriotism", the archbishop of Quebec bought 124 shares in the railway while the Seminary of Quebec bought forty-eight shares and the Ursulines forty shares. William Ryan has found the same pattern of regional clerical support for railways and industrial activities from mills in the Saguenay to factories in Montreal (Ryan, 1966).

There is ample evidence of the sustained involvement of seigneurs in industrial activity. The seigneur of Lotbinière spoke out strongly in favour of railways by comparing them to the sustaining blood of the human body and predicting that "wherever those iron arteries do not carry life there will be decay". Seigneurs saw the industrial potential of their water-power sites, forests, and mines. While some opted to lease or sell mill sites or timber reserves, other seigneurs participated directly in industrial development.

As early as the 1820s, seigneurs like Barthélemy Joliette saw the lumber potential of their seigneuries. Using capital accumulated from seigneurial dues, Joliette built a mill and alongside of it he constructed a church and classical college. In 1837 he built a second mill and a distillery. By 1847 he had constructed one of the first railways in Quebec, which was used to transport timber from his mills to the St. Lawrence (Robert, 1972).

Even more important to industrialization was the attitude of Quebec's political leadership after 1840. From the first years of collaboration between Louis-Hippolyte LaFontaine and Francis Hincks in the 1840s, through the careers of George-Etienne Cartier, Hector Langevin, Joseph-Adolphe Chapleau, and Honoré Mercier, it is clear that the alliance of some of the most important Quebec politicians with railway and industrial interests was a fundamental reality of Quebec politics. This translated into strong Quebec support for a variety of railway enterprises. The Guarantee Act (1849) and Municipal Loan Act (1852) facilitated public subsidies, particularly for the Grand Trunk.

By the 1870s, Quebec, much more than Ontario, was borrowing heavily in British, French and American money markets to build the North Shore railways. In the budget year ending June 1877, the province spent $3 481 670 on railways and $407 176 as charges on the public debt, much of which had been caused by earlier investments in railroads. All other government expenditures for the year totalled under $2 000 000.

Much of Quebec's early industrial production was concentrated in Montreal, and more particularly, along the Lachine Canal. By the late 1840s manufacturers benefitted from improved shipping facilities and used the waterpower of the recently expanded locks to run their flour mills, sawmills, cooperages, shipyards, sugar refineries, and manufactures for nails, beds and chairs, doors and sashes, saws, axes and hammers. In 1856, 1203 workers were employed in waterpowered industries along the Canal. By 1871 forty-four industrial establishments along the canal employed 2613 workers with another 938 employed in the Grand Trunk shops. (McNally, 1982: 117; Willis, 1987: 220).

The shops, basins, sawmill, and engine foundry of Augustin Cantin, Montreal's most important steamboat builder, covered eleven acres around the first lock. Cantin, a native of a small village near Quebec City, mastered the construction of steamships in New York. In 1850 he invested £10 000 to build a drydock; in 1855 his shops turned out seven steamships for domestic and export markets. Employing 200 to 250 men, Cantin's manufacture was one of the first to integrate iron hulls and marine engines (Tulchinsky, 1977: 210).

The Organization of Work

Industrial production, much more than successful entrepreneurship, implied the changing organization of work. In some instances this brought new forms of discipline and management; in other instances it implied work rhythms, work relations and standards of accuracy and regularity that differed sharply from the work traditions of home, farm, or artisan's shop. This process included the loss of artisanal status and the proletarianization of labour.

The apprenticeship system seems to have undergone transformation after 1816. Masters took less parental responsibility for their apprentices and replaced board, lodging, and educative conditions with increased money payments. An increase in the number of apprentices per master implied larger shops, a division of labour in some trades, and the transformation of apprenticeship from a skill-acquiring process into a simple labour contract.

The construction trades serve as a good example since, in the first half of the nineteenth century, a third of all artisans in Montreal worked in construction. But these men found their traditional work challenged on two fronts: by the growing power of the general contractor who often reduced independence or skills required of the carpenter, plasterer, glazier, and mason; and from competition from ever-larger Lachine Canal manufacturers of standardized building products like doors and sashes.

Leather processing—tanning, shoemaking, and production of gloves, belts, saddles, and harnesses—permits observation of different stages of industrial production across an entire sector and in a region outside Montreal. Historically, tanneries were artisan and family operations. Many tanneries were concentrated along rue Saint-Vallier in Quebec City and in the Rolland Tanneries area west of Montreal. Most tanners were proprietors of their own shop, which was usually adjoined to their house. Normally they employed little labour (in 1842 an average of 3.5 people per tannery in Quebec City). The average investment per Quebec City tannery was $7500 (Ferland, 1985:

52). In the early nineteenth century there was a spreading out of these small tanneries and by 1851 there were over 100 across Quebec.

However, the leather industry was changing and migrating west. An 1865 Montreal Board of Trade report emphasized changes in production and markets for sole leather:

> The manufacture of sole leather is becoming concentrated in the hands of men possessing capital and experience. The production last year was largely in excess of the demand and a considerable quantity of stock was shipped to Great Britain... The black or curried leather which seeks a market in Montreal is made chiefly at small tanneries scattered throughout [Upper] Canada.

Some of this change came from the increasing influence of Americans in the Quebec leather industry: their capital, their technology (splitting machines, hide mills, new presses, vats and ovens), and their management skills in achieving vertical integration in production. For example, the Shaw Brothers of Massachusets improved the use of hemlock bark in the tanning process. Exploiting the Eastern Townships' huge hemlock reserves, by 1871 the Shaws had invested $255 000 in their shops and in their hydraulic and steam facilities. They had 126 employees in their Waterloo, Roxton Falls, and Montreal factories. With the exhaustion of local hemlock by the end of the century, large rural tanneries such as Shaws' moved to Ontario.

In shoemaking, artisanal production was changing even before the introduction of machines. In 1849 Brown and Childs opened their shoe manufacture in Montreal. Here, capital, management experience in the organization of labour, and the use of steam and new technology meant further profound changes for Quebec shoemaking.

By 1871 the largest shoe manufacturers in Montreal and Quebec City were producing nearly 500 000 pairs of shoes annually. Production per employee was high. Joseph Poirier's Quebec City manufacture with twenty-three employees turned out 19 000 pairs of shoes a year. Within the shoe factories, there was an increasing mixture of skilled and unskilled labour. Skilled workers, the lasters and leather cutters, worked in the same building as unskilled hand labour and machine operators. A home labour force was increasingly employed.

Industrial work was often repetitive and organized so that cheaper, unskilled labour could be used. From the point of view of employers, women and children were an excellent source of cheap labour. In 1871, 25 percent of boys in Montreal between the ages of eleven and fourteen were in the labour force. By 1871 women represented 33 percent of the Montreal labour force with particular strength in the textile, clothing, and rubber sectors.

The changes in the form and place of work and in the ownership of the means of production were often resisted. Despite the difficulties of organizing strike action and other forms of resistance, labour militancy was particularly strong in the leather, construction, and transportation sectors. Riots and strikes by Irish navvies at Lachine and other St. Lawrence construction sites were periodic through the half century after 1820. In 1844 stone carters threatened to kill their contractor if wages and working conditions were not improved; the employer's carts were destroyed at night and threatening notices posted (Willis, 1987: 97). The bloodiest confrontations in the construction sector occurred at Beauharnois in 1843 where twenty strikers were killed by British troops. The number of strikes increased later in the century with sixty-one strikes from 1843-79 and 102 from 1880-95.

An important strike occurred in 1866 among Quebec City ship labourers. Organized into a benevolent society four years earlier, the ship labourers demanded uniform pay rates for the same category of work. Their struggle was for more than wages, however, and involved an attempt to regain control of the work site. Among their demands was the refusal to use steam-driven machinery for certain kinds of tasks and their insistence on the right to regulate the number of men employed for specific jobs.

Violence occurred regularly between ethnic groups. Along the Lachine Canal, immigrants from Cork and Connaught fought openly while throughout the 1830s and 1840s confrontations, known as the Shiners War, occurred between Irish and francophone workers in Ottawa Valley lumber camps. With completion of the Rideau Canal, Irish labourers moved into forest work, a traditional preserve of francophone farmers for whom winter wage labour was essential for the family economy. Along the Quebec City port and shipyards, ethnic relations among francophone and Irish workers had traditionally been good. The francophones predominated in shipbuilding and the Irish in longshoring. However, with the decline of shipbuilding, francophones moved into longshoring activities. After ethnic riots in 1878 and 1879, the Ship Labourers' Benevolent Society adopted a by-law providing for the employment of equal numbers of francophones and Irish on a job.

Class antagonism, a factor in the formation of unions, emerged in a broad cross section of crafts and trades in the 1830s and 1840s. In these two decades unions were formed by tailors, shoemakers, bakers, carpenters, printers, mechanics, firemen, painters, stonecutters, and milkmen (Palmer, 1985: 30).

By the early 1880s the Knights of Labour were an important force in Quebec. Despite direct interdiction from Archbishop Taschereau who described membership in the Knights as a mortal sin (1886), the Knights program, which emphasized class solidarity, labour's autonomy on the work site and the nine-hour day, had a strong appeal to Quebec workers. Their symbolism and secret rituals, their picnics, galas and parades, their program of self help and temperance reflected family, work site and cultural concerns of many anglophone and francophone workers. Stressing labour's solidarity, the Knights organized female workers.

Although Montreal and Quebec City were the Knights strongholds in Quebec with 8000 to 15 000 people attending rallies, there were assemblies in Hull, Sillery, Buckingham, Valleyfield, Sherbrooke, and Bedford. The Knights of Labour movement was strongest in Quebec in 1886 when it participated in important strikes of coopers, shoemakers, and metalworkers. Unlike most parts of North America where the Knights quickly faded, the Knights in Quebec and New England held out much longer and remained a major force into the 1890s.

Banking and Financial Institutions

Access to capital was crucial for industrial producers who, besides needing exchange facilities, had to invest heavily in a physical plant. Collecting investment capital was not the vocation of the first banks in Quebec. The Bank of Montreal was founded in 1817 and the Quebec Bank a year later to aid the transactions of merchants. It was only as the needs of industrial producers became clearer that banks and other financial institutions moved from exchange functions into various lending and savings capacities. These new functions permitted the capitalists who controlled the banks to collect capital in new forms.

Later in the century, the broader nets of building societies, the stock exchange, insurance companies, and municipal bonds began competing with friendly and national societies for the savings of rural parishes, the white collar workers, and the popular classes. Chartering of the Montreal Stock Exchange in 1874 facilitated, legitimized, and institutionalized the raising of capital in Quebec. Ten of the sixty-three companies listed on the exchange in 1874 were industrial companies (Sweeny, 1978: 184).

Life insurance, another means of accumulating capital, became important in the 1870s. The most important Canadian company, Sun Life, was founded in 1871 by a group of Montreal capitalists. The company quickly amassed huge amounts of capital from its insurance premiums. These were invested first in mortgages but increasingly in public utilities. In 1877 the company began writing insurance in the West Indies and by 1900 it was a force in the Orient, Great Britain, the United States, and Africa. This spread gave the company a huge pool of capital accumulated on a world-wide basis that it could invest in industrial activities in Quebec and elsewhere.

The relationship between investment capital and industrial production, the function of family and kin networks, access to financial institutions and the larger question of dominance in industrial-capitalist society can be seen from the career of Hugh Allan. By his death in 1882, Allan had become Quebec's first monopoly capitalist. Although his empire lacked the rationalization of later industrial organization, Allan was able to use his resources of private and public capital to develop an integrated financial, transportation, and manufacturing complex.

Born into an important Scottish shipping family, Allan emigrated to Canada in 1826. With his father's help, he became a partner in a company that built one of the largest merchant fleets on the North Atlantic. He expanded from this steamshipping base into the industrial economy. Exploiting Montreal's growing metropolitan strength, he moved into the widening markets brought by the transportation revolution and became the chief backer of the original Canadian Pacific Railway syndicate. Allan was also president of the Montreal Telegraph Company (1852) and the Montreal Warehousing Company (1865). In addition, he became a director of other companies: the Montreal Railway Terminus Company (1861); the Canadian Railway Station Company (1871); the St. Lawrence International Bridge Company (1875); and the Detroit River Tunnel Company. He took an active role in the financing of dozens of companies in cotton and wool textiles, tobacco, shoemaking, iron and steel, rolling stock, and paper.

President of the Cornwall Woolen Manufacturing Company and the Canada Cotton Manufacturing Company, Allan was also a founder of the Montreal Cotton Company which, thanks in large measure to the National Policy, declared dividends of 11 percent in 1880, 20 percent in 1881 and 14 percent in 1882. Allan also served as president of the Adams Tobacco Company (1882). He was a director of the Canada Paper Company, one of the first industrial stocks listed on the Montreal Stock Exchange. Pulp-and-paper was another growth industry and it doubled its production twice between 1861 and 1881.

Allan was also active in developing natural resources such as land, cattle, fish, and minerals. President of the Montreal and Western Land Company, the North-West Cattle Company and the Canada and Newfoundland Sealing and Fishing Company, he was also a director of three Ontario mining companies and a Vermont marble company. Coal was the most important mineral resource to industrial capitalists like Allan. It was the energy source for his railways, steamships, and many of his factories. Director of several Maritime coal mining companies, he was president of the Vale Coal, Iron and Manufacturing Company (1873), supplier of coal to many of Montreal's largest industrial consumers.

Financing these industrial activities came in part from the credit and banking facilities of his bank and from six fire, marine, and life insurance companies. His bank, the Merchants Bank, chartered in 1861, quickly established a reputation as Canada's most aggressive bank; by the late 1870s it was second in size only to the Bank of Montreal. Many of its loans were directed to Allan's companies.

Francophone entrepreneurs were well aware of the significance of banks and investment capital, but they found it difficult to compete with the accumulative and international powers of their anglophone counterparts. In 1835 the Banque du Peuple was established and when it was chartered in 1844 it had a capital stock of £200 000. In 1846 francophone and anglophone business leaders established the Montreal City and District Savings Bank. Founded to collect savings from the popular classes for investment by its directors, this bank was promoted by the Montreal Catholic hierarchy as a philanthropic organization.

In the period before 1874, seven small banks were established by francophones to overcome the older banks' discrimination against their communities and to promote local savings deposits, note circulation, and investment. These banks were characterized by their undercapitalization, and their regionalism; in this they had much in common with smaller anglophone banks such as the Eastern Townships Bank.

Table 4.5 Francophone Banks Established before 1874

	Established	Fate
Banque du Peuple—Montreal	1835	Closed 1895
Banque Nationale—Quebec City	1860	Merged 1924
Banque Jacques Cartier—Montreal	1862	Reorganized 1900
Banque Ville-Marie—Montreal	1872	Closed 1899
Banque de St-Jean—Saint-Jean	1873	Closed 1908
Banque d'Hochelaga—Montreal	1874	Renamed 1925
Banque de St-Hyacinthe—Saint-Hyacinthe	1874	Closed 1908

(Rudin, 1985b: 5)

Commercial Capitalism

Merchants had, of course, been an important force in preindustrial Quebec and trade had co-existed comfortably with other preindustrial activities. While nineteenth-century merchants were supported by an increasingly complex commercial network of banking, insurance, brokerage, warehousing, shipping, and legal services, the nature of their local and international trade activities did not change significantly in the transition. What did change were the opportunities for investment of capital accumulated through trade.

Local and regional trade remained the bread and butter of many Quebec coastal traders, urban retailers, and general merchants in the villages. Behind the very visible square-timber and wheat trades were feed suppliers who shipped oats for Quebec City's horses; local producers and merchants who supplied butter, apples, eggs, potatoes, and flour for the timber shanties of the Ottawa, Saint-Maurice and Saguenay; firewood suppliers in Châteauguay or Saint-Jérôme for Montreal stoves; and Eastern Townships pork-dealers for British troops stationed in the province. There was also a small army of tavernkeepers, boarding-house and ferry boat operators, market-stall holders, victualers and pedlars who assured consumer supplies of food, alcohol, medicine, and drygoods. Emphasizing the diversity and scale of trading activities, Serge Jaumain has found that the number of pedlars reported by provincial census takers quintupled from sixty-seven in 1851 to 344 in 1891.

Until the mid-nineteenth century, the square-timber trade remained important although it was ultimately surpassed by the processing of forest products into potash, construction lumber, barrel staves, deals (spruce planks), and paper. Some of the great family fortunes in Quebec, the McLarens of the Ottawa Valley and the Sharples and Prices in Quebec City, originated in the timber trade and sawmilling. The Prices are perhaps the best example of the accumulation of capital in the forest industry.

Arriving in Canada in 1810 as representative of a British timber firm, William Price (1789-1867) exported square timber on his own account to the British navy in the 1820s. By 1833 Price and his partners had individual contracts worth up to £200 000 and were dispatching 100 shiploads of timber a year to Britain. In the 1840s he controlled some 19 940 square kilometres of forest reserve in the Saguenay-Lac Saint-Jean area, as well as in a south-shore township and an important part of two seigneuries. As sawn lumber became more important, Price ploughed his square-timber profits back into sawmilling. His forest concessions supplied his thirty-three sawmills along the Saguenay and both sides of the St. Lawrence.

These mills produced 500 000 planks a year for the British market and huge quantities of sawn lumber for American markets. By 1861, 12 000 settlers in the Lac Saint-Jean area assured Price a dependent source of labour for summer work in his sawmills and for cutting timber in the winter.

Price was a gentleman farmer and his 325-hectare farm near Chicoutimi employed up to 100 workers who supplied his lumber camps with butter, pork, wheat, beef, and sugar beets. In 1860 the local priest reported that Price's farm harvested as much grain as all the rest of the parish (Ryan, 1966: 142). His biographer, Louise Dechêne, is unequivocal in describing his monopoly and character: "Price ruled the region; charitable when his men were docile, he was ruthless towards those who disputed his dominion."

Trade with Upper Canada assumed new dimensions with population growth, completion of the Rideau Canal system (1832), improvement of the Lachine Canal (1840s), and construction of the first railways to Upper Canada (1850s). "Forwarding" became an increasingly important activity for Montreal merchants with hardware, tea, coffee, cotton, woolens, silks, and sugar being shipped to Upper Canada. Upper Canadian products like wheat, flour, oatmeal, butter, pork, square timber, staves, deals, and potash came down to Montreal for local consumption or export. Wheat was of particular importance because by 1851 Lower Canada was importing half of its total consumption, most of it from Upper Canada. In that year almost 4.3 million bushels of Ontario wheat were imported to Quebec. Of the total tonnage passing down the St. Lawrence canals, 78 percent consisted of wheat and flour (McCallum, 1980: 35, 71).

Agriculture

Agriculture, as we have seen, had already been integrated into exchange markets in preindustrial society, and the Quebec peasantry were not strangers to either merchant or seigneurial debt. Perhaps the major transformations of the transition period was greater rural migration both to new agricultural regions and to industrial centres in the province, and to New England as seigneurial lands were filled after 1830. At the same time, there was increasing dependency on industry for goods previously produced locally, such as leather products. This dependence on commodities forced farms to produce specialized agricultural products for market sale. Finally, agriculture was affected by changes in the legal structure of land ownership as seigneurialism was phased out. Outside the St. Lawrence lowlands there was a shift to agro-forestry—an economic system in which farmers were dependent on revenues from the forest industry—and the increasing phenomenon of regionalism.

Wheat exports from Lower Canada declined from 1815 to 1840 because of climatic conditions and attacks from parasites like the Hessian wheat fly. The reduction of wheat exports resulted also from the lack of large herds to produce manure for fertilizing; the expansion of settlement onto grain producing lands; and shifts in production to satisfy growing local markets. The importance of these factors varied across Lower Canada. As regional disparities became more evident there was an out-migration of young people from poorer rural areas, which became the source of much of Lower Canada's and New England's industrial labour.

The Montreal plain seems to have fared the best. It was highly fertile and new land remained available until the 1830s. Saint-Hyacinthe was another lowland area still under development in the first half of the century, offering farm conditions comparable to those of the New France period. In the Quebec City region, Montmagny continued to produce surplus grain.

Conditions in Charlevoix, however, deteriorated as its limited arable land became densely occupied by an expanding population. Seigneurial concessions at Malbaie became larger in the 1820s but since they were concentrated in the unproductive, hilly back-country, farm families had to spread themselves across fishing, forest, and farm occupations. In parts of the Ottawa Valley, population pressure forced farmers to settle on the unproductive flanks of the Canadian Shield.

According to Normand Séguin, it is the dependence of this marginal farming population on cash income from forest work that characterized the agro-forest economy of the Ottawa, Saint-Maurice, and Saguenay Valleys and many communities along the lower St. Lawrence. The Saint-Maurice provides a good example. Here families farmed in the short growing season to produce both their own food and cash crops, like firewood for Montreal and Trois-Rivières, and hay, oats, potatoes and wheat for the local lumber shanties (Figures 4.7 and 4.8). But for family survival on the marginal agricultural lands of the Saint-Maurice, farm production had to be supplemented by males' winter work in the forest.

Figures 4.7 and 4.8 Wood in the Local Economy. The trade in wood is often seen as synonymous with the export trade in square timber. These two photos illustrate the importance of local markets for wood products and emphasize the difficulties of the staple interpretation in explaining the dynamics of economic activity in Quebec. Figure 4.7 illustrates the

firewood market in Trois-Rivières. In the 1820s, for example, 23 000 cords of hardwood were sold as firewood in Montreal. This suggests that about as much wood was consumed in the local market as was exported. The Lambkin Furniture Manufacture represents another industry that developed to serve local markets. It used both waterpower and steam power for its wood-working machinery. The three-story building served as warehouse and showroom while the kiln was located across the street. Using local maple, ash, and pine, a dozen employees produced furniture, caskets, and woodwork for local churches and homes. While modern woodworking machinery and steam power was used, the industry retained some artisanal characteristics. A well-known artist decorated the fancy furniture. Barter, particularly lumber, was used instead of cash to settle many accounts; and the owners doubled as Missisquoi County's first architects.

Forest labour paid $7 to $10 a month in the 1850s and $12 to $22 in the 1880s (Hardy et Séguin, 1984: 131). Much of this wage labour came from adolescent or unmarried males; boys under sixteen and men over forty-five rarely went. Married males aged twenty-two to forty-five generally took forest work only if their sons were too young to work.

Cutting began with the first snows and moved into high gear with the freeze-up, which permitted transportation of food and timber. Until the 1920s when piecework replaced wage labour, cutting teams consisted of five men: two cullers, a team driver, clearer, and piler. By 1865 the lumberjack's traditional axe was being replaced by the two-man crosscut saw. Spruce was the primary product of the Saint-Maurice. Skidded to the banks or piled directly on the frozen rivers, it was driven downstream to the mill or port after spring breakup in mid April.

These regional forest economies were dominated by lumber producers such as William Price who controlled the forests, the transportation systems, the marketing of lumber products, and the labour market. The lumber producers also controlled local consumption through the use of truck payments at company stores. The tradeoff for the peasantry was that, while their labour contributed to the fortunes of Quebec's great timber capitalists, they were able to ensure the social reproduction of their families.

In the agricultural regions of the Montreal plain, the rural economy was also transformed. The wheat boom at the end of the eighteenth century had encouraged the progressive integration of the peasantry into a market economy. While wheat continued to be a major crop, fodder and dairy products for urban markets increased in importance. A social differentiation, already apparent at the turn of the century, became more pronounced as large farmers who benefited most from this market economy began employing their poorer neighbours as labourers (Dessureault, 1986).

The growing body of rural and landless day labourers contributed to the development of rural industries and to the expansion of villages in the Montreal region, particularly in the period 1815-1831 (Courville, 1984).

While there had always been craftsmen such as tanners and blacksmiths in the villages and towns, new commodities were produced in smaller centres. In the Richelieu Valley village of Saint-Charles, for example, hat making and pottery became important occupations while farther up the Richelieu, Saint-Jean became an important centre for china-ware production. The development of cooperage, tailoring and carriage making in other small centres emphasized the growing differentiation of the rural economy.

New crops and more specialization were indications that fundamental changes were occurring in the structure of Quebec farming. By the second decade of the nineteenth century, potatoes had become a staple in the peasant diet. The dairy industry's expansion in response to growing demand from both local urban populations and, later, export markets led to an improvement in Quebec livestock and increased production of fodder crops such as clover and hay. By the end of the century, Quebec had 1992 cheese factories and was, with Ontario, the leading exporter of cheese, which was then Canada's second most valuable export (Pomfret, 1981: 132).

The decline of Quebec wheat production and its disappearance from export markets is part, then, of a larger adjustment to changing economies and markets. However, far from being backward, as Fernand Ouellet has suggested, these shifts in production were rational responses to market realities, enabling farmers to exploit expanding local markets and, later in the century, new British markets for dairy products.

There is clear evidence of a growing landless peasantry that had no choice but to emigrate from some of the oldest rural regions. On the Ile d'Orléans near Quebec City, 41 percent of the heads of families in 1831 were not property owners (Ouellet, 1980: 143). And although traditional peasant strategy had been to keep Quebec farms a viable size rather than subdividing them infinitely among heirs, some farm division did occur in these conditions. Heavy colonization out of the St. Lawrence lowlands was underway by mid-century. Despite strong support from family networks, Catholic clergy, government, and colonization societies, colonists faced serious difficulties. Arable parts of the Shield and the Appalachians were isolated, and colonization roads proceeded only slowly, making it difficult to obtain supplies and to market potash, pork, and butter.

Francophone settlement of unsettled parts of the Eastern Townships was often blocked by the presence of large land companies. With charters giving them ownership over huge tracts, these private companies responded to imperial and shareholder considerations. Whatever their attitude to franco-phones, company officials had little enthusiasm for settlers without capital to buy land. Land settlement companies such as the British American Land Company and the Megantic Land Company simply abandoned their settlement mandates in favour of exploiting their lands' pine and spruce resources through logging and sawmilling.

The Grand Trunk Railway and the Reciprocity Treaty of 1854 stimulated rural settlement in agriculturally-viable townships like Compton, which shipped wool and cattle to American markets (Little, 1978). As a result, many of the francophones who migrated into the region were single males who worked as forest labourers rather than as self-sufficient farmers. This tendency to francophone wage labour in the Townships was accentuated by demand in the 1850s for unskilled labour in new industrial centres like Sherbrooke. By 1871 francophones were a majority in the Townships, although in its institutions, in the visibility of the English language, and in its economic power, the anglophone minority remained dominant.

To the north of the St. Lawrence, colonization occurred in Shield areas along the Ottawa, Saint-Maurice, and Saguenay systems. The Saguenay population grew from 3000 in 1844 to 19 800 in 1871; this represented about 1 percent of the Quebec population. North of Trois-Rivières, 1 200 000 hectares of grassland along the rivers of the Saint-Maurice system were suitable for agricultural settlement. To facilitate exploitation of the region, a 160-kilometre colonization road was built in the Saint-Maurice Valley. Between 1850 and 1875 fourteen new parishes were established in the region. The local population (including Trois-Rivières) grew from 30 000 in 1851 to 50 000 in 1881 (Hardy et Séguin, 1984: 138).

The transition in dairying had important gender implications for the division of labour in farm families. Animal husbandry and the production of butter for family consumption or barter in the local community were traditional responsibilities of farm women in preindustrial Quebec. The growth of export markets, capitalization through investment in herds, buildings, and in new technology such as cream separators; and the shift from the home production of cheese and butter to local manufacturers meant the distancing of women from economic power in dairying (Cohen, 1984).

During the period of the Reciprocity Treaty (1854-66), exports of Quebec butter and cheese to American markets grew rapidly, especially from Huntingdon, Châteauguay and Missisquoi counties. An infrastructure of dairy-production laws, inspectors, and producers' organizations and the improvement of refrigerator and ventilation facilities on trains and ships improved access to British markets for Canadian butter and cheese, and accelerated the shift from production for home consumption to market production. The first Quebec creamery was opened in 1873 and by 1891 there were 112 in the province.

Conclusion

The impact of the transition on Quebec as a whole can be understood by using Saint-Hyacinthe as an example. Great changes occurred here from the mid-1830s to 1881 (Figures 4.9 and 4.10). Within regions, however, and within sectors such as leather processing or agriculture, and even within manufacturing, the process of the transition to industrial capitalism was uneven. The overlapping of preindustrial and industrial, the new power of capital, and changing forms of labour had profound influence on social relations, political life, and institutional structures in Quebec.

Figure 4.9 Saint-Hyacinthe about 1836. In the 1830s Saint-Hyacinthe was a village of 1000 inhabitants. Its size, the forms of labour power, the significance of its parish church, and its intimate relationship to the countryside emphasize its preindustrial vocation. The seigneur, Jean Dessaulles (1766-1835), was the dominant local figure. As well as sitting in the Assembly, he decided the sites for the bridge, market, courthouse, and classical college.

Figure 4.10   A Bird's-eye View of Saint-Hyacinthe in 1881. By 1881 the village had become an industrial city of 5321. Indicative of its transition to industrialization are the urban growth, the railways, the new bridges, dams and water technology, as well as the large clerical institutions evident at the top right. In the foreground, waterpower is being used in the knitting mill and tannery while closer to the railway a foundry smokestack is evident. The city also included a corset factory, a shoe manufacturer, its own bank, and a cathedral.

Bibliography

General Works
Both strongly contested, Fernand Ouellet's *Lower Canada 1791-1840: Social Change and Nationalism* and Stanley Ryerson's *Unequal Union: Confederation and the Roots of Conflict in the Canadas, 1815-1873* are the most provocative starting points for the economic history of the period.

Rural Life
For the rural crisis debate see Joseph Goy and Jean-Pierre Wallot, *Evolution et éclatement du monde rural*, especially the articles by Louise Dechêne and Louis Michel. For the growth of villages see Serge Courville, "Esquisse du développement villageois au Québec: le cas de l'aire seigneuriale entre 1760 et 1854". Agriculture and settlement in the Townships has been described in several places by Jack Little; a good starting place for Little's work is "The Social and Economic Development of Settlers in two Quebec Townships, 1851-1870". Normand Séguin, *La conquête du sol au 19e siècle*, and René Hardy and Normand Séguin, *Forêt et société en Mauricie*, are the major sources for the agro-forest sector. The careers of seigneurs Papineau and Joliette are described in R. Cole Harris, "Of Poverty and Helplessness in Petite Nation", and Jean-Claude Robert, "Un seigneur entrepreneur, Barthélemy Joliette, et la fondation du village d'Industrie (Joliette)".

Urbanization and Class Relations
For cholera, see Geoffrey Bilson, *A Darkened House: Cholera in Nineteenth-Century Canada*. On Irish immigration H.C. Pentland's *Labour and Capital in Canada* should be compared to Donald Akenson, *The Irish in Ontario: A Study in Rural History*.

Business
The Montreal business community is discussed by Gerald Tulchinsky's *The River Barons*. For francophone banking see Ronald Rudin, *Banking en français: the French Banks of Quebec 1835-1925*. Paul Craven and Tom Traves's argument that railways are manufacturers is in their "Canadian Railways as Manufacturers, 1850-1880". For development of the Lachine Canal see Larry McNally, *Water Power on the Lachine Canal, 1846-1900*, and John Willis, *The Process of Hydraulic Industrialization on the Lachine Canal 1840-80: Origins, Rise and Fall*.

Labour
Fernand Harvey's *Le mouvement ouvrier au Québec* describes the Knights of Labour in Quebec. A repertory of strikes can be found in Jean Hamelin, Paul Larocque, and Jacques Rouillard, *Répertoire des grèves dans La province de Québec au XIXe siècle*, while Bryan Palmer's *Working-Class Experience: the*

Rise and Reconstitution of Canadian Labour, 1800-1980 gives a useful overview of the Canadian situation. For examples of carters and shoemakers see Margaret Heap, "La grève des charretiers à Montréal, 1865", and Joanne Burgess, "L'industrie de la chaussure à Montréal: 1840-1870—le passage de l'artisanat à la fabrique". Much of the material on tanning is taken from Jacques Ferland's *Evolution des rapports sociaux dans l'industrie du cuir au tournant du 20e siècle*. Women in dairying is described in Marjorie Cohen, "The Decline of Women in Canadian dairying".

Politics,
Institutions,
and Social Life
in Transition,
1816-1885

Important social, political, religious, institutional, and cultural change accompanied the transition to industrial capitalism in Quebec. Despite the presence of an assembly, political power in 1816 was still largely synonymous with the governor's executive prerogatives. Of importance in enforcing authority, Lower Canadian institutional structures were rudimentary.

The rebellions of 1837-38 and the restructuring of Canadian public life in the 1840s were a watershed in Canadian political development. In Quebec constitutional history, the period ended the struggle between legislative and executive power. Responsible government, the party system, and the alliance of centrist political elements in Upper and Lower Canada were evidence of the assertion of the legislature's power over the executive and the installation of the main elements of the British cabinet system.

This achievement of bourgeois democracy on the British model was accompanied by other important political changes. In the 1840s the first significant elements of federalism in the political and administrative structure of the united Canadas appeared. Education, justice, and local government assumed their Ontario and Quebec particularities. Federalism came to fruition in Confederation. By the 1880s the Riel crisis and other Macdonald government policies confirmed that Quebec had only a minority status in the Canadian state and that its provincial government was simply a local administration.

The final important political element of the period 1816-85 was the formation in Quebec of a centralized and bureaucratized state. Justice, education, and the administration of crown lands, local railways, municipalities, and colonization gave Quebec greatly expanded powers over isolated regions.

Bourgeois democracy, federalism, and the formation of the bureaucratic state corresponded to changing social relations. By the 1880s, the preindustrial autocracy—the colonial bureaucracy, seigneurs, clerical elite, and great merchants—had ceded power to industrial capitalists and their allies in the Quebec bourgeoisie. Far from being reactionary, the latter used their new political power to reshape preindustrial structures into forms that responded to the economic and social interests of the new dominant groups.

As part of the realignment of classes after 1838, an important element in the Quebec bourgeoisie moved into alliance with the Roman Catholic Church, which emerged from the rebellions in a stronger position. The common ground would be local autonomy and a loosely-defined nationalism that could serve both clergy and bourgeoisie. The social and economic result of the alignment among the elite in Lower Canada was vigorous state sponsorship of transportation and industrial development. This alignment also extended the church's authority to shape social and educational institutions for the popular classes.

The function and power of the Catholic Church changed dramatically in the transition. At the end of the preindustrial period, the Lower Canadian church was weak. Its human resources were declining; its religious, property, and civil powers were in question under British administration. In the countryside, it faced an increasing challenge from the petty bourgeoisie over ideological, social, and taxing power.

The church had been a consistent supporter of established authority, both in the French and British regimes. This support was particularly precious in 1837-38 and was symbolized by Bishops Lartigue's and Signay's description of insurrection and violence as "criminal in the eyes of God and of our Holy Religion". Its role was particularly important in defusing popular unrest. In the countryside, parish priests received clear instructions from the bishops to support established British authority and divine-right monarchy. As parish priests of Montreal, the Sulpicians had strong influence on Irish Catholics and were a key force in blocking the channelling of Irish popular discontent to the Patriotes. Lord Durham recognized the importance of this intervention:

> The priests have an almost unlimited influence over the lower classes of Irish; and this influence is said to have been very vigorously exerted last winter, when it was much needed, to secure the loyalty of a part of the Irish during the troubles.

Other fundamental elements of social organization, particularly the law, landholding structures, and political, educational and social institutions, took new form in the 1840s and 1850s. Quebec civil law and seigneurialism were reformed to emphasize the individual, freehold property, and freedom of contract and labour. New attention was focused on directing and controlling the popular classes, both rural and urban. A universal education system, a province-wide judicial fabric of courthouses, rural police and jails, the implementation of municipal structures, and new forms of taxation facilitated the subjugation of Quebecers' minds and pocketbooks to a bureaucratized and centralized state.

Culture was an important force in this changing structure. It may at first seem paradoxical that nationalism, on one hand, was encouraged by elements in the church that rejected the values of the French Revolution, and, on the other hand, by francophone leaders who supported Quebec's integration into the larger Canadian state. The answer lies in the changing Quebec elite and its need to manage popular ideology. Through family, tavern, *rang*, friendly society, labour union, and neighbourhood the popular classes resisted being told what to think; in opposition to this, lay and clerical intellectuals formulated a unifying national ideology. This ideology took its roots in Catholicism, the French language, the preindustrial family, and the idealization of rural life. Women, in the enclaves of both convent and domestic life, became important deputies in propagating this ideology.

Political Struggle

The early decades of the century were characterized by political and social struggle between the preindustrial elite that controlled the executive and the francophone professionals who dominated the Assembly. In the press and Assembly, the governor and executive council came under increasing attack from lawyers, notaries, doctors, innkeepers, and small merchants. Of the members of the Assembly in the pre-rebellion period of 1792-1836, 77.4 percent were merchants or professionals (Ouellet, 1980: 188).

The Assembly challenged the executive for control of patronage in the bureaucracy, militia, and judiciary. An 1829 report noted that of thirty-nine magistrates in Montreal, twenty-two were natives of Great Britain, seven were foreigners, three were English Canadians, and only seven were French Canadians. The same committee accused Robert Christie, chairman of the Quarter Sessions, of dismissing magistrates at will, "of acting as a spy upon the conduct and votes of the Members of this House", and of bringing "contempt upon this office of the Magistracy."

With military and canal construction forming the largest building projects of the period, government contracts were important factors in the local economy. At the same time, provisioning the British army produced some of the largest supply contracts for local merchants. Other elements in the bourgeoisie resented the large, anglophone land companies that by the 1830s controlled development in the Eastern Townships. Attacks on the monopoly and settlement practices of these companies raised the issues of colonization and French Canadian nationalism and thus appealed to both the church and the landless peasantry.

Status was added to the bad blood of contracts, patronage, and power. Ethnic slurs became common coin as prominent francophone notaries, lawyers, surveyors, and doctors found themselves far down the local colonial pecking order. Precedence in this society, and the order that was used at official gatherings, was that of England: royalty, clergy, nobility, royal household officials, military, professional classes, artisans, labourers (Senior, 1981: 39). But more was at stake than the defensive action of what Fernand Ouellet calls a class looking "for someone to blame": the basic issue was power in the industrializing state (Cited in Cook, 1969: 54).

Strong evidence of consensus on financial, regulatory, and developmental policy such as roads, bridges, canals and railways can be detected. Alan Dever has shown that 82 percent of the motions for economic development in the Assembly passed unanimously and he concludes that "conflict was the exception rather than the rule" (Dever, 1976). Many members supported the efforts of millers, urban landowners, and manufacturers to lift preindustrial restrictions on the free movement of property and labour. In short, the

Assembly often opposed the great commercial capitalists by positing local control and industrial development. Some anglophones in the Assembly were members of the parti canadien and later the Patriotes—Marcus Child of Stanstead, Ephraim Knight of Missisquoi, James Stuart and Robert Nelson of Montreal. Some of them, John Neilson, W.H. Scott and E.B. O'Callaghan, represented francophone ridings.

After 1840, this consensus in favour of economic development was clear in the all-party support given to canal, railway and industrial development. Etienne Parent, editor of *Le Canadien*, emphasized (1846) that the francophone bourgeoisie's future was tied to industrial capitalism:

> ... the industrialists are the lords of America; and their claim to nobility is better justified and more enduring than that of your noblemen in the old world. Neither misfortune nor revolution can destroy them. It is through industry's struggle against hostile elements that countless cities and empires have been conquered, not with sword and bloodshed, but with spade and sweat. For this, gentlemen, industry must be honoured, not just through words and gestures but through action.

Until the 1830s, British parliamentary democracy was perhaps the common goal with republicanism and nationalism as recurring themes; there was less consensus on separation of church and state, on reform of the Custom of Paris, and on the abolition of seigneurialism. Anticlericalism led to confrontations with the Roman Catholic Church. The issue of universal primary education remained an open sore between the church and francophone bourgeoisie until the 1840s. In the first decades of the century, attempts to establish a hierarchical British system of education failed. The 1824 churchwardens' law was an attempt to obtain secular influence over church finances while respecting clerical sensitivities. It gave churchwardens control over local primary schools and the right to use one quarter of the *fabrique's* funds for school construction. An 1829 law went further and separated education from local clerical influence by entrusting school authority to civil officers—to the members of the Assembly and an elected syndic (Chabot, 1975).

Control of the peasantry was particularly worrisome to the church. Local doctors and notaries contested the powers of parish priests. In 1831 a prominent priest warned that "it is time to organize ourselves before the nationalist and liberal effervescence turns everyone's head. Already they are speaking out against the priests and episcopal authority in the legislative assembly." The ideology of these local professionals and merchants was rendered more dangerous by their growing numbers in relation to the clergy.

In its struggle in the political arena, the bourgeoisie who controlled the Assembly concentrated on three main demands: responsible government, control of the civil list (most taxes that were needed to pay local officials required Assembly approval), and an elected legislative council. Until the 1830s these fundamental political reforms were demanded within the cadre of

British constitutional tactics—attempts to impeach the chief justice, petitions to Westminster, blockage of government bills. For their part, British authorities, frustrated by the actions of the popularly-elected Assembly, drew on their autocratic political powers: sessions were suspended, elections were rigged, the Assembly's nomination of Papineau as speaker was refused, and opposition newspaper editors were jailed. In the escalating political crisis, the Riot Act, the army and, ultimately, martial law were the means used to impose authority.

As the issues of educational policy, taxation, control of the bureaucracy, and reform of the landholding and judicial systems became more critical in industrializing society, the stakes became higher. In Westminster, the Union Bill (1822) was introduced into the British Parliament. Proposing to unite Upper and Lower Canada and to abolish French as an official language, the bill's terminology such as "all written proceedings of the (Assembly and Legislative Council) shall be in the *English* language and none other," left no doubt as to the future of French Canadians and their bourgeoisie in a united Canada.

Although never passed, the bill was a milestone in the evolution of what became the Patriote movement. John Neilson, a Scot and editor of the *Quebec Gazette*, was among those who joined the reform movement. He wrote to Papineau: "What fate have the inhabitants of this country to hope for from people who proceed in such fashion?" Protest delegations were sent to England and some 50 000 Lower Canadians signed petitions opposing the bill.

The Rebellions

By the late 1820s, Patriote leader Louis-Joseph Papineau was becoming more nationalist, more republican, and more critical of British constitutional practice. In the early 1830s rallies, marches, secret societies, riots, and radical newspapers like *La Minerve* and the *Vindicator* made it clear that the struggle of the bourgeoisie in the Assembly could spill out into larger revolutionary potential. Following the July 1830 Revolution in France, law and medical students scaled the wall of Montreal's most prestigious classical college, le Collège de Montréal, hung a teacher in effigy, and left the tricolour of the French Revolution on the school flagpole.

In 1835 revellers broke windows at the Seminary of Montreal and threw into the courtyard an effigy of the superior wearing the ears of an ass. In the 1830s Saint-Jean Baptiste day was a rowdy, nationalist festival that celebrated French Canada's patron saint with revolutionary songs and toasts to the United States.

Social unrest was not limited to the bourgeoisie. Francophone artisans and labourers in Montreal, Quebec City, and the Ottawa Valley had to compete with cheap Irish labour and with new forms of labour organization that included large work sites, company stores, and contract day labour.

The Quebec peasantry faced failing local economies, regional disparities, emigration, and increasing dependence on wage labour in the forest. In 1825, censitaires petitioned that seigneurs were violating seigneurial law by refusing to make concessions, by stripping land of timber before conceding it, and by increasing the rates of seigneurial dues. On Papineau's own seigneury, only ten of his censitaires were not in debt to him in 1832 and during the 1830s he used the courts to obtain judgments and enforce payment (Baribeau, 1983: 138). In 1838 the Sulpicians reported that the annual arrears of their rural *censitaires* on the Island of Montreal averaged a total of £433 over the past thirty years. On another seigneury in the Montreal area, two-thirds of the censitaires were in arrears by the late 1830s.

The peasantry had a long tradition of poaching, evading tithes, and cheating on seigneurial dues. Debts, the lack of land for their children, and the possibility of famine in the 1830s made their mood potentially dangerous.

Throughout the period imperial, provincial, and municipal authorities took measures to control the popular classes of countryside and city. The British Combination Acts (1800), Master and Servant Laws, and provincial legislation concerning the desertion of apprentices (1802) and worker sabotage (1841) impeded union formation and strikes. In 1821 special police regulations in Montreal required workers to give fifteen days notice before quitting their employment (Tremblay, 1983).

In the same period, tavern, market and lighting regulations were tightened. Leisure time was perceived as a particular threat. Between 1817 and 1826 Montreal magistrates forbade not only charivaris, gaming at city markets, and the firing of guns to celebrate birthdays, but even skating and sledding within the city.

At the same time, the struggle between the Patriotes and the executive intensified. Particularly in Montreal, magistrates were increasingly forced to call out the troops. A particularly bloody riot broke out in 1832 in Montreal's West Ward where the Patriotes nominated Daniel Tracey, editor of the *Vindicator* and recently released from jail for libel. There was no secret ballot in this period and voting occurred over several days. After recurrent clashes, the Riot Act was read, the troops opened fire, and three French Canadians were left dead on St. James Street (Figure 5.1). While Governor Aylmer described it as an "accidental circumstance", Patriotes renamed St. James Street the "Street of Blood" (Senior, 1981: 20).

The Patriotes' fate was increasingly linked to Louis-Joseph Papineau's leadership and ideology. Papineau's grandfather was an artisan, while his father's professional success as a notary and surveyor enabled him to purchase a seigneury. Papineau studied law but spent most of his life in politics. Personality difficulties, incapacity to provide forceful leadership in an armed rebellion, and ideological confusion over the relative importance of Catholicism, the bourgeoisie, and seigneurialism marked his career. These ambiguities over social, religious, and nationalist goals were also present in many of his colleagues and shaped the first rebellion in 1837 into goals that were essentially socially conservative and nationalist.

Figure 5.1   The Election Riots of 1832. As the political system imposed in 1791 became increasingly paralyzed by constitutional deadlock between assembly and legislative council, British authorities turned increasingly to garrison troops. According to military historian Elinor Senior, the use of troops became "almost a normal military operation during Montreal elections" (Senior, 1981: 72). As well as being used in elections in 1832, 1844, 1846, and 1847, the Riot Act and troops were used during strikes in 1843, for the civil disturbances of 1849, and in the religious riots of 1853. The imposition of martial law, with its suspension of ordinary government and justice, was more serious. Virtually unused in England, martial law was applied in Lower Canada for several months during the rebellions of 1837 and again in 1838. Legal historians like Jean-Marie Fecteau see a parallel between the application of martial law and the War Measures Act, which was applied in Quebec in 1970 (Fecteau, 1987: 495).

Deflecting Patriotes who wanted to stir latent popular hostility into a common front against the church, seigneurs, great merchants, and British authoritarianism, Papineau concentrated on the great commercial capitalists. His attacks became increasingly ethnic. Ultimately, he defended the church, Quebec civil law, and the seigneurial system as bastions of his definition of the "national" cause.

> ...in Papineau's scheme of thought the social equilibrium would rest upon two fundamental institutions, so far as these could be restored to their original meaning: seigneurial tenure and French common law. The first seemed essentially favourable to an equal distribution of landed property, when the seigneur was conceived of as the guardian of social equality and

as an insurmountable obstacle to capitalist speculation. It possessed, moreover, what seemed to Papineau a further great advantage that of maintaining the individuality of Lower Canada in the face of the surrounding Anglo-Saxon bloc. Thanks to the French common law, the indispensable support of the seigneurial regime, Lower Canada would be ready to develop in the true sense of its traditions (Ouellet, 1964: 12-13).

In February 1834, the Assembly, complaining that it had been "insulted" and "trampled under foot" by the governor, passed the Ninety-Two Resolutions. Expressing support for American republicanism, the resolutions threatened impeachment of the governor. Although the passage of the resolutions cost the support of many moderates, 80 000 Lower Canadians signed petitions supporting the resolutions and in elections held later in 1834, Patriote candidates won seventy-seven of the Assembly's eighty-eight seats.

By 1835 the Tories were holding mass meetings and forming vigilante groups: the British Rifle Corps, the Montreal British Legion, and the Doric Club. In both Upper and Lower Canada, William Lyon Mackenzie and Papineau leaned toward militancy. Liaison was established with British reform groups like the Chartists. A paramilitary group, the Fils de la Liberté, was formed, and mass rallies were held at which the crowd waved revolutionary flags and danced around the liberty pole.

Lord Russell's rejection of the principles of the Ninety-Four Resolutions brought the political crisis to a climax. With warrants out for their arrest in the fall of 1837, Patriote leaders fled to the countryside where revolutionary activity centred in the Richelieu Valley and Two Mountains areas. On October 23, a six-county Patriote rally in Saint-Charles denounced executive oligarchy and called for the popular election of magistrates and militia officers. When Bishop Lartigue's pastoral letter was read in Montreal on October 24, 1200 patriotes massed in front of his cathedral singing the Marseillaise and chanting "Down with the mandement" and "Long live Papineau".

The first important confrontation with British troops took place on November 23, 1837 in the Richelieu Valley community of Saint-Denis. In an all-day battle 800 men beat back British troops. However, the church's condemnation of revolution, Papineau's weak military leadership, the failure to marshal peasant support, and ineffective military organization hindered sustained Patriote resistance. After a British victory in Saint-Charles on November 25 the rebellions subsided in counties on the south shore of the St. Lawrence.

In Montreal, the church hierarchy feared all-out attack. However, Montreal remained quiet and it was to the north in the Two Mountains area where resistance was sustained. On December 14, some 2000 troops attacked Patriotes barricaded inside the church at Saint-Eustache; fifty-eight Patriote defenders were killed. In the sack that followed, sixty houses and barns were burned and two days later the Patriote village of Saint-Benoît was torched and looted.

The rebellions of 1838 were more revolutionary in their goals. With Papineau in exile, the more radical Robert Nelson took leadership: "Papineau has abandoned us for selfish and family motives regarding the seigneuries and his inveterate love of the old French laws. We can do better without him..." (Ouellet, 1980: 312). On February 28, Nelson entered Canada near Alburg, Vermont with 160 men. Before being forced back into the United States by local militia, Nelson declared Lower Canada a republic and issued a Proclamation of Independence calling for separation of church and state, and state expropriation of the Clergy Reserves and the lands of the British American Land Company.

Confessional schools would be abolished, French and English would both be official languages, the Chartist goals of universal suffrage, secret ballot and freedom of the press were affirmed; and the death sentence was abolished. Native peoples were to enjoy the rights of all other citizens. The most important difference between the goals of 1837 and 1838 was on the land question and the social relations of seigneurialism. The Proclamation stated that "Seigneurial tenure is hereby abolished as if it had never existed in this country. Every person who bears arms or furnishes help to the Canadian people in its struggle for emancipation is discharged from all debts (...) due to seigneurs for seigneurial arrears."

With the failure of border missions such as Nelson's incursion, secret military lodges—the Frères Chasseurs—were established across western Lower Canada in July 1838. In the Richelieu area around Saint-Denis 1500 men took the oath of Chasseurs, and uprisings across Lower Canada were planned to coincide with renewed rebellion in Upper Canada (Senior, 1985: 165). The actual outbreaks were minor: in early November there was insurrection in the Beauharnois, Napierville, and Châteauguay areas where attacks focused on seigneurs.

The insurrection was limited in region and duration. It may have been dampened by the strong opposition of the church, by Lord Durham's grant of an amnesty to all but eight of the 1837 leaders, and by strong military force. The estimated 2500 Chasseurs faced regular troops backed by local militia units, including the 2000-strong Montreal Volunteers, the St. Regis Indians and troops from Upper Canada (Figures 5.2 and 5.3). After several skirmishes through the southwestern counties, the rebellions were over.

After the first rebellion in 1837, martial law was proclaimed, the Canadian constitution was suspended, and Lord Durham was named Governor of all British North America. Unlike the leniency that followed the first rebellions, the punishments the authorities imposed after November 1838 were severe. Some 850 Patriotes were arrested, 108 were courtmartialed of whom ninety-nine were condemned to death. Ultimately, twelve were hanged and fifty-eight deported to Australian penal colonies. The legislature of Lower Canada was suspended and replaced by an appointed Special Council that ruled from 1838 to 1841.

Figure 5.2 Rebels as painted in November 1838 by Jane Ellice. Without arms, military training, or support from the Indians, organizing a military uprising against British forces was problematic. Of the 150 to 300 men who occupied the seigneur's manor in Beauharnois, only half had muskets; the rest carried pikes and clubs.

Figure 5.3 Grenadier Guards. By July 1838, British authorities had 4704 rank and file troops and 527 officers in Lower Canada. As well, 3000 infantry, a troop of cavalry, and three artillery companies were stationed in Upper Canada.

Effects of the Rebellions

The rebellions have traditionally been marginalized from Lower Canadian political development. Unsuccessful, un-British, and nationalistic, they are interpreted as diverting Canadians from constitutional solutions and subjecting Lower Canadians to an authoritarian and anti-francophone regime. French Canadians, this Whig interpretation continues, took years to overcome the rebellion legacy. They did so only by compromises, by a new ethnic alliance symbolized by Baldwin and LaFontaine, by working in a bicultural partnership that was at the base of the emerging Canadian party and federal system, and by working within the British constitutional framework: "the organic vitality of the British constitution in which freedom wears a Crown" (Monet, 1969: vii).

The rebellions, however, must be seen as an integral part of a political chain of resistance, authoritarianism, and bourgeois democracy. The Quebec Act and Constitutional Act had left Lower Canada with a preindustrial institutional structure. The rebellions served to clean house, purging some members of the francophone bourgeoisie, giving short-term power to the authoritarian Special Council, and preparing the terrain for a profound adjustment of judicial, landholding, social, educational, and religious institutions.

The rebellions were part of the accession to political power by elements in the Lower Canadian bourgeoisie who would subordinate seigneurialism and preindustrial French law to economic development, local autonomy, and the formation of a centralized bureaucratic state. This group saw that many of their social and economic goals were synonymous with those implemented by the Special Council. Charles Poulett Thompson, Lord Sydenham, who was sent out in 1839 as the first governor of the united colony, was not from the preindustrial elite. He was an aggressive administrator whose family had important merchant, industrial and mining interests in the Baltic and in South and Central America. Sydenham's goals were to restore stable British government, to modernize administrative structures, and to make Canada attractive for British investors.

Within a short period it was clear to both British authorities and to industrial capitalists like Francis Hincks that legitimation and political stability could occur only with the collaboration of an important element in the francophone bourgeoisie. And, although the preindustrial or Papineau/Viger faction in the bourgeoisie refused the compromises inherent in political activity under the Union Act, the wing led by LaFontaine was soon participating actively. With the legacy of the Special Council and the help of Upper Canadian allies, they were able to co-opt the preindustrial elite and to put in place the political, economic, and social institutions of Quebec industrial society.

The Role of the Special Council

The Special Council that governed the province from 1838 to 1841 made fundamental changes in Lower Canada's institutional structure. The state took a new, active role in organizing and financing social and educational institutions. New institutions for the urban proletariat such as the Montreal Lunatic Asylum were established (1839), while across the province dozens of schools, Catholic colleges, literary societies, and institutions for indigents, orphans, widows, foundlings, and the elderly or sick were funded. The Special Council responded to local demands for transportation improvement by subsidizing bridges, roads, and the Chambly Canal. Longstanding complaints concerning seigneurial land in Montreal were regulated, with landowners being given the option of commutating their seigneurial lands into freehold tenure.

Another complaint of local capitalists had been the insecurity of their capital because of the lack of a public registry system in which land sales, mortgages, and encumbrances would be publicly recorded. This was remedied with the Registry Act of 1841 that required that all conveyances be registered in county registry offices. Important municipal and judiciary ordinances also served to increase central control over the countryside. For example, circuit courts for small-debt claims were established in the Montreal, Trois-Rivières and Quebec districts while rural police were established in the Montreal area.

The Special Council moved quickly to reassure the Catholic clergy, which feared the worst from Durham and the authoritarian regime. Religious communities were forced to give a full accounting of their property and social services, but they were treated respectfully. While the ordinance concerning its property in Montreal was being drawn up, the Superior of the Seminary of Montreal and his lawyer met for eight consecutive days with Charles Buller, Durham's first secretary. The Superior described the resulting ordinance as "the most Catholic and Papist law that it [Britain] had sanctioned in over three hundred years".

The Special Council recognized the Catholic Church's important social role and accorded it new corporate powers and reinforced property rights. At the base of these privileges was the reality that the church's capital and ideological influence were to serve the state. New Catholic orders were permitted into Lower Canada; rights of religious institutions to hold property without taxes (in mortmain) were clarified; seigneurial lands held by religious orders were to be fully compensated in their transformation to freehold tenure; and male religious communities like the Sulpicians were permitted to expand their numbers.

Preindustrial institutions that had served the elite well were to prove inadequate for an industrializing society. For example, the Collège de Montréal, a classical college for bourgeois youth, could no longer respond to the educational needs of an industrial city like Montreal with its growing wage labour force. There were new sources of discontent and resistance, with increasing stress on traditional family support structures and a growing urban wage labour force. Nor was the peasantry amenable to new forms of taxation and state control. The result was a fundamental restructuring of the institutions of law, landholding, education, welfare, and health. The structure of state and business changed as new bureaucracies, management and work-site systems evolved.

Seigneurialism and Law

The industrial activities of seigneurs like Barthélemy Joliette had shown that seigneurialism was compatible with industrial activities like sawmilling, railways, and town development. However, industrial producers objected to seigneurial monopolies over waterpower sites and over mills to which peasants had to bring their grain and to restrictions on the free transfer of property. Looking to new urban and export markets, they wanted to build flour mills, woolen mills, and sawmills without seigneurial interference and dues. As early as 1816 industrial miller William Fleming challenged the milling monopoly of the seigneurs of the island of Montreal by building a mill at Lachine. And urban speculators, particularly in Montreal, objected to paying *lods et ventes* as a surcharge on improvements they made to their properties.

Seigneurial land blocked industrial expansion in other ways. Redpath's sugar refinery, for example, was on a seigneurial domain and, even though it straddled the Lachine Canal on the outskirts of Montreal, the land was used for grain storage and pasturing of the seigneur's animals. Until seigneurial law was changed, seigneurs could not be forced to release their land for industrial use. Immediately following the rebellions, the Special Council introduced free tenure principles into property relations in Montreal by making commutation voluntary (1840). Legislation in 1854 and 1859 extended these principles across the province and made them universal and increasingly mandatory.

Industrial producers' demand for an end to seigneurial rights and for a "free" market for land and labour led inevitably to attacks on the legal system. Legal reform became a central element in the formation of a modern, centralized Quebec state. Reflecting its preindustrial origins, the Custom of Paris integrated property rights into a seigneurial, family, and religious framework; since individual property rights were often not absolute, the alienation of land was often complicated. From the standpoint of universality, it was important to have an English translation of the code since some anglophones, particularly in the Eastern Townships, did not use French civil law.

In their demand for a new legal culture, large capitalists called for a legal system in which all individual creditors would receive equal treatment. To protect their capital in landed property, they demanded changes in mortgage and registry regulations and restrictions on the property privileges of women, children, and artisans. The pressure to revise preindustrial legal codes was clear in a Quebec law journal, the *Revue de législation et de jurisprudence* (1846).

> The conquests which modern society has made in politics, science, the arts, agriculture, industry, and commerce necessitate the reform of the old codes which directed ancient societies. Everywhere, one feels the inadequacy of laws made for an order of ideas and things which no longer exists, and the need to remodel ancient systems and of promulgating new ones, in order to put ourselves at the level of society's progress (Fecteau, 1986: 135).

As with the changes to seigneurialism, it was George-Etienne Cartier who masterminded codification. The codification commission of old colleagues, René-Edouard Caron, Charles Dewey Day, and Augustin-Norbert Morin submitted eight reports in the early 1860s, which were referred to a special legislative committee chaired by Cartier. One year before Confederation the new code went into effect. Among other reforms, it clarified contract law and gave new definitions to master-servant relations (Cairns, 1987). Concurrently with codification, Cartier presented two bills (1857) that aided the development of a uniform, centralized legal system. These bills reorganized the Lower Canadian court system, established nineteen judicial districts, provided for court houses and jails and clarified application of the legal system to be applied in the Eastern Townships.

Educational Institutions

Important social institutions were created by the state in the early industrial period. Most Lower Canadians did not know how to read or write. School acts in the 1840s shaped a school system based on religion, and established a church/state partnership in education. In the Catholic sector, newly-arrived religious communities such as the Christian Brothers provided teachers, while orders long established in Quebec, such as the Congrégation Notre-Dame, greatly expanded their pedagogical activities. In 1853 11 percent of the teachers in Catholic schools were clerics; by 1887 this had risen to 48 percent. The number of elementary school students had risen to 178 961 in 1866.

While the popular classes were being introduced to elementary education, the expansion of higher education in Quebec reinforced the solidification and reproduction of the bourgeoisie. Professionalization of agronomy, engineering, law, and medicine served to separate the lower classes and women from scientific knowledge, access to capital, and power in the sector of industrial production. Université Laval was established in Quebec City in 1852 and opened a Montreal campus in 1876; the Ecole Polytechnique, a school of applied sciences, was formed in 1873 and affiliated with Laval in 1887. Anglophone universities benefited from the industrial capital of the Molsons, Redpaths, and Macdonalds (tobacco). McGill University's arts faculty was established in 1843 and by the end of the century McGill University had five faculties. Anglophones in the Eastern Townships were served by Bishops University (established in 1851).

Medicine provides a good example of professionalization in Lower Canada. Before the mid-nineteenth century, most doctors, as was the case with lawyers and notaries, learned their trade by apprenticeship. By mid-century, doctors established their professional credentials and expanded their power over hospitals and competitors such as midwives. In 1847 the provincial College of Physicians and Surgeons was established. Universities were central elements in the legitimization of the profession. McGill University began granting medical degrees in 1833 while francophone doctors were trained at l'Ecole de médecine et de chirurgie (1843) and at Laval University's Faculty of Medicine (1852). A second anglophone school was established at Bishops in 1871.

Medical students in the francophone schools were largely from bourgeois backgrounds and graduates of the classical college system. Of Laval medical students, 93 percent (1865-1930) came from Quebec. Laval, known for its recruitment of students from rural Quebec, had 72 percent of its students (1870) coming from Quebec City and eastern Quebec. While 82 percent (1872-1905) of Bishops' medical students were from Quebec's anglophone community, only 30 percent of McGill medical students (1849-1939) came from Quebec (Weisz, 1987).

Religious Institutions

The church played an increasingly important role in controlling the popular classes. In preindustrial Quebec, churches had not been immune to civil disobedience. Drinking, heckling, and obstructing services was apparently such that a law "for the maintenance of good order in churches, chapels and other places used for public worship" was passed in 1821. Churchwardens were empowered to arrest loiterers, tipplers, or disturbers of the peace and to bring them before magistrates. If necessary, magistrates could appoint constables to assist the churchwardens. The physical power of the church was in decline before the rebellions of 1837-38: from 750 Catholics per priest in 1780, there were, by 1830, 1834 Lower Canadian Catholics per priest (Gagnon et Lebel-Gagnon, 1983: 377).

At Petite-Nation where the first settler arrived in 1805, the seigneury was without a resident priest until 1828. In the early years, the seigneur fed, lodged, and provided a chapel in his manor house for the visiting missionary priest. Once the parish was established, the priest complained that parishioners refused to pay the tithe and that he was reduced to "scratching among the stumps" (Baribeau, 1983: 125; Harris, 1977: 347).

Urban conditions were not better. In the 1830s, one-third of adult burials in Montreal were conducted without a religious ceremony. Only 36 percent of the parishioners at Montreal's parish church bothered to take Easter communion, the most important religious service of the year, while at the Recollets' Church in the Montreal suburbs, pew-holders petitioned against the behaviour of their rougher compatriots and "the ridicule of the irreligious" who obstructed their services.

The apparatus of the Catholic church expanded rapidly after 1840. The number of priests in Quebec escalated quickly, and according to Louis-Edmond Hamelin, the number of faithful per priest dropped from 1834 in 1830 to 1080 in 1850 and 510 in 1890 (Gagnon et Lebel-Gagnon, 1983; Linteau, Durocher and Robert, 1983: 200). Male religious communities increased in membership from 243 to 1984 over the period. The Congrégation Notre-Dame which never had more than eighty members in the seventeenth and eighteenth centuries, saw its membership grow fivefold between 1830 and 1870 (Danylewycz, 1987). By 1891 the Congrégation was running ten schools in Montreal alone. New dioceses were established across the province: Trois-Rivières (1852), Saint-Hyacinthe (1852), Rimouski (1867), Sherbrooke (1874), Chicoutimi (1878), and Nicolet (1885).

The membership of female religious communities, which had remained steady in the decades before 1840, doubled in the 1840s and by 1881 had reached 3783. In the second half of the nineteenth century, twenty-five female religious communities (nine of which were French in origin) were established in Quebec (Figure 5.4), while in the same period twelve male orders, all French, were established in Quebec.

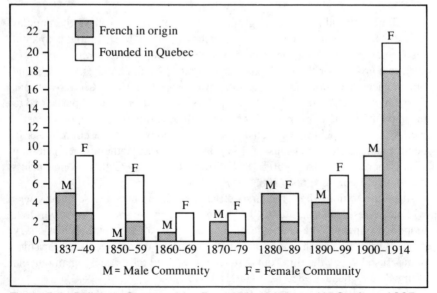

Figure 5.4 Religious Communities Founded or Implanted in Quebec, 1837-1914 (Danylewycz, 1986: 47).

In imposing social and educational institutions on industrializing Quebec, male and female religious communities could draw on their preindustrial experiences with communal living, authority, discipline, surveillance, and their understanding of the relationship of isolation, work, and prayer. As well as the nuns, priests, and brothers who had taken religious vows, lay self-help, burial, friendly, and philanthropic societies like the Dames de la Charité and Saint-Vincent-de-Paul were encouraged. Brigitte Caulier's work shows the sharp growth of Montreal burial societies after 1820 (Figure 5.5).

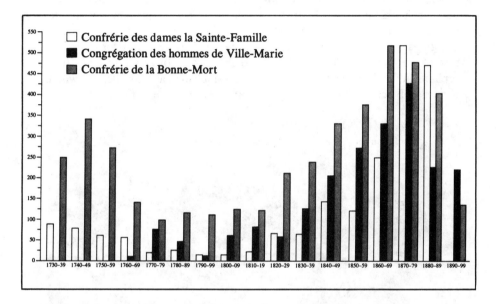

Figure 5.5 Membership in Three Roman Catholic Burial Societies in the Parish of Montreal. Burial societies provided their members with coffins, transportation, and a funeral mass. In one such society, contributions in the 1860s ranged from thirty to sixty cents a year. These societies accumulated an important capital, which authorities might invest in a refuge, asylum, or other social work (Caulier, 1986: 82).

The extent of urban poverty and suffering in Montreal was, however, overwhelming. A nun who visited the Montreal immigrant sheds in 1847 was shocked to find 1500 cholera victims, two to a bed, "suffering and abandoned". In 1848, 332 of the 650 immigrants lodged in the sheds died before being moved to alternate shelter. In the great Montreal fire of 1852, 1100 houses were destroyed. To serve these expanding social needs, the church found itself responsible for hospitals, orphanages, maternity hospitals, daycare centres, houses of industry, food depots, hospices and asylums for the indigent, elderly and insane (Lapointe-Roy, 1987).

The Seminary of Montreal (Figure 5.6) is an example of the enormous problem of staffing. This seminary was charged with the administration of three seigneuries, as well as overseeing the parish of Montreal, an Indian mission, a college, and several convents. The seminary also had the responsibility to direct the expanding Catholic social services in Montreal. But for all this the seminary had only twenty priests (1840), two of whom were over seventy years old. Despite a seemingly impossible situation, the seminary was instrumental in rebuilding the parish church of Notre Dame, as well as establishing St. Patrick's Church for the Irish and new suburban churches in popular neighbourhoods. Elementary schools were a major concern and the seminary subsidized teaching orders such as the Christian Brothers and Congrégation Notre-Dame. The seminary also offered land for construction of a House of Industry; sponsored the upkeep of thirty to forty Irish orphans in the Grey Nuns orphanage; and established a "poor depot" where nuns distributed flour, potatoes, peas, and firewood.

Figure 5.6   Grand Séminaire and Collège de Montréal (1876). The importance of the Roman Catholic Church's educational and institutional function in industrializing Quebec is clear from this picture of the Sulpicians' new seminary and classical college. Modelled on the architecture of seminaries in France, it was built on the Sulpicians' mountain domain in the 1860s with capital derived by the religious community from the commutation of its seigneurial land into freehold land. In the Grand Séminaire (the left half of the institution), 7529 priests were trained between 1840 and 1940. As a classical college, the Collège de Montréal served as a preparatory school for the Montreal-area male elite. Its male and essentially clerical faculty taught the French classical program of syntax, methods, literature, rhetoric, and philosophy. Both institutions taught anglophone as well as francophone Catholics.

The subordination of the Sulpicians to the Bishop of Montreal was an important part of the institutional history of Montreal. The epitome of a preindustrial institution, the Sulpicians were seigneurs and titular parish priests of Montreal. In the 1820s the Sulpicians singlehandedly supervised construction of their new 4968-seat parish church, Notre Dame, and in the 1830s and 1840s they operated their social services and supervised female religious communities in a quasi-independent fashion. Although they retained their power in the training of priests and in the parish of Montreal, they were increasingly subject to control by the state and in the 1860s, they lost important powers to Ignace Bourget, the Bishop of Montreal. This was symbolized by the division of their Montreal parish. In 1886 Pope Leon XIII named Montreal an archdiocese and it was archbishops like Edouard-Charles Fabre and Paul Bruchési who dominated religious life in the city.

These deeply conservative bishops worked to suppress religious disturbances. They tried to repress sexuality and popular culture, and relegated women to separate spheres. The bishops opposed theatres, lotteries, mixed pilgrimages, amusement parks, carnivals, baby contests and dancing by young people. Girls were not to attend public gatherings, nor were women to wear jewellery or watches.

Paul Deschamps, farm tenant on a religious domain on the outskirts of Montreal, had the following clause in his lease (1886): "the lessee promises not to tolerate dancing or any other disorder in his house. In addition he will not permit the farm or woodlot to become a *rendezvous de plaisir* nor allow any picnic—even for a charitable cause."

Religiosity did seem to increase and Louis Rousseau has discerned a new popular attitude to religion as early as 1839. The first pastoral retreats were held in that year and in 1841 30 000 faithful in the Montreal area went to Mont Saint-Hilaire for the dedication of a cross. While in 1839 only 36 percent of the parishioners at Montreal's Notre Dame Church took Easter communion, only 3 percent of the Catholic population of the diocese of Montreal did not take Easter communion in the 1860s.

The Achievement of Bourgeois Democracy

In the aftermath of the first rebellions, Lord Durham had been ordered to examine the causes of unrest and to propose political solutions. In his 1839 report, Durham differentiated between the rebellions in Upper and Lower Canada. He observed social conflict as an important factor in Upper Canada but interpreted the Lower Canadian struggle as an ethnic struggle of "two nations warring in the bosom of a single state". With roots deep in Whiggism, and having been largely influenced during his Canadian visit by Tories and great merchants who detested French Canadians, Durham was harsh with their culture, which he described as "stagnant". As a Whig he had a particular dislike for French law and Roman Catholicism: "There can hardly be conceived a nationality more destitute (...) than that which is exhibited by the descendants of the French in Lower Canada, owing to their peculiar language and manners. They are a people with no history and no literature."

But behind the strong ethnic bias and the views of Edward Gibbon Wakefield in favour of heavy British immigration, there was careful attention to questions of capital, labour, and land and an insistence on the need for what he called "industrial progress". Here, the Lower Canadian bourgeoisie, artisans, and industrial producers found their Assembly speeches echoed by Durham.

> A very considerable portion of the Province has neither roads, post offices,
> mills, schools, nor churches. The people may raise enough for their own
> subsistence, and may have a rude and comfortless plenty, but they can
> seldom acquire wealth... Their means of communication with each other,
> or the chief towns of the Province, are limited and uncertain.

Durham's ideology was, of course, anathema to the Papineau wing that linked nationalism to French law, seigneurialism, and Roman Catholicism. But the LaFontaine/Cartier element of the bourgeoisie sensed the possibilities of industrial capitalist development. To them, ethnic collaboration and the integration of Lower Canadian nationalist goals with the larger Canadian economic reality was an acceptable political tradeoff. Within months of the Durham Report, LaFontaine was corresponding with Francis Hincks of Toronto and agreeing that he did "like the principles of government laid down in the report". For his part, Hincks represented Upper Canadian promoters like Welland Canal developer, William Merritt, grain dealer William Pearce Howland, and merchant Isaac Buchanan.

Durham's two most important proposals were to unite Upper and Lower Canada and to let the colony conduct its own internal affairs by the granting of responsible government. Authorities in London rejected his proposal for responsible government but acted quickly to unite Upper and Lower Canada. By the Union Act of 1840 the reunited Canadas were granted a legislative assembly in which Canada East (Lower Canada) and Canada West (Upper Canada) each had forty-two seats. This appearance of equality was in fact a denial of representation by population. Lower Canada had a significantly larger population, 650 000 compared to Upper Canada's 450 000. This policy ensured the political superiority of the minority anglophone population.

The obvious potential of a bicultural political alliance under the Union Act quickly broke down attempts at ethnic isolation. In his Terrebonne election manifesto, LaFontaine called for the opening of the resources of the interior, the abolition of seigneurial tenure, and the development of canals. Although LaFontaine was defeated in the elections of 1841, his program brought him into alliance with the Upper Canadian reform group led by Robert Baldwin. The latter found LaFontaine a seat in a Toronto riding and over the next years the two men established a binational party. By 1842, with their Reform Party controlling the Assembly, Baldwin and LaFontaine were invited into the government. Although it lost the election in 1844, the Reform Party had become a central political fact in Canadian politics, a legacy inherited by Cartier and John A. Macdonald in the 1850s.

The Reform Party's first goal was to win responsible government. Control over local resources, markets, and the state bureaucracy would facilitate creation of a suitable environment for the industrial capitalists: canals, railways, expanding financial institutions, a stable labour force and a supportive state. This struggle for local autonomy coincided with the growing demand in Britain for free trade; the decline of mercantilism led to repeal of the Corn Laws and Navigation Acts in the 1840s and a re-evaluation of the cost, function, and political organization of the empire.

In 1847 Lord Elgin was named Governor General. Although a francophobe and critical of French Canadian use of British constitutional practice, Elgin was prepared to accept the principle of responsible government that had already been applied in colonies like Nova Scotia. When the Reformers won two-thirds of the seats in the 1847 elections, Elgin called on Baldwin and LaFontaine to form a government.

Despite legislation permitting exiled rebels of 1837-38 to return home and the naming of French as an official language, it was Lord Elgin's signing into law of the Rebellion Losses Bill granting indemnity to Patriotes who had lost property during the Rebellions that emphasized the full implications of responsible government. This act enraged conservatives. On April 25, 1849 a Tory mob marched on Parliament, the symbol of responsible government.

> The Assembly was still sitting at nine o'clock when a volley of stones came crashing into the chamber through the vaulted windows and a dozen ruffians erupted into the hall, swinging sticks at the gaslights. In a moment, the chamber floor was crowded with rioters. One threw rocks at the clock; another, mounting the steps of the Speaker's chair right under Morin's nose, pronounced, "I dissolve this French House"; another began to hack the throne to pieces. Perry pulled down a portrait of Papineau and trampled it under foot; someone else seized the splendid mace and hurled it out a window to the excited crowd. Some members, who had hurried out to the library, now ran back to announce that fire had broken out....By then the flames were licking the walls about the roof while the rioters were running around the building, singing, and yelling, celebrating the ruin of French domination. They had turned away the firemen and cut their hose. At midnight the huge fire still raged high into the black sky (Monet, 1969: 337-8).

The annexation movement provoked another crisis in 1849. Calling for "a friendly and peaceful separation from British connection and a union upon equitable terms with the (United States)", the annexation manifesto won support from some industrial producers and from leading Montreal merchants with a continentalist viewpoint. At the same time, the Rouges, a party whose essential program was separation of church and state and the secularization of Quebec society, used its newspaper *L'Avenir* to promote annexation. However, popular support of annexation was weak with only a determined few believing that French Canadian nationalism had a future with Montreal Toryism or in a larger American union.

The political reality was that the Reformers held a strong central position. Anglophone Tories on the right were isolated while the Rouges faced perennial trouble gaining strong popular support. In 1844 they had founded the Institut Canadien and from then until 1877, when Wilfrid Laurier made peace on behalf of Quebec liberals, they faced unceasing opposition from the church. The church had powerful means beyond the pulpit and confessional to suppress opponents. Rouges like book merchant Edouard-Raymond Fabre found ecclesiastical sales dropping. Groups like the Institut Canadien found it difficult to obtain meeting halls, most of which were controlled by the church. Radicals like Médéric Lanctot found the bishop ranged against him, and Rouge lawyers and notaries found that lucrative ecclesiastical business went to their political opponents.

When Joseph Guibord, a member of the Institut Canadien, died in 1869, his wife, unable to obtain a Catholic burial, buried his remains temporarily in the Protestant cemetery and took the case to court. For five years the church resisted. It was not until after her death that the highest court, the Privy Council in England, resolved the case. In November 1875, 1235 soldiers accompanied Guibord's remains to the Catholic Côte-des-Neiges cemetery, where, under court order, he was buried. Guards were posted and the coffin was protected by cement while Bishop Bourget declared that the grave was separate from consecrated ground.

The Rouges were divided over industrial development. In the ruralist tradition of Papineau, some attacked railways and insisted on the alliance of seigneurialism, French law and nationalism. However, a majority seems to have accepted Etienne Parent's argument that industry was the means of conserving French-Canadian nationality (Bernard, 1971: 31). The ideological stresses of the Rouges and the weakness of their political base made them easy prey for the Reform pragmatists with their comfortable relationship with the Upper Canadians, their alliance with the clergy, and their effective use of state patronage. The Rouges grappled with integrating Papineau's ruralism, idealism and dreams of independence with the reality of industrialization and federalism. At the same time, the Reformers offered workable compromises: the maintenance of a francophone bloc within a larger binational party and an emphasis on political and institutional separateness within a nebulous, but developing, federal system. In their first cabinet, Baldwin and LaFontaine established a dual prime ministership with Baldwin becoming attorney general for Canada West and LaFontaine taking the same post in Canada East. Each section also had its own minister of public works and a solicitor general.

The Reform Party was increasingly professional in its attention to Lower Canada's regional and political realities. It encouraged party newspapers such as *La Minerve* in Montreal and *Le Journal de Québec* in Quebec City, and subsidized local colonization, railway, and canal projects. In Quebec City, Hector Langevin was emerging as a careful, conservative politician with the necessary links to the journalism, clerical, and local capitalist circles. Elections and government contracts were carefully supervised; all appointments of judges, militia officers, customs officials, school inspectors, prison chaplains, and postal workers crossed the desk of the local party chief.

The Reform Party paid close attention to the anglophone majority in Montreal and the Eastern Townships. Leaders like Alexander Galt, John Rose, and Thomas D'Arcy McGee were given important positions in both party and government. Strident French-Canadian nationalism was quietly abandoned in favour of bicultural rhetoric. Anglophones were assured that French Canadians had British hearts and that Canada was blessed to have two great civilizations. Nowhere was this rhetoric more evident than in the negotiations leading to Confederation when the anglophone minority of Lower Canada was given strong assurances concerning Protestant schools, the division of school taxes, and a fixed number of ridings in the Eastern Townships. In both Montreal and Quebec City, political leaders like LaFontaine, Cartier and Langevin cemented their party to the major industrial interests by accepting directorships, contracts, and party contributions.

By the late 1850s the Reform Party had essentially become the Conservative Party. One of the Party's strengths was its alliance with the Catholic clergy. The issue was not religiosity but the social and political significance of official religion. In the 1840s the Reformers had supported colonization, temperance, and clerical influence over the Saint-Jean-Baptiste Society. Its education and social legislation was always worked out after consultation with the clerical hierarchy. Also, in particularly sensitive areas such as the law, seigneurialism, and Confederation great care was taken to obtain clerical support.

Leaders were particularly careful when they saw any evidence of popular unrest. The capital was moved away from Montreal's turbulence, and new courts, police, and support from the church were used to control the countryside. In 1849 when widespread rural rioting broke out against compulsory schooling and school taxes, the Reformers reacted with alacrity. Charges of arson and criminal conspiracy were immediately laid and justices of the peace dispatched to trouble spots. LaFontaine demanded stronger support from church officials to get rural obedience. When the curé of Ile Bizard called for submission to the school law, his parishioners threatened to burn down his house. Schools were burned, and priests, tax-collectors, and schoolmasters threatened. Bishop Bourget responded by visiting the troubled parish and ordering the parish church locked until the law was obeyed.

Médéric Lanctot and his Grande Association de Protection des Ouvriers du Canada posed a particularly dangerous threat of political action by the popular classes. It brought strong reaction from industrial capitalists, clergy, and Conservative politicians. The son of a Patriote notary who had been transported to Australia, Lanctot was attracted to the Institut Canadien even before he became a lawyer in 1860. He was soon locked in bitter battle with the bishop and at the same time he opposed the project of Confederation. With a strong base among workers in Montreal, Lanctot established a newspaper, *L'Union Nationale*, and was elected alderman and prepared to take on George-Etienne Cartier.

Lanctot's labour sympathies were a particular threat to the industrial capitalists who backed the Macdonald/Cartier party. The Association of Workers incorporated European socialist principles and demanded Prudhomme-type councils to ensure improved working conditions and equality before the law. The association was supported by twenty-five labour groups in Montreal; it participated in two strikes, opened bakery cooperatives, and drew 15 000 people to its rallies. Cartier's campaign was supported by the church and by the city's most powerful industrial capitalists. He was nominated by William Molson, and Bishop Bourget issued two pastoral letters urging voters to respect the status quo.

Confederation

The unofficial federalism and party system that had emerged from the Union Act broke down by the late 1850s under the pressure of regionalism, increasing ethnic tensions, and the demands from Britain that Canada assume a larger share of her defense and administration costs. At the same time, expanding government economic programs in canal, railway, and industrial development made maintenance of a strong central government essential.

Lower Canadian Conservatives were early and enthusiastic supporters of movement to federation. At the 1864 negotiations in Charlottetown and Quebec City, Lower Canadian delegates did not fight hard on specific issues and, despite the fierce opposition of the Rouges, they accepted a highly centralized state. Protection of sectional interests was largely delegated to an upper house that did not exercise financial control and whose members were appointed for life by the central government. Nor did they reject the federal power of disallowance or the naming of the provincial lieutenant governor by the central government.

The most important Lower Canadian member of the government, Cartier, had become, despite his Patriote background, an inveterate anglophile and supporter of British institutions. He broached the idea of a new "political nationality" in which "British and French Canadian alike could appreciate and understand their position relative to each other. They were placed like great families beside each other, and their contact produced a healthy spirit of emulation." Rouge leader Antoine-Aimé Dorion was enraged at Conservative acquiescence in Confederation, but because he was excluded from the negotiations, his power was limited. Accusing French Canadians of being "fast asleep", Dorion charged that Confederation would simply be "Legislative Union in disguise". Since the Conservative majority in the Assembly was more than adequate to approve the federation resolutions, Rouge attacks could be largely ignored.

Unlike Ontario, Quebec made little attempt to emphasize its autonomy in provincial and economic matters in the first decades after Confederation. Leaders like Cartier, Langevin, and Joseph Cauchon had built their careers on the duality of British institutions like responsible government and the cabinet system and an ad hoc federal system that was now formalized in Confederation. Younger Conservatives like Joseph-Adolphe Chapleau subscribed to the rhetoric of their elders. Although he speculated privately that Quebec's role in Confederation was to "carry water to the mills of others", his public pose was a defender of the federal system which, he insisted, protected "the autonomy of our Province".

Although they spoke in favour of provincial autonomy, Quebec's Conservative leaders were centralists. Most of them supported double representation by which politicians could sit simultaneously in the provincial and federal legislatures. Prime Minister Macdonald's correspondence to Langevin leaves no doubt as to subordination of Quebec's legislation to that of Ottawa.

> I have read [Premier] Chauveau's bill with not a little astonishment. It gives the local legislature infinitely greater power than we have here or the Lords or Commons have in England. The Bill will not do at all but you need not say anything to him about it. I will draft a Bill which I think will hold water and do all that is necessary and will give it to you when you come up.

The financial terms of Confederation reinforced Quebec's subservience to Ottawa since over half of the province's income was in the form of a federal subsidy. As Quebec finances drained away in railway subsidies, Ottawa began warning Quebec of the implications. In 1879 Alexander Galt wrote to Premier Joly of Quebec that "you have a most difficult task before you, if the Province is to be saved from bankruptcy. If you fail, then Confederation must give way to a legislative union."

The most important attack on the increasing centralization of the Canadian state came from Judge Thomas J.J. Loranger. Confederation, he wrote, seemed to be working to the detriment of French Canada: "Political union, which, for other nations means increased force, natural development and concentration of authority, means for us, feebleness, isolation and menace, and Legislative Union, political absorption!" In opposition to the increasing power of Ottawa, Loranger emphasized the autonomy of the provinces, the independence of the lieutenant governors and argued in favour of what became known as the compact theory.

> In constituting themselves into a confederation, the provinces did not intend to renounce, and in fact never did renounce their autonomy. This autonomy with their rights, powers and prerogatives they expressly preserved for all that concerns their internal government; by forming themselves into a federal association, under political and legislative aspects, they formed a central government, only for interprovincial objects.

These aspirations for provincial autonomy had little political influence before 1887. Confederation had locked Quebec into a federal state in which, for the moment at least, the most important powers lay with the central government. In accepting the subordination of Quebec to Ottawa, the Conservatives were only following the centralizing economic logic of Canadian industrial capitalism. Caught up with the National Policy and the rush for capital and western trade, the province's bankers, shippers, and industrial producers had little time for constitutional niceties, Riel, or federal-provincial relations. The Liberal opposition in Quebec, never a serious threat to the Conservatives until it made peace with the church in 1877, was still unable to shed its vestiges of rougeism and create a winning political coalition. Only with Honoré Mercier's accession to the premiership in 1887 would Quebec politicians begin to exploit effectively the issue of provincial rights.

Social Life

The growth in the power of the Roman Catholic Church, manifestations of popular resistance, religious and ethnic clashes, and the development of neighbourhoods segregated by class and ethnicity were bench-marks of important changes in social relations during the transition.

Popular housing in Quebec City suburbs developed near the shipyards and tanneries along the Saint-Charles River (Figure 5.7). By the late 1850s popular suburbs were developing in Montreal along the Lachine Canal and to the north-east of the old city. In Pointe Saint-Charles, the railway shops and canal-side factories had a range of industrial employees: labourers, foremen, ironworkers, rope makers, carpenters, mill workers, guards, paint-shop workers, bolt makers and coppersmiths. Until tramways were extended into this area in the 1870s and 1880s, workers had to live near their work site. Some of these popular class suburbs were ethnically mixed (Sainte-Anne and Pointe Saint-Charles for example), while farther along the canal Sainte-Cunégonde and Saint-Henri were predominantly francophone.

Although some company housing was built, the common pattern was that of subdivisions in which the better-paid skilled workers financed their single-family dwellings or, more often, duplexes and triplexes. Those without access to capital became boarders or tenants. The development of tenancy was an

Figure 5.7 Saint-Roch, 1866. The Saint-Roch suburb of Quebec City was a popular-class community without public lighting, water or sewers until the second half of the nineteenth century. Saint-Roch was characterized by small proprietorship and, although labourers worked in the nearby shipyards, many artisans worked in shops near their homes. The household raised animals and produced food to meet part of its requirements. The housing and outbuildings in popular class urban communities were constructed of wood. Major fires occurred regularly and their catastrophic dimensions on these communities are evident from this photo. The Saint-Roch fire of 1845 destroyed 1630 houses and 3000 workshops, boutiques, and outbuildings (Dechêne, 1981). This suburb was again ravaged in 1866. The popular class Saint-Laurent and Sainte-Marie suburbs of Montreal were devastated by a major fire in 1852.

important facet of the transition as is illustrated by the increase in the number of leases contracted before notaries (Figure 5.8). In preindustrial Montreal of the 1740s, fewer than 30 percent of households leased accomodation, but by 1825 almost 70 percent were tenants, many of whom signed leases before notaries (Massicotte, 1987). David Hanna estimates home ownership in Montreal at 32 percent in 1847 after which it declined rapidly to 14.7 percent in 1881. He attributes this as a factor of the "shockingly swift proletarianization of the labour force in mid-century" (Hanna, 1986: 77-78).

Until the 1840s, Saint-Henri was a tanning and shoemaking village separated from Montreal by the open countryside of the Sulpicians' seigneurial domain. In 1825 its population was 466 with 63 percent of the declared occupations in the leather trades: tanning, cobbling, saddlemaking. Lachine Canal expansion, and road and rail construction, along with subdivision of the seigneurial domain and local country estates into industrial estates and popular housing, placed Saint-Henri in the path of industrial development.

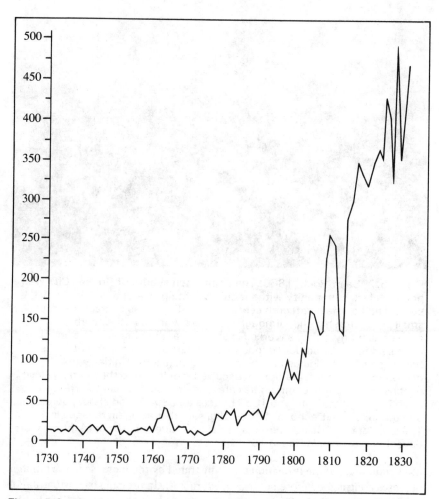

Figure 5.8   Number of Leases in Montreal Notarial Archives, 1731-1831 (Massicotte, 1987: 92).

By the 1850s leather production in artisanal shops was ceding to "putting out", by which shoes were stitched by men and women working at home. By the 1870s both the putting-out system and artisanal shoemaking were declining fast in the face of a fifty-employee shoe factory, a steam-operated tannery with eighty employees and two brick manufacturers. In 1871 Saint-Henri's population was nearly 2500. Between 1879 and 1881 Saint-Henri reached another industrial plateau with the construction of huge industrial abattoirs, the Williams sewing-machine factory, and the Merchants' Cotton Mill. The two latter factories employed large numbers of women (Lauzon and Ruelland, 1985).

Seventy-four percent of Saint-Henri residents were tenants. Onézime Bourelle and his wife, Philomène Mire, were what might be considered a typical working-class couple in their community. Married in their home village of Saint-Isidore in 1859, they had worked in New England before settling in Saint-Henri where Bourelle found work as a policeman and later in the Redpath sugar refinery. With a household of nine, the Bourelles rented a four-room, second-floor flat in a wooden building of four apartments. One of the tenants, a milkman, paid extra rent for the backyard stable in which he kept seven cows. Each apartment had access to the courtyard where tenants had separate outside toilets and storage sheds. The Bourelles had neither a garden nor animals but their landlord, who occupied one of the apartments, kept a pig in the courtyard.

Bourgeois housing in Montreal was a response to class demands for communities isolated from popular housing and industrial activities. The housing of bourgeois neighbourhoods was characterized by single-family dwellings, different building materials, and larger lots. The francophone bourgeoisie built fashionable greystone homes up Saint-Denis and Saint-Hubert streets, while farther west their anglophone counterparts moved into the Square Mile, villa, terrace and rowhouse subdivisions near the Mount Royal estates of the great Montreal capitalists. In one streetcar suburb, near what today is the Montreal Forum, of ninety-four purchasers over a twenty-five-year period after 1860, ninety-three had anglophone names. Property-owners in this subdivision had six months to erect fences and to plant trees along their property fronts. Their deeds restricted land use to private residences; dictated fireproof roofs and the use of stone and brick building materials; and prohibited construction within twelve feet of the street.

Like housing, cultural life was a function of class. In Saint-Hyacinthe girls of the local elite spent their school holidays riding, walking in the woods, visiting friends, partying, flirting, making lace, and playing the piano. In the summer of 1876 the Dessaulles family took the train for a holiday on the Maine coast at Old Orchard Beach.

Despite her apparently frivolous lifestyle, fourteen-year-old Henriette Dessaulles had a sharp, critical mind as is evidenced by her disdain for the convent, priests, and retreats.

> March is a time of tedious and ridiculous goings-on at the convent. If you are good, you earn a tissue-paper rose which you go and deposit solemnly in front of a tall ugly statue of St. Joseph. Every week you exchange your roses for a lily branch—made from the same dirty paper—that has a certain number of flowers on it according to how many roses you have earned. At the end of the month we all carry in procession our supply of lilies to poor old St. Joseph who looks as foolish as ever. I'm not blaming him because I realize he was *made* to look like this (1 March 1875).
>
> The retreat continues. All of it bores me except the silence which I relish... No, really, this [priest] is laughable with his way of seeing

baseness everywhere, of talking only about the ugly side of human nature and of death and eternity, and with his senseless descriptions of the punishments that await us! (4 October 1875)

He [Curé Prince] is much better at blowing his nose noisily in his red handkerchief than at hearing girls' confessions. I even think he has no idea creatures like us exist. For him there are priests, nuns, old parents, and perhaps boys (31 January 1876). (*The Diary of Henriette Dessaulles*, 32, 68-9, 91)

In Montreal, the bourgeoisie established curling, cricket, tandem, and hunt clubs, while males of the urban popular classes played lacrosse, hockey and baseball. Horseracing, wrestling, boxing and cockfighting drew large crowds. Swimming, previously confined to the dangerous and frigid St. Lawrence, became immensely popular with the opening of public baths in the 1880s. When a bath on a waste weir of the Lachine Canal was opened, 3296 men and boys came to swim in the first four days. Aside from overcrowding, which led to twenty-minute restrictions for swimmers, municipal authorities made a gesture for public morality by insisting that "frequenters of public baths wear bath trunks." Skating was another popular sport and by the 1870s private pay-rinks had been opened on vacant lots across the city. Other popular recreational activities included parades, sledding, picnics, circuses, band concerts, fireworks, and music halls. After 1853 Viger Gardens with its three acres of trees, its greenhouse, fountains, walks, and free public concerts became the most popular park in Montreal.

Montreal life posed particular problems for women, especially those who could not fall back on family networks. Their responsibility in the preindustrial family for preparation of food, care of domestic animals, and provision of clothing had different dimensions in an urban, industrial society that emphasized wage labour, tenancy, the exchange economy, and consumerism. Until pressure from city fathers during the 1860s made it increasingly difficult, urban families persisted in keeping animals: horses, cows, poultry, and pigs. The latter two were of particular importance in the diet of the popular classes. The decline of pigs after 1861 emphasizes the effect of municipal regulations on the popular classes' family survival strategies. Urban families were forced to buy rather than to produce meat.

Table 5.1 Animals in Montreal, 1861-1891

	Horses	Milk Cows	Pigs	Poultry
1851	2077	1528	1877	n/a
1861	2892	2160	2644	n/a
1871	3530	1837	831	n/a
1881	4479	1658	180	n/a
1891	6751	1290	92	9589

(Adapted from Bradbury, 1984: 15)

Widows and unmarried or deserted women without capital faced desperate material conditions. While preindustrial society had also been patriarchal, cultural norms in industrializing society imposed new forms of appropriate female behaviour that subordinated independent economic action to family ideals. The number of female family heads was large: in 1881 30 percent of women in Montreal over the age of forty were widows. Generally without capital or wage-labour experience, they took work in which they used their domestic skills: cleaning, washing, cooking or running boarding houses or taverns.

> When Widow McGrath lost her husband, she was left with three children aged 4 to 9. She took in two other widows, one with an 11-year old child. Two of them worked as a washerwoman, one sold goods at market. Between them they kept five pigs, probably eating some, and raising cash by selling others (Bradbury, 1984).

Shopkeeping, peddling, and hawking were important female occupations. Women were not allowed to enter taverns as clients but they could act as proprietors.

Popular Resistance

Popular resistance was often manifested in the transition period. In the early part of the century, traditional signs of community control such as charivaris were evident in Montreal. Popular mores were offended in 1821 by the marriage of an older widow to a younger man. A crowd of 500 gathered outside the newlyweds' house in Montreal and, after a battle with the constables, they extorted from the couple a money contribution to the Female Benevolent Society.

Mobs, riots and strikes were regular features of urban life, while arson and riots became regular parts of the popular celebration of holidays. By Confederation, Queen Victoria's birthday had become an important occasion for civil unrest in Irish neighbourhoods of Montreal.

> ...armed with bludgons and stones, they escaped the vigilance of police who were too busily engaged at the Champs de Mars. They arrived at the Bonsecours market and commmenced an onslaught on the French Canadian street arabs who reside in that locality. Stones and sticks flew about in all directions until the arrival of a few policemen dispersed the juvenile delinquents (*Montreal Gazette*, May 25, 1867).

Taverns were an important part of the popular culture of Quebec males, and Montreal was reputed to have a tavern for every 150 inhabitants (DeLottinville, 1981-82: 12). In addition to drinking, taverns served as centres for other forms of popular recreation—gambling, billiards, music, and political debate. The tavern also acted as an alternative to the new social control structures of industrializing Quebec: employer paternalism, the Catholic and Protestant

Churches, trade unions, police and friendly and national societies like the Y.M.C.A. and the Saint-Jean-Baptiste Society.

Judicial records show a broad variety of social deviance within the popular classes. Crimes associated with drunkeness (drunk, disorderly, disturbing the peace, delirium tremens) accounted for 5358 (4313 men, 1045 women) of the 11 135 Montreal arrests in 1870. The largest occupational groups among the arrested were labourers (2121), vagrants (895), prostitutes (843), carters (727), shoemakers (302), clerks (235), and tavernkeepers (170). Some measure of work-site resistance early in the transition period can be gleaned from "crime" statistics for servants. The four most important crimes, representing eighty-two of 114 arrests of servants in Quebec City, 1816-20, were for desertion (38), absence without leave (18), poor conduct (14), and disturbance, nuisance and damage (12) (Lacelle, 1987: 52).

Election disturbances were endemic and the Riot Act and bayonet were never far from the poll box. In the particularly bitter 1844 election, a brewery worker was knocked unconscious, stripped, and he wakened to "find himself naked except his legs". In Quebec City and Montreal, anti-Catholic speeches by the ex-monk Alexandre Gavazzi brought Irish Catholics into the streets and left ten dead. During the 1885 smallpox epidemic, whole neighbourhoods in Montreal resisted violently as public health officials tried to vaccinate the population. The Archbishop of Montreal ordered his priests not to interfere with doctors and to reassure their parishioners.

Conclusion

Quebec in 1885 was a very different world than that of 1815. The purging of 1837-38, parliamentary democracy, a new federal system, and the alliance of the clerical hierarchy and francophone bourgeoisie with the industrial producers left the province in the hands of conservative elements, forces that would effectively control Quebec well into the twentieth century.

Bibliography

Nationalism
Aside from the works of Fernand Ouellet noted in chapter four and his *Louis Joseph Papineau: A Divided Soul*, political events before the rebellions can be examined in Alan Dever, "Economic Development and the Lower Canadian Assembly, 1828-40", and in Stanley Ryerson, *Unequal Union: Confederation and the Roots of Conflict in the Canadas, 1815-1873*. For the origins of Quebec nationalism see Ramsay Cook, *French-Canadian Nationalism: an anthology*.

The Rebellions

For interpretations of the rebellions, consult Jean-Paul Bernard, *Les rébellions de 1837-1838*. Details of the rebellions themselves can be found in Elinor Senior's two books, *British Regulars in Montreal*, and *Redcoats and Patriotes: The Rebellions in Lower Canada*. The legal elements of the rebellions are treated by Jean-Marie Fecteau in "Mesures d'exception et règle de droit: les conditions d'application de la loi martiale au Québec lors des rébellions de 1837-1838", and F.M. Greenwood, "The Chartrand Murder Trial: Rebellion and Repression in Lower Canada, 1837-1839". For treatment of the rebels see George Rudé, *Protest and Punishment: The Story of the Social and Political Protesters Transported to Australia, 1788-1868*.

Union and Confederation Period

Politics of the Union and post-Confederation periods are described in Jacques Monet, *The Last Cannon Shot: A Study of French-Canadian Nationalism 1837-1840*; Jean-Paul Bernard, *Les Rouges: libéralisme, nationalisme et anticlericalisme au milieu de XIXe siècle*; and Brian Young, *George-Etienne Cartier: Montreal Bourgeois*. Of particular use for institutional development is J.M.S. Careless, *The Union of the Canadas: The Growth of Canadian Institutions 1841-1857*.

Religion and Education

For the clergy see Serge Gagnon et Louise Lebel-Gagnon, "Le milieu d'origine du clergé québécois 1775-1840: mythes et réalités". For the history of the church, *L'église de Montréal. Aperçus d'hier et d'aujourd'hui*, particularly the article by Louis Rousseau, is of great help. Essential for education questions and the clergy is Richard Chabot, *Le curé de campagne et la contestation locale au Québec de 1791 aux troubles de 1837-8*. Literacy is treated in Allan Greer, "The Pattern of Literacy in Quebec, 1745-1899", while the education of women is the subject of two volumes by Nadia Fahmy-Eid and Micheline Dumont, *Maîtresses de maison, maîtresses d'école: Femmes, famille et éducation dans l'histoire du Québec* and *Les couventines: L'éducation des filles au Québec dans les congrégations religieuses enseignantes 1840-1960*.

Law

For judicial institutions and codification see Jean-Marie Fecteau, "Régulation sociale et répression de la deviance au Bas-Canada au tournant du 19e siècle" Evelyn Kolish, "Le Conseil législatif et les bureaux d'enregistrement (1836)"; and John Brierley, "Quebec's Civil Law Codification Viewed and Reviewed". Of special interest is the July 1987 issue of the *McGill Law Journal* (33,3) devoted to Quebec legal history.

Social

Urban social structure and economic strategies of the elite are discussed in Jean-Paul Bernard, Paul-André Linteau, and Jean-Claude Robert, "La structure professionelle de Montréal en 1825"; Paul-André Linteau and Jean-Claude Robert, "Land Ownership and Society in Montreal: an Hypothesis"; and Louise Dechêne, "La rente du faubourg Saint-Roch à Québec, 1750-1850".

The social history of nineteenth-century Montreal's popular classes is treated in several articles by Bettina Bradbury: "The Family Economy and Work in an Industrializing City: Montreal in the 1870s"; "The Fragmented Family: Family Strategies in the Face of Death, Illness and Poverty, Montreal, 1860-1885"; "Pigs and Boarders: Non-wage forms of Survival among Montreal families, 1861-81"; and "Women and Wage Labour in a Period of Transition: Montreal, 1861-81". For extensive coverage of women at work see Marie Lavigne and Yolande Pinard, *Travailleuses et féministes: Les femmes dans la société québécoise*. Of particular interest for its analysis of both Montreal housing and the building trades is David Hanna, *Montreal: A City Built by Small Builders, 1867-1880*.

Popular culture is treated in Peter DeLottinville, "Joe Beef of Montreal: Working Class Culture and the Tavern". For labour see Robert Tremblay's two articles: "La grève des ouvriers de la construction navale à Québec (1840)", and "Un aspect de la consolidation du pouvoir d'Etat de la bourgeoisie coloniale: La législation anti-ouvrière dans le Bas-Canada, 1800-1850". For servants, see Claudette Lacelle, *Urban Domestic Servants in 19th Century Canada*. For the economic and social life of a colonization community, see Normand Séguin, *La conquête du sol au 19e siècle*; this can be compared to Claude Baribeau's *La seigneurie de la Petite-Nation 1801-1854*.

For bourgeois social activity see Alan Metcalfe, "The Evolution of Organized Physical Recreation in Montreal, 1840-1895". *Hopes and Dreams: The Diary of Henriette Dessaulles 1874-1881* is an important source for the life of the female elite.

Industrial Capitalism, 1886-1933

The maturing of industrial capitalism in Quebec was made possible by the use of new forms of energy, particularly electricity; by technological advances; and by the rapid expansion of manufacturing. Most important, ownership of the means of production became increasingly concentrated. Monopolies came to dominate transportation, finance, and leading manufacturing sectors such as textiles. This concentration of capital and ownership in the Quebec economy was part of the development of a concentrated pan-Canadian bourgeoisie that was centred in Montreal and Toronto.

American capital became important in the Quebec economy, particularly after the First World War and at the same time, the developing resource industries became increasingly dependent on American markets. It was in this period that branch plants and resource towns became important features of the Quebec landscape.

Industrial capitalism brought new forms of organizing production, labour, management, and of cost accounting. Large corporations emerged with interlocking directorships and centralized management systems. During the transition period of the nineteenth century, small workshops and skilled artisans had remained important. However, by the turn of the century, industry was increasingly large, mechanized, and specialized. The world's largest railway shops with a labour force of between 4000 and 8000 were located in the Canadian Pacific's Angus Works in Montreal (Ramirez, 1986: 13). At the same time, productive trades such as the blacksmith were transformed into service trades such as the garage operator.

By the beginning of the twentieth century, farming had lost its position as the largest employment sector. While farming itself did not change much, increasing numbers of young people left farming and fishing for work in mines, forests, or factories. By the 1930s, electricification, the radio, the automobile and expanding rail networks had made the consumer products of industrial society accessible to almost all regions of the province.

Before the National Policy was adopted in 1879, industrial activity had been widely dispersed across the Maritimes and Central Canada. The concentration of manufacturing in Central Canada after the 1880s was of great benefit to southern Ontario and the Montreal region. By 1919 four-fifths of Canada's manufacturing production occurred in Ontario and Quebec.

While Montreal's rapid population growth and the expansion of its financial and manufacturing power testified to its strength in the province's economic life, other industrial activities developed across the province in regions with mining, forest, and waterpower resources (Figure 6.1). Some of these activities were outside the direct influence of Montreal and were dependent on Toronto or New York. At the same time, industrial development was uneven, leaving important pockets dominated by small service towns, traditional farming, and marginal contact with consumer society. The contrasts among these several Quebecs were emphasized by the Depression and world war.

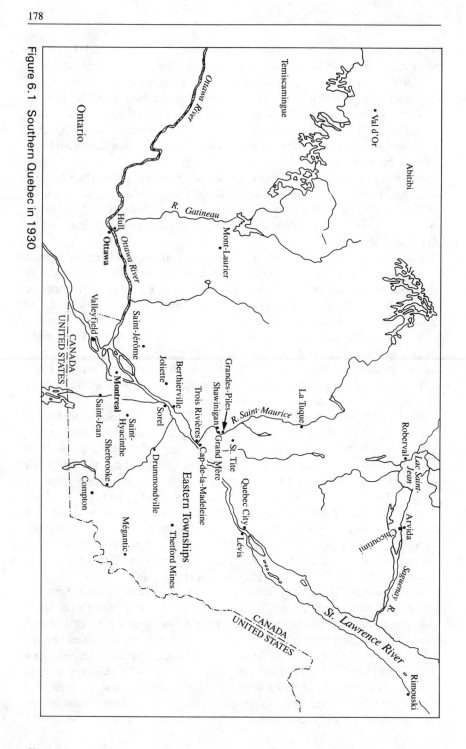

Figure 6.1 Southern Quebec in 1930

The rapid growth of literacy, new forms of rail, road, telegraph, telephone, and postal communication between town and country, the changing form and ownership of the means of production, and the growing influence of capital and the state led to changing social relations. The anglophone bourgeoisie separated itself from daily contact with Quebec society. In Montreal, new anglophone municipalities like Westmount and the Town of Mount Royal cut themselves off physically from the larger city (Figure 6.2). At the same time, in company towns across Quebec separate neighbourhoods, tudor-style homes, and curling clubs testified to the separate existence of local managers and engineers.

Figure 6.2 Mount Stephen Avenue in lower Westmount in the Early 1900s. A traditional bastion of the anglophone bourgeoisie, Westmount dates from the last two decades of the nineteenth century, and from building booms in the decades before and after the First World War. Westmount attracted the great anglophone capitalists to estates near the top of the mountain while professionals, managers, and merchants built their homes down the slope in Lower Westmount. Of particular note in the photo is the use of brick and wood lathing as building materials in these semi-detached houses and the City Beautiful influence evident in the trees, sidewalks, and house position on the lots.

The absence of a Roman Catholic church in Westmount contrasted sharply with the plethora of Protestant churches while its lawn-bowling and tennis clubs, the architecture of its public buildings, its park and library infrastructure emphasize its British traditions. Westmount's class and ethnic separateness was further emphasized by its resistance to annexation to Montreal. While twenty-three suburban municipalities were annexed to Montreal during 1883-1918, Westmount, like its francophone counterpart Outremont, remained separate.

For labour, particularly during the First World War, consumerism, gains in wages and working conditions were counterbalanced by continuing problems of public health, particularly high infant mortality rates among urban franco-phones. Along with health problems, desperate unemployment and the strug-gle for mere survival during the Depression were a reality as were the deepening class strictures and inequalities of industrial society.

The nineteenth-century tradition of community and shop-floor solidarity, symbolized institutionally by important Quebec support for the Knights of Labour, was superseded in the twentieth century by conservative institutions of international and Catholic unionism. Immigration, insecurity, and the power of conservative Catholic ideology led to increased ethnic and shop-floor division among workers and, until the 1930s, little public support for progres-sive movements.

Working-class women were restricted to the lowest-paying jobs and were subject to blatant wage discrimination. While unmarried women were re-cruited for clerical jobs, this work became increasingly segregated, menial, and low-paying in the rapidly expanding office hierarchy. This feminization of clerical work accelerated during the labour shortage of the First World War. Unmarried women were directed to the gender ghettoes of teaching and nursing, both of which were subject to proletarianization under the guise of professionalization. At the same time, the professionalization of medicine reduced the power of midwives, a traditional female occupation.

Population

Quebec's population increase from 1 359 027 in 1881 to 2 874 662 in 1931 did not keep pace with the rest of Canada, particularly because of the growth of the Prairies. As a percentage of the Canadian population, Quebec fell from 31.4 percent in 1881 to 27.7 percent in 1931. By the 1920s almost one-third of the Canadian population lived west of Ontario. The West had only a small francophone population and little contact with Quebec. In the four western provinces in 1941, there were only 138 000 residents whose mother tongue was French. Only 5 percent of these had been born in the East (Joy, 1972: 45). This reality gave poignancy to the language and school crises affecting francophone Catholic minorities in the West.

Despite the importance of immigration into Quebec in the early twentieth century, francophones continued to represent 80 percent of the province's population across the period. There was a dramatic fall in the birth rate from fifty per thousand in preindustrial Quebec, to 41.1 in 1884-85, and to 29.2 in the period 1931-35. Although Quebec still had Canada's highest birth rate, much of the province's natural increase was restricted to certain rural families. Of Quebec's married women born in 1887, 20.5 percent had more than ten children. These women produced more than 50 percent of the children of their generation (Collectif Clio, 1982: 249).

An important factor in population growth was the fall in the death rate to 11.4 per 1000 in 1931-35 (Charbonneau, 1975: 44). Diarrhea was the leading cause of death of children at the turn of the century, while tuberculosis was the leading cause of death among adults. Martin Tétreault has shown that infant mortality (the death of children in their first year) was specific to class and ethnicity. In 1900, for example, the death rate among francophone Catholic infants in Montreal was almost three times that of the city's Protestant infants (Table 6.1). The construction of a water filtration plant in Montreal, the general pasteurization of milk, and public health programs brought the death rate down significantly in the 1920s. However, even at the end of the Second World War, more than 100 of every 1000 children died before their first birthday.

Table 6.1 Infant Mortality in Montreal, 1885-1914 (per 1000)

Year	Francophone Catholics	Other Catholics	Protestants
1885	408.9	189.5	198.3
1890	249.4	204.6	146.2
1895	259.0	199.6	172.3
1900	282.5	235.4	102.8
1905	255.4	198.7	174.4
1911	225.6	179.3	140.6
1914	182.3	195.0	115.8

(Tétreault, 1983: 512)

Another significant demographic factor was the proportion of unmarried females. The marriage rate stabilized at about seven marriages per 1000 women in the period 1884-1930. Across the province about 20 percent of women aged forty were not married, with the proportion being highest in the Montreal area. Marta Danylewycz notes that in many counties of the St. Lawrence plain around Montreal, "where land shortage was endemic and the rate of outmigration high, 25 to 35 percent of the women never married"; in Montreal itself, "at least one woman in three was still a spinster at age forty" (Danylewycz, 1987: 52). From the 1880s until at least the 1920s, an increasing percentage of these unmarried women entered religious orders.

The period was marked by sharp increases in urbanization. The urban percentage of the Quebec population increased from 36.1 percent in 1901 to 63.1 percent in 1931. The growth of Montreal was a major factor in this urbanization, with the city's population doubling between 1896 and 1911. It reached 818 577 in 1931, which represented 28.4 percent of the province's population. This compared to Quebec City's slower growth from 63 090 in 1896 to 78 710 in 1911 and 130 594 in 1931.

Montreal's dominant urban position must not overshadow the significant expansion of other urban centres in Quebec. The province counted twenty-four towns and cities with populations over 2500 in 1901 and forty-four in 1931. Much of this development occurred in resource areas along the St. Lawrence, Saint-Maurice, and Saguenay rivers as well as around Montreal. In Chicoutimi County, for example, pulp and paper mills opened at the turn of the century. As the region's port, rail, waterpower, and mill facilities expanded, population growth in the county was almost entirely urban. From a county that was only 17 percent urban in 1881, Chicoutimi was 62 percent urbanized by 1921 (Figure 6.3).

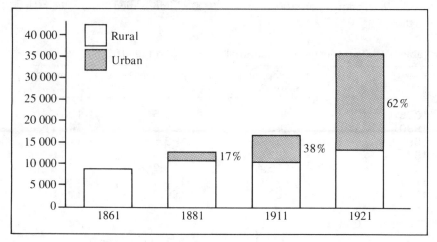

Figure 6.3   Urbanization in Chicoutimi County, 1861-1921

Urbanization was accompanied by an increasing concentration of the province's declining anglophone population in the Montreal region and by 1941 some 70 percent of Quebec anglophones lived on the island of Montreal (Rudin, 1985: 37). By 1911, all traditional anglophone counties in the Eastern Townships except Brome reported francophone majorities (Joy, 1972: 28). The anglophone population of Quebec City continued to decline, representing only 7 percent of the city's population in 1901. While a majority of Quebec anglophones were still British or Irish in origin, European immigration began to change the ethnic balance, particularly in Montreal. By 1931 Montreal was 63.9 percent French in origin, 21.8 percent British/Irish, and other groups made up 14.3 percent. A factor in the lower British/Irish population of Montreal was their concentration in developing suburbs. For the province as a whole, only 15.1 percent of the population was British or Irish in origin and 5.9 percent neither French nor British/Irish (Figure 6.4).

Chapter Six

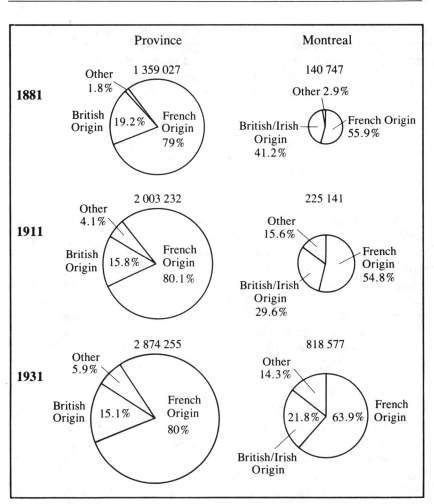

Figure 6.4 Ethnic Composition of the Province of Quebec and Montreal, 1881-1931 (based on Bernier et Boily, 1986: 43)

Quebec, and particularly Montreal, was a favourite immigrant destination in the first three decades of the century. Between 1901 and 1930, 632 671 immigrants gave Quebec as their destination. The heaviest immigration occurred in the period 1911-15 when an annual average of 46 491 people arrived.

Although there had been a Jewish community in Montreal since the 1760s, it grew rapidly only after 1890. From 2473 in 1891, the Jewish population of Montreal reached 28 807 in 1911. Although some Jews were professionals, manufacturers, or merchants, many first-generation Montreal Jews were workers in the garment industry. In 1931, 1608 Jewish males were working as tailors in Montreal and 1232 women as sewing-machine operators. The 1931 census showed that of the employed Jewish population, 42.1 percent worked in manufacturing, 35.1 percent were employed in commerce, and 5.1 percent declared a liberal profession (Bernier and Boily, 1986: 208).

Nobel prize winner Saul Bellow has recounted his childhood in Montreal of the 1920s:

> In our family, my parents spoke Russian between themselves. The children spoke Yiddish with their parents, English among themselves, and French in the streets . . . I never even was aware of what language I was speaking. I made no distinction whatsoever and simply used the appropriate language for the person with whom I was speaking. I was confident in what I was. That's how I lived.

Italians became important in Montreal urban life in this period. Early in the century, many were recruited in Italy as sojourners, and worked as seasonal labourers for railway or tramway construction sites. In 1903, for example, the Canadian Pacific Railway hired over 3500 Italians, mostly through Italian hiring bosses like Antonio Cordasco (Harney, 1979: 74). Two out of three Italian workers were unskilled. Many of the CPR's employees were young, and much of the work was seasonal. Some of these sojourners settled in Montreal and established families, usually with Italian wives. Montreal's first Italian parish was established in 1905 to serve an Italian community that increased from 1398 in 1901 to 13 922 in 1921 (Ramirez and Del Balso, 1980: 43).

While these ethnic groups were visible and important, they must not be overemphasized in Montreal's demographic profile, which was dominated by francophones. Lucia Ferretti's study of the east-end working-class parish of Sainte-Brigide's reiterates the nineteenth-century characteristics of Saint-Henri shown by Gilles Lauzon (Ferretti, 1985; Lauzon, 1987). Family and household patterns in Sainte-Brigide's make clear the class and ethnic homogeneity among francophones, and the formation and reproduction of a Montreal francophone working class. Francophone workers respected class proprieties and married the offspring of their francophone peers. Of the working-class marriages in the parish church, 61 percent were among people born in Montreal. The remaining 39 percent came largely from rural areas in the Montreal region, particularly from the island of Montreal itself or from the Lower Laurentians. Others migrated from urban working-class communities like Saint-Roch in Quebec City. New arrivals in the parish frequently found work and lodging within family or village networks.

Although rural migration to cities dominated, colonization was again promoted as a panacea for overpopulation during the 1930s. The clay belt of Abitibi was favoured over the Lac Saint-Jean or Gaspé regions. As in the nineteenth century, the clergy, the state, and rail and resource interests promoted communication, resource development, and the parish and service infrastructure of this back-to-the-land movement. Although some 45 000 people moved into colonization areas in the 1930s, two-thirds later abandoned colonization (Trofimenkoff, 1983: 240). In Abitibi, for example, dairying, hay, and blueberries were of some importance, but most of the population gravitated to the mining centre of Rouyn-Noranda, which had a population of 5471 in 1931.

This colonization to marginal areas reminds us of the increasing encroachment of settlement and resource industries upon areas occupied by native peoples. In 1857, the province's 3910 Montagnais-Naskapi were separated into twenty-three different bands. Depletion of fish and game led to famines such as the one in 1892, which reduced the population of Fort Chimo from 350 to 200. In 1900 the Montagnais population was, at best, stable at about 3500. In the early 1900s the Montagnais relied on purchased foodstuffs to support their winter trapping expeditions. Increasingly dependent on a money economy, many acted as hunting and fishing guides for wealthy whites.

The Hurons at Lorette had an infant mortality rate of 331 per 1000 and the reserve suffered from outmigration in the period 1900 to 1930. Hunting became less important and agriculture had disappeared from the reserve by the end of the century in favour of handicrafts and factory work. The last Huron speaker died in 1912 (Helm, 1981: 173).

An Industrial Capitalist Economy

The importance of industrial activity and the centrality of capital make the term "industrial capitalism" apt to describe Quebec's early twentieth-century economy. While financial institutions and many traditional manufacturing sectors remained Canadian, significant American capital was invested in Canadian mining and smelting and pulp-and-paper industries. There are problems in assessing the role of foreign capital. Theoretically, American investment in pulp-and-paper grew from $20 000 000 in 1897 to $74 000 000 in 1914 (Bernier and Boily, 1986: 142). But it is difficult to assess how much of this was American capital and how much was simply the reinvestment of accumulated profits from Canadian operations.

Development of hydro-electric resources in the southern part of the province was a central factor in the maturation of Quebec's industrial capitalist economy. Four rivers provided massive power potential: the St. Lawrence west of Montreal, the Ottawa and its tributary the Gatineau, the Saint-Maurice, and the Saguenay. By 1933 almost half of Canada's total electric capacity of 8 000 000 horsepower was located in Quebec (Armstrong and Nelles, 1986: Table 36).

Two important political decisions influenced Quebec's development of hydro-electric power in the period before the 1960s. Unlike Ontario, Quebec

did not nationalize hydro-electric power. Equally important, private companies were permitted to concentrate on commercial clients, giving them prefer-
ential treatment over residential service. Many of these companies had
arrangements with important industrial consumers. Three-quarters of Quebec's hydro-electric power in the 1930s was sold to the wood, paper and
aluminum industries or was exported, while pricing structures discouraged
consumption by small industries, farms, and residences. In 1931 domestic
service in Quebec represented only 3.5 percent of provincial hydro-electric
consumption, compared to 17.4 percent in Ontario (Armstrong, 1984: 224;
Armstrong and Nelles, 1986: 299).

Canadian generating and transmission technology was first developed in the
1890s at Niagara Falls, Ontario. In 1898 the Shawinigan Water and Power
Company was formed to exploit the forty-one metre drop of the Saint-Maurice
River at Shawinigan (Figure 6.5). Using American capital, the Shawinigan
generating station and dam became the world's second largest hydro-electric
centre, Niagara being the largest. By 1903 hydro lines capable of carrying

Figure 6.5 Shawinigan 1914. The importance of electricity in Quebec's
early twentieth-century economy is evident in this photo. As well as the
dam and generating facility, the aluminum smelter (established 1901) is
apparent on the top of the hill to the left of the dam. With war demands, its
annual production rose to 8332 tonnes in 1915. In the bay below the
generating station is the Belgo-Canadian Pulp and Paper Mill, which
produced eighty-two tonnes of pulp a day in 1902; in 1904 the mill began
producing paper and by 1926 it produced 635 tonnes of newsprint a day.
Near the generating station were also located a brickyard and cable (1902)
factory. Shawinigan's chemical factories are in the background (1911)
[Groupe de recherche sur la Mauricie, 1985].

Chapter Six

50 000 volts had been built across the 134 kilometres that separated the site from Montreal. In 1905 the company's total capital was $10 600 000 (Armstrong and Nelles, 1986: Table 10). Shawinigan experienced a further boom during the First World War when electrical consumption and local chemical production, particularly carbides, expanded enormously.

Aside from inexpensive power and the availability of forest resources, industries in centres like Shawinigan benefited from cheap labour. Already dependent on seasonal forest work, the Saint-Maurice population was categorized to industrial investors as a pool of passive, happy wage-labourers who were obedient to their priests.

> Nowhere in the world can more favorable labour conditions be found than in the province of Quebec and in the region of the Shawinigan Water and Power Company in particular. A happier and more satisfied people can probably not be found on the face of the earth. The satisfaction of the French Canadian people is a factor of great importance for employers in this region; this value of human happiness is directly attributable to the wise and good direction of their 'father confessors', the Catholic priests. For centuries in this region, the first principle of the habitants' religion has been to be satisfied with their lot. Local unions are moderate and reasonable in their demands... Another important factor for labour availability is the proverbial size of the French Canadian family. Since they all must eat, they must all work, and so the factory has abundant female and male labour on its doorstep; since they all must work, the wages asked for are extremely low (Shawinigan Water and Power Company brochure, 1930).

In the period 1896-1914 thirty new parishes were opened in the diocese of Trois-Rivières compared to seven between 1870 and 1896 (Ryan, 1966: 91). While local francophones served as unskilled labour, skilled workers, company managers, and professionals were recruited in Britain and in the anglophone community. In 1911, 6.5 percent of Shawinigan's population was anglophone, a much higher percentage than in other Saint-Maurice communities.

The Expansion of Industry

The province's largest mills developed in the Canadian Shield and Appalachians where direct access to spruce forests and hydro-electric power was available. Here, American capital was central in the development of pulp-and-paper towns along the Ottawa, Saint-Maurice, and Saguenay rivers. Like other pulpwood-producing provinces, Quebec was concerned about the export of pulpwood and moved to force the manufacture of newsprint in the province. It did this with differential crown land fees and in 1910 it followed Ontario's lead in forbidding the export of pulpwood. By the First World War, Canada was the world's largest producer of newsprint, with 86.4 percent destined for American markets. Despite a drop during the Depression, pulp-and-paper held its position as the largest Canadian export, representing 24 percent of the country's exports in 1954.

Mining became increasingly important in the first half of the twentieth century. Quebec's gold and copper became of world importance in the 1920s (compare, for example, gold and copper production in 1920 with that of 1930 and 1940 in Table 6.2) with development of mines in the Abitibi region around Rouyn-Noranda. By 1930 Noranda Mines had built a copper smelter and concentrator in Noranda and a refinery in Montreal. The rise of gold prices during the Depression served to stimulate gold production. Asbestos mining was controlled by American companies like the Johns Manville Corporation. Production of asbestos fibre in Eastern Townships communities like Thetford Mines expanded rapidly in the twentieth century with 70 percent of it being exported to the United States. Before the First World War, asbestos was exported especially for use as roofing material. Its qualities of fire resistance and low conductivity made it an important war material, and in the 1920s it found new markets in the expanding automobile industry, particularly as brake linings.

Table 6.2 Value of Quebec Gold, Copper, and Asbestos Production, 1910-1940 (in dollars)

Mineral	1910	1920	1930	1940
Gold	3000	19 000	2 930 000	39 122 000
Copper	112 000	154 000	10 426 000	13 530 000
Asbestos	2 556 000	14 735 000	8 390 000	15 620 000

(Armstrong, 1984: 221)

Like copper and asbestos, aluminum was an increasingly important material in the electrical, war, and automobile industries. Alcan, the major producer of Canadian aluminum, was founded as a Canadian branch plant of the Aluminum Company of America in 1902. The company helped develop the massive hydro-electric resources of the Saguenay River in the 1920s and built a smelter. Its company town, Arvida, was named after company president Arthur Vining Davis. By 1936 Alcan, largely owned by the Davis family, was the world's second largest aluminum producer.

The value of Quebec manufacturing doubled between 1900 and 1919 and the number of workers in manufacturing increased from 101 600 in 1901 to 125 400 in 1921 (Roby, 1976: 19). In Valleyfield, for example, the Montreal Cotton Company mill developed the largest concentration of textile machinery in Canada: by 1907 Valleyfield had over 5000 textile workers (Ferland, 1987: 61).

While the First World War stimulated Quebec industry, the Depression was characterized by an acceleration of bankruptcies and mergers. Two large munition factories were built in the Montreal area while shipbuilding expanded in Montreal, Quebec City, and Sorel. Nor was it just the transportation and iron and steel sectors that benefited. The Wood Manufacturing Company, a Montreal producer of twine, tents, and flags, saw the value of its common stock triple during the First World War.

Transportation, traditionally a central element in the Quebec economy, was subject to two marked changes in the period: expansion into resource regions and consolidation. Two new transcontinental railways, built early in the century, had important regional ramifications for Quebec. The National Transcontinental, part of the larger Grand Trunk Pacific system, ran from Moncton to Winnipeg, and crossed the St. Lawrence at Quebec City. Opening of the Quebec Bridge at the end of the First World War gave Quebec City a direct rail link to the south shore of the St. Lawrence and from there to ports open year-round. West of Quebec City, the railway reached La Tuque, followed the Upper Saint-Maurice Valley for 192 kilometres, and continued into the Abitibi region and into Northern Ontario.

In 1903 contractors William Mackenzie and Donald Mann began grouping Quebec railways into their Canadian Northern Railway system: the Lower Laurentian Railway, the Quebec and Lake St. John Railway, and the Quebec, New Brunswick, and Nova Scotia Railway. Despite some success, such as their five-kilometre tunnel through Mount Royal in Montreal, the Mackenzie-Mann syndicate was bankrupt by the First World War. Nationalization of the two new transcontinental lines left Canada with two major systems, the publicly-owned Canadian National Railway and the private Canadian Pacific Railway, each with its head office in Montreal. By 1923, the Canadian National system, which was composed of the residual assets of 221 different railway companies, had 35 000 kilometres of rail and 99 169 employees (Stevens, 1973: 311).

Food and beverage processing, much of which had undergone an early transition to industrial production, remained Quebec's most important manufacturing sector across this period. It represented 23.6 percent of the value of manufacturing production in 1880, 17 percent in 1910, and 19.3 percent in 1939. Distribution to national markets of the products of the mills, breweries, canneries and sugar refineries was assured by the expanding transcontinental rail system.

In 1911 the St. Lawrence Sugar Company's Montreal plant produced between 20 and 25 percent of Canada's sugar. Ogilvie Mills of Montreal, a flour milling company started in 1801, was reputedly the world's largest private flour company in 1900; in 1920 it controlled over 100 western grain elevators and seven mills with a daily capacity of 19 000 barrels (Sweeny, 1978: 199). Not all food and beverage production was for export markets. In Montreal, the Viau Biscuit Company's annual sales of $1 000 000 (1913) came largely from local consumption while regional distillers like Melcher's of

Berthierville satisfied the attraction of Quebecers for gin. The sector also spawned important ancillary Quebec industries such as bag, barrel, bottle, and can manufacturers.

Agriculture became less central in the Quebec economy. The percentage of the Quebec labour force engaged in agriculture declined from 45.5 percent in 1891 to 19.3 percent in 1941. The dairy industry remained important, with cheese exports to Britain climaxing in 1904 and then declining in the face of New Zealand competition. Cheese production, which was concentrated in the Eastern Townships, fell significantly in the early twentieth century. On the other hand, butter production, in response to new manufacturing technology, refrigerated rail transportation, and growing domestic demand increased threefold.

Table 6.3 Factory Butter and Cheese Production in Quebec, 1901-41 (in tonnes)

Year	Butter	Cheese
1901	11 193	36 650
1911	18 922	26 441
1921	22 104	24 655
1931	31 660	11 776
1941	34 666	17 737

(Séguin, 1980: 123)

Despite improvements in the dairy industry, Quebec agriculture did not modernize during this period. Colonization into the Shield was still encouraged by clerical nationalists fearful of emigration to the United States, although the total number of farms levelled off. The growth of the pulp-and-paper industry maintained the traditional agro-forestry sector. More important, the average size of Quebec farms remained stable, indicating a lack of concentration into larger, more profitable units, and farm mechanization lagged far behind other Canadian provinces.

While another consumer industry, tobacco, increased in importance, the leather sector declined. The tanning and saddlery industries migrated to Ontario as Quebec hemlock (used in the tanning process) was exhausted and as hide production became tied to the Ontario meat packers. The number of tanneries in Quebec City fell from twenty-seven in 1901 to twenty-one in 1911 and the number of shoe manufacturers fell from thirty-five to twenty-six in the same period. This decline was accompanied by a drop in shoeworkers in Quebec City, from 3838 to 2987. In 1871 Montreal had dominated Canadian saddlery production with twenty-three saddle manufacturers, mostly small. What was left of this dying industry by the turn of the century was largely in Ontario (Ferland, 1985: 147-8).

Shoemaking remained diverse in both its organization and capitalization, which is a reminder that not all sectors of the Quebec economy underwent centralization or concentration. Concentration in the shoe industry came in the production of the machines used in shoe assembly. Here a virtual monopoly was held by an American company. In 1912 the United Shoe Machinery Company of Massachusetts built a branch plant in Montreal to produce shoe-assembly machines for the Canadian market of which it controlled 95 percent (Ferland, 1985: 187). The company leased its machines and aggressively defended its proprietary rights. Concentration in the shoe-assembly machines tended to protect small Quebec manufacturers since shoe producers had no choice but to rent rather than to invest in shoe-assembly equipment (Bluteau et al., 1980: 111).

While a few giant shoe manufacturers, such as Ames-Holden of Montreal, produced over 2 000 000 pairs of shoes annually (1921), they represented only 9 percent of Canadian shoe production. Twenty-nine percent of production came from manufacturers who produced fewer than 100 000 pairs annually.

The Quebec garment industry was characterized by low capital investment, limited technology, and dependence on cheap, female piecework labour. In the late nineteenth century, social change, urbanization, the evolution of new work and consumer patterns, along with new marketing phenomena (department store and catalogue-sales outlets) stimulated Quebec's "ready-to-wear" clothing industry. Canadian clothing production increased 400 percent in the last three decades of the century. Although Quebec City had 1300 workers in the garment trades in 1891, the industry was traditionally concentrated in Montreal.

Based on standard sizes, clothing production branched out from an early concentration on men's clothing (work shirts, overalls, coats) into blouses, underclothes, and coats for the women's market. Unlike the generators of the hydro-electric station or the boilers of a foundry, the technology of the garment industry—the sewing machine, button-holer, and steam iron—was inexpensive and did not have to be concentrated on a single work site.

At the H. Shorey Company in Montreal, only 130 of the 1530 employees on the 1892 payroll worked on the company's premises (Steedman, 1986: 153). While the cutting, pressing, and finishing was accomplished by male tailors and workers in the Montreal factory, piecework was distributed to women in the city or surrounding countryside. In 1935 a pair of pants sewed in out-work brought $0.25 to its female producer; the same pair of pants produced in a union factory had a labour cost of $1.50 (Lavigne and Pinard, 1983: 129). Low fixed capital costs meant that the industry remained open to entrepreneurs and less subject to concentration than the highly capitalized sectors.

Iron- and steelworks remained an important sector. In Trois-Rivières, the Canada Iron Furnace Company built what was reputed to be Canada's largest furnace. In 1908 its 800 workers produced 40 000 train wheels, 20 000 tonnes of pipe, and machinery for the pulp-and-paper industry. Production of transportation equipment increased in importance, particularly in Montreal where the Canadian Pacific's Angus railway shops were opened and the British-owned Vickers Company opened its Maisonneuve shipyards in 1912. War contracts were of great importance in this sector, prompting expansion of Quebec foundries and engineering companies. Over 15 000 people worked at the Vickers shipyards during the First World War, while Davie Shipbuilding of Lauzon built submarines, submarine chasers, and steel barges.

Financial Institutions

Industrial capitalism in Quebec as shown by Gilles Piédalue, Wallace Clement, and Robert Sweeny was characterized by vertical and horizontal concentration in the early twentieth century (Piédalue, 1976; Clement, 1975; Sweeny, 1978). An important part of this concentration was the expansion of Canadian financial institutions into both local and foreign industrial investments. For example, the need for transmission lines, tracks, and telephone exchanges made utilities like the Montreal Light, Heat and Power Company, the Montreal Street Railway, and Bell Telephone important industrial borrowers.

Canada's largest bank, the Bank of Montreal, shows the mixing of industrial and financial capital. It was active in the financing of the Canadian Pacific Railway, Bell Telephone, the Laurentide Paper Company, and Dominion Textile. George Stephen, president of the bank, headed the CPR syndicate while in the 1890s the bank's principal stockholder was Montreal's leading tobacco manufacturer, William Macdonald. In 1930 the Bank of Montreal shared three directors or more with ten companies including industrial concerns like Canada Steamship Lines, Consolidated Mining and Smelting Company, Dominion Rubber, Bell Telephone, and Dominion Textiles. Among financial institutions it shared directors with Sun Life; particularly important was the bank's alliance with Royal Trust with which it shared eleven directors in 1930 (Piédalue, 1976: 378). This consolidation within Canada was accompanied by rapid overseas expansion of the Bank of Montreal into Newfoundland, the Caribbean, and Central and South America; by 1926 it was the largest financial institution in Mexico (Sweeny, 1978: 19).

Bank mergers were an important element of this concentration. The number of Canadian banks dropped from fifty-one in 1875 to twenty-one in 1918, and eleven in 1925. Sherbrooke's Eastern Townships Bank with seventy-seven branches was acquired by the Canadian Bank of Commerce in 1912. Among the regional banks, only the two francophone-controlled banks, the Banque Canadienne Nationale (the result of a government-managed merger of the Banque d'Hochelaga and the Canadienne Nationale in 1923), and the Banque Provinciale remained. For its part, the Bank of Montreal acquired three old

Montreal banks (the Bank of British North America, the Merchants' Bank, and Molson's Bank) and at the outset of the Depression had assets totalling $965 000 000 (Rudin, 1985: 120; Sweeny, 1978: 20).

The Sun Life Assurance Company illustrates the expansion of a Montreal financial institution from a local capital base into an international operation. This company also illustrates the fusion of industrial and financial capital in Quebec. Life insurance began in Canada only in the 1870s, particularly with the growth of an urban, white-collar labour force. Founded in 1871 by Montreal merchant and industrialist capitalists, Sun Life soon had agents across Canada and throughout the world, particularly within the British Empire. In 1877 the company began writing insurance in the West Indies and by 1900 it was a force in the Orient, Great Britain, the United States, and Africa. In collecting insurance premiums, Sun Life amassed huge amounts of capital, which it invested first in mortgages and increasingly in industrial stocks.

As early as 1900, company secretary T. B. Macaulay emphasized to his board of directors the importance of utilities and other industries based on hydro-electric power: "We should do well to ask ourselves whether the securities of some of the corporations which depend on this new and rising power [electricity] may not be just as desirable as those which depend upon [steampower] which has already reached its zenith" (Sweeny, 1978: 241).

Making millions from public utility bonds in Ontario and the American Midwest, Sun Life invested $50 million in First World War Dominion and Imperial bonds, and during the Second World War it was the largest subscriber to Canadian war bonds. In the 1920s Sun Life took over dozens of Canadian and foreign insurance companies. By the end of the 1920s its assets totalled over $400 million and its office staff numbered 1500; the company's Montreal head office was the largest office building in the British Empire.

Despite their experience in societies around the world, Montreal capitalists were often ignorant and even suspicious of Quebec society. This contrasts sharply with the nineteenth century when Montreal capitalists like the Molsons, Allans, and Redpaths understood Quebec society and knew how to profit from it. This distancing between the Montreal capitalists and their own backyard left important territory that both Americans and local entrepreneurs benefited from.

Besides the regional banks, an important savings and loan co-operative, the Caisse Populaire movement, was established. Using European co-operatives and savings and loan bank models, Alphonse Desjardins opened the first Caisse in his Lévis home in 1901.

The Caisses were run as co-operatives with every member having a vote. They had the double social and nationalist aim of encouraging farmers and workers to save and of collecting capital that would be available to franco-phones. They both collected savings deposits and made loans; in the period

1915-20, the average loan was $182. The Catholic clergy were enthusiastic supporters of this movement and many Caisses were associated formally with parish churches, which helped their expansion. By 1920, 206 had been established across Quebec and in francophone communities in Ontario and New England; these were grouped into ten regional federations.

The Depression of the 1930s ended Montreal's primacy as a financial centre. In the 1920s, 70 percent of stocks sold in Canada were handled on the Montreal Stock Exchange, but by 1933 the Toronto exchange had 55 percent of the market volume (McCann, 1982: 96). Aside from the increasing financial and industrial strength of Toronto as the metropolis of industrial southern Ontario, the decline of the Montreal exchange was accelerated by the preference of American investors for the Toronto exchange where almost all of the financing of the expanding mining sector, especially gold, took place.

Labour

In industrial capitalist Quebec the nature of work was changed by the declining importance of agricultural work, by fluctuations resulting from world war and depression, and by the state, church, and employers combining to suppress labour resistance. At the same time, there is strong evidence from the work of Jacques Ferland and Jacques Rouillard of vigorous labour resistance in certain sectors (Ferland, 1975; Rouillard, 1981).

Despite industrialization, work in Quebec remained seasonal for many workers, and not just in the forest sector. Longshoremen, the construction trades, and sailors could not expect to work more than seven or eight months a year. Machinists, ironworkers, and mechanics in Quebec City came back to the docks in late February and March to prepare ships for the season. In October it was a tradition that many workers from the Quebec suburb of Sillery would take the train to Lac Saint-Jean where they worked in the forest. Shoe manufacturers shut down for four to six weeks in the slow season. Of the CPR's Italian employees in Montreal in 1900-1930, 50 percent worked less than six months for the company and 19 percent worked a month or less. The instability and de-skilling of labour is clear from Bruno Ramirez's analysis of CPR employment records.

> [Italian machinist T. D.] was first hired in July 1917 as a machinist [. . .] one week later he was switched to a bolt threader job and then laid off during a staff reduction. In February of the following year, he landed another skilled job, this time as a boiler maker, but in less than two months he was laid off again in another staff reduction. Three days later, he got himself hired as a bolt threader and one month later he climbed to a machinist job. But the path to downward mobility could be a precipitous one, and one year later T. D. found himself once more at the bottom working as a labourer. . . . in November 1920, he started moving up the occupational ladder again, first as a "foundry helper," then as a "skilled

helper." His path was halted by another reduction in staff. It took another two years before T. D. was back in the employ of CP [as a machinist]. A few months later he had slipped down again, and was working as a rivetter (Ramirez, 1986: 24).

Across the first half of the century, improvements in working conditions came only slowly. Personal income per capita in 1926 was $363 in Quebec, compared to $278 in New Brunswick and $491 in Ontario (Armstrong and Nelles, 1986: 286). Many skilled workers in Quebec City had won the fifty-four-hour workweek by 1909 while women and children worked sixty hours a week. Although a provincial law in 1912 reduced the workweek in the textile industry to fifty-five hours, the law was not applied.

Through the first quarter of the century, child labour continued to be important in the manufacturing sector with fines and corporal punishment being used to control this juvenile labour force. Although Quebec was a leader in Canada with its 1909 industrial accident legislation, the government consistently failed to provide sufficient budgets to monitor infractions to its factory act. Factory inspection remained haphazard, with overworked inspectors having little power to improve plant ventilation, sanitation, or safety. There were 131 industrial deaths reported in Quebec City during the period 1904-14. Construction was particularly dangerous (Figure 6.6). On the other hand, both the federal and provincial governments were active in passing legislation to impose arbitration of labour conflicts (Dickinson, 1986).

Figure 6.6 Collapse of the Quebec City Bridge, 1916. Modelled on the Firth of Forth bridge near Edinburgh, Scotland, the Quebec Bridge collapsed twice during construction. On August 29, 1907 thirty-five of the seventy-four workers killed were Mohawk steelworkers from Kahnawake. On September 11, 1916 the central span collapsed while being hoisted into place. Ten men perished in the river: "the mass twisted on its side as though in pain", an observer recalled, "and plunged to the bottom in a great cloud of spray [...] Bodies were shaken down like apples from a tree, to fall splashing into the river. One man fell from a great height like a mannequin or wooden doll."

As elsewhere in Canada, the Depression had an effect in Quebec that went far beyond unemployment; farm bankruptcy, acute social distress, and hunger were common. The collapse of markets for export resources such as pulp-and-paper and asbestos led to intense hardship across entire regions of the province. Despite popular myth as to their self-sufficiency, farmers were not spared and, in 1931, 35 000 Quebec farmers were reported to be bankrupt (Lévesque, 1984: 21). In Montreal alone 48 percent of family heads (1931) had annual incomes of less than $1000, the minimal survival income for a family. A 1933 study of the city's unemployed showed that only 55 percent of unemployed adults had an adequate diet (Figure 6.7).

Figure 6.7 Eviction in Montreal during the Depression. A city of tenants, Montreal was also characterized by a labour force of which one sixth were unskilled labourers. This double vulnerability was made even harsher by the low per capita expenditure of $39.60 (1926) on social services, compared to $54.50 in Toronto (Copp, 1974: 146). The conjuncture of tenancy, limited social services, and unemployment assumed massive social dimensions during the Depression and by 1933, 38 percent of the city's francophones were on relief. Many were simply forced into the streets (Copp, 1974: 146; Horn, 1972: 307).

Women at Work

While women continued to be responsible for domestic work and mothering, they were of growing significance in Quebec's paid labour force. The percentage of women in the Quebec labour force rose from 21.6 percent in 1911 to 25.4 percent in 1931 and 27.4 percent in the wartime year of 1941

(Table 6.3). Nor must increased participation in wage labour hide work done by women in other sectors. Many women contributed what Leonore Davidoff calls a "hidden investment" through labour in non-industrial family enterprises such as a farm, store, rural post office, or workshop.

Table 6.3 Division of Female Labour (percent) in the Principal Occupational Sectors, Montreal 1911-1941

Sector	1911	1921	1931	1941
Manufacturing	40.1	33.5	23.4	29.6
Domestic	32.6	20.2	29.3	26.9
Office workers	—	18.5	18.9	19.9
Professional services	9.6	14.2	11.6	10.0
Commerce	13.9	8.8	8.4	10.0
Transportation	2.7	3.6	4.4	1.5
Percent of total labour force	21.6	25.2	25.4	27.4

(Lavigne et Pinard, 1983: 127)

In the labour shortage of the First World War, Quebec women moved into labour sectors traditionally reserved for men: munitions, steel, cement production, and transportation (see Figure 6.8). Female labour was synonymous with cheap labour, with females' wages at about half those of males: 53.6 percent of males' wages in 1921 and 51 percent in 1941. Competition from clerics contributed to keep teachers' salaries low (Table 6.4). A female teacher's starting salary of $625 in 1920 compared to her unmarried male counterpart's salary of $900; a married male started at $1200. Male Protestant schoolteachers averaged nearly $2000. Female teachers in urban schools, it is estimated, earned a little more than half the salary of the male caretakers of their schools (Lavigne and Pinard, 1983: 126; Thivierge, 1983: 176; Danylewycz and Prentice, 1986: 75).

Figure 6.8 Women's lunchroom in a Montreal munitions factory

Table 6.4 Percentage of Lay Female Teachers, Male Teachers, Nuns, and Brothers in Catholic Schools, 1900-1950

Year	Lay Females	Lay Males	Nuns	Brothers
1900	55	2.3	32.5	10.2
1910	51.4	2.5	33.7	12.4
1920	48.1	3.3	35.4	13.2
1930	45.6	6.1	35.1	13.2
1940	44.2	6.6	35.1	13.5
1950	47.4	8.0	32.7	11.0

(Thivierge, 1983: 172)

As elsewhere in Canada, the proletarianization and ghettoization of female work was characterized by an increasing number of women employed as elementary school teachers, nurses, telephone operators, office clerks, and store clerks. The Banque d'Hochelaga had only one female employee in 1901 and six in 1911. By 1921 in the bank's head office, "where the deskilling of jobs was most advanced", women represented one-third of the work force of 179 (Rudin, 1986:65). By the 1930s Sun Life had eighty-seven females in its stenography pool, which was yet another sign of the specialization and degradation of female work at the company. Across Dominion Square from Sun Life, Canadian Pacific Railway grouped its twenty female stenographers and typists into one office in 1935 (Lowe, 1986).

As part of the feminization of clerical labour and as a service to the growing labour demand, private secretarial schools developed. Attracting mainly female students, these schools emphasized the office tasks of typing and stenography, while accounting and bookkeeping were taught largely to the male students. In the retail sector, part-time labour and employer paternalism as evinced by staff discounts, company picnics, Christmas bonuses, and a modicum of job security, were effective means of keeping salaries low.

Far from being intellectual work that offered women good working conditions and opportunities for social advancement, elementary school teaching in Quebec was, according to Alison Prentice and Marta Danylewycz, a distinct element in the proletarianization of female labour (Danylewycz and Prentice, 1986: 61). Subject to increasing bureaucratization and inspection, female teachers worked in poorly ventilated, ill-equipped, and overcrowded classrooms. Rural teachers were expected to clean the classroom, shovel snow, and light fires. Isolation, fatigue, physical breakdown, and poverty in old age were conditions that had less in common with the professions than with the working class.

The proletarianization of nursing and the declining importance of midwifery were associated with the professionalization of medicine, the growth of clinical training for doctors, and the increasing dominance of male doctors in hospital administration. Birthing, traditionally a preserve of the midwife, became a male domain as midwives were formally excluded from using new obstetrical techniques that emphasized use of the forceps, induced labour, surgical deliveries, and anesthesia. In 1886 at the Montreal Maternity Hospital, an important obstetrical teaching hospital attached to McGill University, the midwife was replaced by a resident physician. In 1917 midwives were reminded by the Quebec College of Physicians and Surgeons that they were forbidden to use forceps.

Professionalization of nursing occurred in the 1890s with residences, probationary training, supervision by doctors, and diplomas replacing the earlier practical form of training. The first nursing school in Quebec was opened by the Montreal General Hospital in 1890 with the first nursing courses in French being offered at Notre Dame Hospital in 1897. By 1909 there were seventy nursing schools in Canada. The number of graduate nurses in Canada rose from 280 in 1901 to 5600 in 1911 and 20 462 in 1931 (Urquhart and Buckley, 1965: 44).

Labour Organizations

Until late in the Depression, Catholic ideology defined workers' rights within the framework of the social doctrine of Pope Leo XIII's *Rerum Novarum* (1891), which stressed the social value of manual labour within a hierarchical order. Opposing class struggle and international unions with their principles of religious neutrality, Catholic social activists posited the defense of French Canada's language, culture, and religion against perceived international communist and socialist threats.

In the first half of the twentieth century, Roman Catholic authorities participated directly in the Quebec labour movement. In 1907 the first Catholic union was formed in Chicoutimi under the sponsorship of the Bishop of Chicoutimi, while in 1909 the provincial council of bishops warned of the "false and dangerous principle of religious neutrality in trade unions". Priests intervened personally in important industrial disputes, as when they arbitrated the tramway strike in Montreal (1903) and the shoe industry strike in Quebec City (1911). Labour organizers, particularly Communist or American union organizers, had no doubt as to the role of the church. Rather than a mediating force between capital and labour it was an ideological arm of the former. Joshua Gershman, who organized a general strike of 10 000 francophone garment workers, understood the power of the church at the local shop level.

> Very fine workers; the girls were really good operators and finishers. We got them in those days an increase of $3.50 a week which was a big thing. The shop was very happy and satisfied. Monday, a week after we settled the strike, five girls with the shop chairlady, a French Canadian girl, beautiful person, came down together with the shop committee. The girls,

brought *me* back, not the boss, the increases they got in the new pay envelope and they said we have been to Church yesterday [. . .] and we were told by the priest that this is dishonest money, and they begged that I should return the money back to the boss. We had to go visit the parents of these girls and convince them that it's O.K., that it's all right to belong to the union. . . Many parents agreed with us but the Church really worked against us (Abella, 1977: 200).

In 1911 the Ecole sociale populaire was established to expound and propagate the church's social doctrine through brochures, study groups, and retreats. Under the leadership of a Jesuit, Joseph Papin-Archambault, the church trained priests to lead social action in their parishes and in unions. The Catholic union movement expanded rapidly after 1915 and in 1921 a confederation of Catholic unions was formed—la Confédération des Travailleurs Catholiques du Canada (CTCC). By 1931 the CTCC had 121 locals and 25 000 members.

One of the major goals of the CTCC was to unite workers by religion rather than by class and to protect francophones from international influence. In 1925 the treasurer of the CTCC and Catholic activist, Alfred Charpentier, established the Groupe Jeanne d'Arc des retraitants pompiers. The goal of this benevolent association of firemen was, in Charpentier's words, to "raise the moral fibre of firemen [. . .] to study and spread the social teachings of the church with a view to disaffiliate them from the International union. This is why I put our group under the patronnage of Joan of Arc who drove the English out of France" (Charpentier, 1971: 71).

Catholic unionism was one element in the ethnic, religious, and shop and trade division of labour in Quebec. In 1902 the expulsion of the Knights of Labour from the Trades and Labour Congress of Canada emphasized the growing power of international unionism. Within Quebec, international unions grew rapidly in the pre-war period and by 1914 they reported 30 000 members in Montreal and 3000 in Quebec City (Harvey, 1980: 146). The Depression was less propitious for the international unions and by 1933 once powerful unions like the United Mine Workers and the Amalgamated Clothing Workers were in ruins.

Out of the craft union movement and Montreal's workers clubs came the Quebec Labour Party, part of the Canadian Independent Labour Party movement. Its social democratic program included compulsory and free education, expansion of public libraries, old age pensions, health insurance, workers' compensation, and a ban on child labour. In the federal election of 1906 the party did succeed in electing Alphonse Verville, head of the plumbers union and President of the Trades and Labour Congress, in the Montreal working-class riding of Saint-Marie. However, the party had no long-term success in Quebec.

The passivity of Quebec workers has been overemphasized. Bitter strikes broke out, particularly in the transport, textile, and clothing sectors. There were at least forty strikes and lockouts in the Quebec cotton textile industry between 1900 and 1908 (Roback, 1985: 169). Jacques Ferland has shown the division among skilled and unskilled labour in examining 110 labour conflicts in the textile and leather industries between 1880 and 1910. While skilled workers went on strike in unilateral fashion, broader, multilateral strikes were evident among unskilled workers (Ferland, 1987).

Women were prominent in labour resistance. The garment and textile sectors, both of which depended heavily on female labour, were among the areas with the most frequent strikes. Despite clerical opposition, francophone women crossed ethnic lines to join their Jewish counterparts in garment industry strikes. In 1924 female workers went on strike for two months at the Eddy Match factory in Hull over management's attempt to reduce salaries and to replace female supervisors with men. Female teachers faced tight control from their school boards, but Catholic and Protestant teachers were able to work collectively and formed women's teachers associations for improved pensions and working conditions (Danylewycz and Prentice: 1986, 76).

Resistance took different forms. Within Catholic unions, shop leaders and labour militants struggled with priests for control of their unions and ideology. There is also evidence that women who were isolated and not unionized protected themselves with collective action. In 1929 four female teachers in Cap-Chat closed their school when the school board did not pay their salaries on time, and in Alma four years later ten of twelve female teachers left their classrooms under the same conditions. Marîse Thivierge concludes that these examples of collective action "demonstrate the awakening of combativeness of female teachers who were conscious of being exploited. However, these actions were of short duration and of uncertain influence..." (Thivierge, 1983: 181).

Strikes often failed in the face of federal and provincial labour legislation, the police, and management's powers in the work place. The federal and provincial governments suspended strikes by forcing workers into arbitration. Regular troops and the militia were used while railways permitted the rapid introduction of scabs and private security forces. In 1903, a strike by 2000 Montreal longshoremen was being described as a "civil war". Troops from Toronto were used to supplement the Montreal militia while 1000 workers were imported by the shipping companies as scab labour from Britain (Roback, 1985: 169).

These obstacles continued across the period. An organizer in the garment industry described his difficulties during the early 1930s: "It was the time of the Bennett regime, our union was raided by the police many times. Workers were terrorized on the picket line by police and by gangsters hired by the police. Jewish manufacturers behaved very badly" (Abella, 1977: 200). Of 287 strikes in the City of Montreal during 1901-21, 115 resulted in total rejection of employee demands. Only forty-nine of these strikes were successful, mostly in the area of skilled workers (Copp, 1974). Although labour department statistics are unreliable in counting short strikes and those in Roman Catholic unions, Table 6.5 gives an indication of the major Quebec strikes.

Table 6.5 Labour Conflicts in Quebec: 1901-45

Years	Number of Strikes	Number of Workers Involved	Person Days
1901-05	131	30 516	382 275
1906-10	106	32 311	459 080
1911-15	75	30 120	492 586
1916-20	186	63 728	1 475 220
1921-25	115	30 374	739 499
1926-30	74	21 446	313 901
1931-35	105	39 282	289 762

(Bernier and Boily, 1986: 325)

When 3000 Quebec City shoemakers went on strike against the imposition of a 30 percent pay reduction in 1925, they rejected the arbitration efforts of their chaplain and his suggestion that they return to work with a 10 percent wage cut. Workers demanded justice and paraded before the factories with photographs of the archbishop, Saint-Joseph, and the Virgin. Using Americans as trainers, the owners hired 1500 new workers and, at the same time, introduced new machines that required less skilled labour. The failure of the strike after four months crippled progressives in the Catholic union movement and it was only in the 1930s that militant Catholic unionism re-surfaced.

Conclusion

In the early twentieth century, Quebec's industrial economy was increasingly based on electrical power, the development of natural resources, and factory production. The period saw the rise of great corporations, interlocking directorships, and company towns. Through branch plants and American capital, important sectors of Quebec's industrial production were integrated into the American economy.

Despite this, much of the economic power in Quebec was controlled by anglophone capitalists in Montreal and Toronto. With pan-Canadian and international perspectives, they ignored much of Quebec outside Montreal.

The francophone bourgeoisie did not control significant amounts of capital. They did dominate the state apparatus and, at the regional level, continued to control financial, commercial, and industrial power.

From the shop floor, to the pew, to the classroom, to the teller's wicket, most Quebecers found themselves subject to strict controls. To reinforce its paternalism, capital used immigrant, short term or seasonal labour along with the isolation of company towns. The church remained a strong ideological ally of capitalism. While resistance by gender, union, and regional groups was present, the popular classes were handicapped as they coped with world war, the Depression, urbanization, public health problems, industrial work, consumerism, and ethnic division.

Bibliography

Industrial Capitalism
For financial institutions see Gilles Piédalue's thesis: *La bourgeoisie canadienne et le problème de la réalisation du profit au Canada, 1900-1930.* Also important is Robert Sweeny, *A Guide to the History and Records of Selected Montreal Businesses before 1947.* For banking see Ronald Rudin, *Banking en français: The French Banks of Quebec, 1835-1925.* For hydro-electric development see John H. Dales, *Hydroelectricity and Industrial Development. Quebec 1898-1940.* For the forest industry see René Hardy and Normand Séguin, *Forêt et société en Mauricie.*

Labour
For Quebec labour see Fernand Harvey, *Le mouvement ouvrier au Québec*, and two books by Jacques Rouillard, *Les syndicats nationaux au Québec de 1900 à 1930* and *Histoire de la CSN, 1921-1981.* Another general survey is Leo Roback, "Quebec Workers in the Twentieth Century", while Andrée Lévesque, *Virage à gauche interdit: Les communistes, les socialistes et leurs ennemis au Québec, 1929-39*, treats the left effectively. For female office work see Ronald Rudin, "Bankers' Hours: Life Behind the Wicket at the Banque d'Hochelaga, 1901-21", and Graham Lowe, "Mechanization, Feminization, and Managerial Control in the Early Twentieth-Century Canadian Office". For the proletarianization of female teachers see Marta Danylewycz and Alison Prentice, "Teacher's Work: Changing Patterns and Perceptions in the Emerging School Systems of Nineteenth and Early Twentieth Century Central Canada."

Strikes are discussed in Jacques Ferland's "Syndicalisme 'parcellaire' et syndicalisme 'collectif': Une interprétation socio-technique des conflits ouvriers dans deux industries québécoises (1880-1914)" and Evelyn Dumas, *The Bitter Thirties in Quebec.* Of use for the leather industry workers is M-A.

Bluteau et al., *Les cordonniers, artisans du cuir*. Of interest for the union-ization of female teachers is Marîse Thivierge, "La syndicalisation des institutrices catholiques, 1900-1959". For labour in the garment industry see Irving Abella, "Portrait of a Jewish Professional Revolutionary: The Recol-lections of Joshua Gershman".

Social Groups

The attitude of the clergy to industrialization is examined in William Ryan, *The Clergy and Economic Growth in Quebec (1896-1914)*. Perhaps the best source for the history of the urban working class is Terry Copp, *The Anatomy of Poverty*. Paul-André Linteau's *Maisonneuve: Comment des promoteurs fabriquent une ville* provides a good case study of the development of an industrial community. Much more than a study of women in religious orders, Marta Danylewycz, *Taking the Veil: An Alternative to Marriage, Motherhood, and Spinsterhood in Quebec, 1840-1920*, treats work and the family. For a history of the Jews in Quebec see Pierre Anctil and Gary Caldwell, *Juifs et réalités juives au Québec*, while Italians are treated in Bruno Ramirez and Michael Del Balso, *The Italians of Montreal: From Sojourning to Settlement;* padronism is treated in Robert F. Harney, "Montreal's King of Italian Labor: A Case Study of Padronism". For Italian labour see Bruno Ramirez, "Brief Encounters: Italian Immigrant Workers and the CPR, 1900-30."

Church, State,
and Women
in Industrial
Capitalist Society,
1886-1933

During the period 1886-1933, conservative forces had a strong hold on society. For much of the period, provincial politics were dominated by the Liberal Party which, under both Lomer Gouin and Louis-Alexandre Taschereau, established comfortable relationships with both the Montreal capitalists and the Catholic clergy. While region, class, and gender served to divide its opponents, conservative leadership was able to utilize effectively the church and nationalism. With ideological power in the hands of clerics and nationalists such as Edouard-Charles Fabre, Paul Bruchési, Lionel Groulx, Jules-Paul Tardivel, and Henri Bourassa, reform elements were greatly handicapped. The church's institutional power over education and social life was at its greatest in this period. Urban progressives, feminists, and political radicals were often co-opted into essentially conservative activities or were hived into marginal political groups and ethnic ghettos.

One of the important results of the maturing of industrial capitalism was that Quebec was composed of increasingly segregated economic and social worlds (Figures 7.1, 7.2, 7.3). Capitalists with interests across Canada and around the world, immigrant communities in Montreal, mining regions like Abitibi, fishing villages in the Gaspé, and traditional farmers shared the province and yet they were worlds apart. These elements of ethnicity, class, and regionalism were accentuated by different union, educational, and social institutions, and as we will see, also by the efforts of the province's political leadership. It was these conditions that fostered the contradictory social and political forces that included populism, corporatism, profound conservatism, social democracy, and urban reformism.

The social and economic position of women in Quebec was subject to continuing paternalism in the family, market, church, and state. The Catholic Church retained its strong influence over women's reproductive, domestic, and paid-work activities and intervened directly in the attempts of women to form autonomous organizations. The political and legal rights of women were inferior to those of men. Women did not have the provincial vote and were absent from government and the state bureaucracy. They were denied access to almost all higher education facilities and were marginal to the power structure of Quebec's corporations, universities, and traditional male professions.

In the skilled jobs increasingly reserved for them—nursing, teaching, secretarial work, and telephone operators—job training had larger ideological implications that prepared young women for their social role as wives and mothers. Once married, women were expected to exemplify wifely, motherly, and homemaking virtues and, except for leadership in philanthropic, religious, and national societies, were permitted little access to institutional or political leadership.

The particular role of female religious communities in Quebec's hospitals and schools was, for many Catholic women, an important alternative to

Figure 7.1 A farmer in Charlevoix

Figure 7.2 St. Lawrence Boulevard around 1914

Chapter Seven

Figure 7.3 Sainte-Catherine street at Phillips Square, 1930

These pictures emphasize the existence of several Quebecs in the early twentieth century. With its ox, thatched roof, hay crop, equipment, and wooden barn, this Charlevoix farm (7.1) retained many elements of preindustrial society into the twentieth century. In 1926 there were 1585 mechanized tractors on Quebec farms, compared to 12 286 in Ontario and 50 136 in the prairie provinces (Urquhart and Buckley, 1965: 391).

St. Lawrence Boulevard (7.2), or the "Main" as it is known, has been a kaleidoscope of Montreal's ethnic diversity since the late nineteenth century. A 1913 street directory shows the presence of the garment district, a tobacco factory and a brewery, and a variety of ethnic shops, one of which was the first Steinberg grocery store. Horse-drawn tramways were introduced onto the street in 1864, opening new working-class suburbs like Saint-Jean-Baptiste, while in 1892, as is evident in the photo, the system was electrified.

Farther west at Phillips Square was the centre of anglophone Montreal (7.3). The cars and tramways emphasize the changing form of transportation and the transformation of the walking city. The chauffeurs waiting by their limousines hint at the wealth of some shoppers. To the right is Morgan's Department Store (now The Bay) constructed of red sandstone brought from Scotland as ballast. In the background, an addition is being made to the Toronto-owned Eaton's, which had bought out the local Goodwin's Department Store. The two department stores are separated by the Anglican Christ Church Cathedral, while across from the church and just out of the photo was Henry Birks, Canada's most important jeweller.

marriage. To Marta Danylewycz, the 133 female religious communities, established between 1840 and 1960 in Quebec, represent particular forms of autonomous female activity and cannot be dismissed simply as evidence of the domination of women by male clerics. "Women", Danylewycz argues, "did not stumble blindly into convents" (Danylewycz, 1987: 159). Rather, religious communities were an important institutional means for women to achieve social, personal, and intellectual advancement and offered a celibate existence as an alternative to motherhood.

The convent was also an important source of material security for unmarried women; the largest number of entries into female religious communities occurred in 1930, one of the most critical years of the Depression (Lavigne et Pinard, 1983: 279, 283). The importance of female religious communities in Quebec society is evident from Table 7.1, which shows that the 13 579 nuns in 1921 represented 9.1 percent of the population of single women over age twenty.

Table 7.1 Women in Religious Communities in Quebec, 1851-1921

| | Number of Nuns | Percentage of | |
		Females over 20	Single Females over 20
1851	650	0.3	1.4
1871	2320	0.9	4.1
1881	3783	1.1	4.4
1901	6629	1.5	6.1
1911	9964	1.9	8.0
1921	13 579	2.2	9.1

(Danylewycz, 1987: 17)

The Church

With a population that remained 86 percent Catholic in 1941, Quebec was subject to profound clerical influence in all aspects of early twentieth-century life. The financial relationship among the church, state, and industrial capital is apparent from Table 7.2.

The power of the church hierarchy over social and intellectual life remained strong and showed itself in the area of Sunday activities and laws concerning theatres and cinemas. Secular officials were careful with clerical opinion. In 1893, for example, when the Italian battleship *Etna* visited Montreal, Mayor Desjardins refused to meet the ship's officers. He argued that he did not want to meet representatives of a state that oppressed the Pope. In addition to its direct influence on labour through Catholic unions (see Chapter 6), the church expanded its influence over women, youth, the Caisse Populaire movement, universities, and other educational institutions and social services.

Table 7.2 Sulpician Investments in Bonds, Debentures and Shares Worth over $40 000, 1882-1909

Investment	Type of enterprise	Amount ($)
Richelieu and Ontario Navigation	Shipping	169 000
Sorel, Quebec	Municipality	142 000
Champlain and St. Lawrence	Railway	94 000
Port Arthur, Ontario	Municipality	90 000
Sault Ste. Marie, Ontario	Municipality	89 000
Dominion Cotton Mills	Textile	85 000
Hamilton Power Co.	Utility	73 000
Iberville, Quebec	Municipality	49 000
Lake of the Woods Milling	Milling	43 000
Montreal Light, Heat & Power	Utility	42 000

(Young, 1986: 212-13)

The church was particularly able to use its control over education to recruit the best students to the clergy. In the March 1986 edition of *L'incunable*, Jean-Ethier Blais effectively described the entry of François Hertel into the Jesuits.

> The important event [of his years at the Séminaire de Trois-Rivières] was his decision to become Jesuit and therefore priest and teacher. Hertel drifted into this decision without really understanding what he was doing, caught up by this immense machine which we call destiny. The basic principle of the period was that, whoever did not rise up forcefully against a religious vocation, was made for it. Hertel entered the Jesuits then, negatively one could say, *volens nolens* by the moral authority of his confessor [... this] all occurred in an atmosphere of moral rectitude, and, strange as it may seem, of liberty.

The parish, the central framework of social life of Quebec communities, kept pace with demographic growth, particularly in expanding urban areas. The number of parishes in the diocese of Montreal increased from 152 in 1881 to 215 in 1941 (*Eglise de Montréal*, 1986: 182).

The parish of Saint-Alphonse at the Baie des Hahas on the Saguenay illustrates the steady development of the institutional infrastructure of a rural parish. Early in the twentieth century, the village became an important port for the shipping of aluminum, pulp, and cheese. In 1901 churchwardens bought a new cemetery site for $800. In 1902 a public hall with a sacristy and a special room for young girls was built. In 1908 churchwardens donated land worth $3600 for construction of an orphanage. In 1923 repairs to the church cost $40 000; a new presbytery was added in 1926 at a cost of $25 000 and a year later a boys' academy costing $77 220 was constructed (Potvin, 1957).

Catholicism in Quebec in the early twentieth century was more than symbolic. Its omniscient institutional presence was accompanied by ideological rigour. Church fathers continued to emphasize church going, particularly confession. Patients at the Hôpital de la Miséricorde were obliged to attend chapel three times a day. In 1912 parishioners in urban parishes of Montreal took communion an average of twenty-two times a year while rural parishioners in the Montreal area averaged twenty-eight times (Hamelin and Gagnon, 355). Through fraternal self-help societies and publications, the church exerted a strong influence on morality (Figure 7.4).

Figure 7.4 Brochure published by the Franciscans. Asking to be protected from the ''plagues of modern life'', publications such as this singled out alcoholism, undisciplined education, theatre, cinema, divorce, and non-confessional clubs. Also of note is the idealization of small-town life.

The same strength was apparent in daily life in the countryside. In the village of Saint-Justin, subject of an 1898 study by Léon Gérin, families had religious images in their bedrooms. Daily prayers were a custom and family pews were full for Sunday mass. Feasts and holy days were strictly observed and at Easter, attendance at mass was virtually universal (Gérin, 1968: 114). When radio came to Belle-Anse in the Gaspé, whole families tuned in to the daily rosary recitation. Sociologist Marcel Rioux concluded that Catholicism "was such an integral part of the personality of the Belle-Anse villagers—of their system of values—that the principles on which it was based were never enunciated; it was something which was understood and no one considers that it could be otherwise" (Rioux, 1961: 44). Farm organizations and Caisse Populaires were another source of clerical influence over social and economic life in the countryside. When the Union Catholique des Cultivateurs was established in 1924, the power of chaplains in the movement ensured that its action would be directed at social and moral reform rather than at secular politics.

In their *Histoire de catholicisme québécois*, Jean Hamelin and Nicole Gagnon show the importance of popular religion in early twentieth-century Quebec and the fine line that separated the sacred and profane. Pilgrimages were important means of channelling popular religious practices and recreation into sanctioned and supervised forms. In 1903 a Quebec City typographer reported that he and his wife took three excursions a year out of Quebec City, two to visit kin and the third as a pilgrimage. In Saint-Justin, women of the village undertook an annual pilgrimage as their primary sortie from the village. These pilgrimages were carefully supervised. The Archbishop of Montreal forbade women to participate in mixed, overnight trips.

The three most important pilgrimage sites in Quebec—Sainte-Anne-de-Beaupré, thirty-five kilometres east of Quebec City, Cap-de-la-Madeleine near Trois-Rivières, and St. Joseph's Oratory in Montreal—all had origins as popular shrines in the early years of French colonization. Run by the Redemptorists, the Basilica at Sainte-Anne-de-Beaupré had an increase in the number of its visitors from 113 560 in 1895 to 256 610 in 1923 (Hamelin and Gagnon, 1984: 349). St. Joseph's Oratory was erected on the site of a popular shrine that had existed since the seventeenth century. It became North America's most important urban shrine with the faith healing of Brother André, an illiterate caretaker at the shrine. Despite opposition from Catholics hostile to faith healing, a small shrine was built on the site in 1904; in 1924-25 the church hierarchy sponsored a Basilica and in 1982 Brother André was beatified. Between 1898 and 1930, twenty-three new pilgrimage sites in Quebec were established (Hamelin and Gagnon, 1984: 352).

Clerical Ideology

Higher education, with its close links to intellectual life, the clergy, and the professions, was a traditional area of particular clerical interest. In response to chamber of commerce pressure, Quebec's first business school, the Ecole des Hautes Etudes Commerciales, was established in 1907. Premier Gouin met with the archbishop of Montreal and promised that, although the school would at first be independent, it would be affiliated with Laval University and its religious authority at the first opportunity. The archbishop was given a voice in the naming of the business school's first professors, two of whom were priests.

The Montreal campus of Laval became the autonomous University of Montreal in 1920. Mgr. Georges Gauthier, auxiliary bishop of Montreal, was rector. A Sulpician was named the first dean of philosophy while the department itself became what Hamelin and Gagnon describe as "a fief" of the Dominicans for forty years.

The classical college system remained at the core of Catholic secondary school education. The establishment of these colleges, their curriculum, and faculties were tightly controlled by the clerical hierarchy. Like the parish, the colleges reflected the province's changing demography. Originally located primarily in small comunities, eighteen of the twenty-nine colleges established between 1920 and 1939 were in Montreal and Quebec City. And fifteen of these were established for girls (Galarneau, 1978: 59).

The most important Quebec intellectual of his generation was Canon Lionel Groulx, profoundly conservative and dedicated to soil, family, and the church. He touched Quebec's political and ideological nerve by questioning the values of the industrial capitalist society and by pointing out the dangers of the decline of rural Quebec. His emphasis on an idyllic, preindustrial, and self-sufficient past had broad appeal in an industrializing and urbanizing society in which anglophone capital played an increasing role.

> One of the characteristics of the Canadian family is to be a work co-operative and a small society almost independent in the economic domain. The family budget aims at family self-sufficiency for all needs. Everyone works and makes his contribution so that from the work of all we have the wherewithal to feed and clothe ourselves.

Questioning Confederation at the very time of the conscription crisis, Groulx wrote of a nostalgic past and a messianic future based on Catholic martyrdom and virtues that had been lost by the Conquest, by compromise with the British, and by betrayal by the Quebec bourgeoisie. His emphasis on racial homogeneity and moral purity coincided with other right-wing intellectuals' attacks on Jews and Jehovah's Witnesses in the 1930s and with the attraction to some Quebecers of Italian, Portuguese, and Spanish fascism. Groulx gave currency to his solution of a strong French and Catholic Quebec through his chair in Canadian History at the University of Montreal and through the influential monthly *Action française*.

Despite this institutional and ideological strength, traditional clerical prerogatives were threatened by bureaucratization and the growth of state power in the twentieth century. Clerical power was threatened also by the Depression with its new scale of public assistance, and with the intrusion of new Canada-wide social programs. Bernard Vigod summarizes the Church's attitude to social issues and state interference in the 1920s as one of "insecurity" (Vigod, 1978: 180).

Quebec's Minority Status in Canada

In the transition period, leaders of the francophone political bourgeoisie like La Fontaine and Cartier had assiduously developed credentials as political brokers between the emerging industrial capitalist interests and traditional Quebec. One important result of their power in the mid-nineteenth century had been the structuring of many of the province's fundamental social and political institutions in a framework of an industrializing but conservative and Catholic society. The reproduction of this political stance and the tensions it generated formed the core of the Quebec political system until the end of the Second World War.

This political elite successfully reproduced itself both in terms of families and values. Lomer Gouin, provincial premier from 1905-20, was the son-in-law of former premier Honoré Mercier. Gouin's successor as premier 1920-36, Louis-Alexandre Taschereau, was the son of a supreme court judge and nephew of Canada's first cardinal. At the same time, their nationalist opponent, Henri Bourassa, was grandson of Louis-Joseph Papineau. This elite governed with a sense of *noblesse oblige*. For them, democracy was still "in the experimental stage" and needed a guiding hand: "the task", Premier Taschereau told a student audience in 1930, "rests with a certain class of aristocracy. Not the aristocracy of blood, lineage, or money, but the aristocracy of learning, science and knowledge" (Vigod, 1986: 163).

Confederation had integrated Quebec into an increasingly larger political state. With the addition of Saskatchewan and Alberta in 1905, Canada had nine provinces and in 1949 Newfoundland became the tenth. A series of linguistic and ethnic crises, from the execution of Métis leader Louis Riel in 1885 to the conscription crisis of the First World War, emphasized Quebec's vulnerability in this federation.

The collapse of the vision of a viable French Canadian presence in the West and the failure of Quebec members to block the execution of Riel was followed by the Manitoba schools crisis in the 1890s, and the growing force of anti-Catholic and francophobe elements in Ontario and New Brunswick. Each incident emphasized Quebec's minority position in the federal system and the fragile status of francophones outside the province.

In 1896, Wilfrid Laurier's election as Prime Minister on a platform of "sunny ways" placed him on a political tightrope in which the defence of French Canadian interests depended on a strong French Canadian presence in Ottawa and a vigorous Liberal Party. Laurier's successor as Liberal leader, William Lyon Mackenzie King, emphasized the importance of his Quebec lieutenant, Ernest Lapointe. Part of Liberal strategy was to foster the image of the Conservative Party as hostile to francophones. However, "sunny ways" or faith in British institutions, the good will of anglophone allies, and strong, non-threatening leadership from Laurier or loyal Quebec lieutenants could not ultimately soften the reality that Canada had a growing English-speaking majority.

In each political crisis (the Boer War (1899), Northwest Schools (1905), Ontario's Regulation XVII (1911), and the conscription crises of the two world wars) Quebec's views were inevitably subordinated to the majority. It also became clear that in the view of the English-speaking majority, Confederation had not established "two nations" but rather a federation in which Quebec was only one voice among many provinces.

The place of francophones outside Quebec was made perfectly clear in Eastern Ontario where francophones were a majority in certain border counties. In Prescott County, for example, francophones represented 71 percent of the population in 1901 but officials had no intention of granting permanent status to French schools. According to Chad Gaffield, Ontario school officials saw French-language schools in the county as "ephemeral, a necessary but temporary phenomenon to be tolerated on the way to the goal of uniform, unilingual schooling" (Gaffield, 1987: 29, 34).

It is overly simplistic to see Quebec's minority status only in terms of linguistic questions. For example, establishment of the Supreme Court of Canada in 1875 subjected Quebec's civil law to judges trained in the common law tradition. Even judges appointed from Quebec to the federal court did not defend the civil-law tradition. According to Snell and Vaughan, "none of the early Quebec members of the Supreme Court were militant defenders of the civil law [... and none saw] any great threat to that tradition from a close working proximity to common-law influence" (Snell and Vaughan, 1985: 130).

Canada's role in the British Empire was an ongoing source of difficulty for politicians from Quebec, particularly after the 1890s as Britain sought Canadian support in imperial matters. At Queen Victoria's Diamond Jubilee in 1897, British officials began to pressure Laurier to contribute to the cost of the British navy. In the Boer War (1899-1902), many Canadians of British origin insisted that Canada support the British in conquering the Boers in South Africa. Despite the strong resistance of many francophones—many of whom saw themselves in much the same position as the Boers—7000 Canadian troops served in the war.

The First World War further divided Canada. By 1917 any unity that had existed at the outbreak of war had broken down with the growing casualties that led to the conscription crisis. In 1917 a bipartisan Union Government was established to implement conscription. In Quebec anti-conscription riots, the failure of 40 percent of conscripted men to report for duty, and the election in 1917 of only three Union Government supporters (all from predominantly anglophone ridings) emphasized strong French Canadian resistance to the English Canadian majority.

Provincial Autonomy

This sense that the province was isolated in Confederation, with its institutions and language under attack from the majority, led to an increasing Quebec separateness from the rest of Canada on social and moral issues. Quebec politics from 1886 to the Depression were characterized by increasing attention to the minority status of French Canadians in Canada, and by a growing emphasis on provincial rights and on the Quebec government as the defender of French Canada's religious, language, and cultural traditions. "Sunny ways" was increasingly contested by hardening theories of provincial rights.

In the post-Confederation period, Cartier's and La Fontaine's provincial heirs were Conservatives like Joseph-Adolphe Chapleau and Liberals like Honoré Mercier. They were caught between two forces: the conflicting interests of a conservative Catholicism with roots deep in the Church, small-town bourgeoisie, and peasantry; and the exigencies of maturing industrial capitalism. Provincial politics in the decades after Confederation were marked by instability, bitter political division between centrists and the Catholic right, and deepening provincial debt to subsidize railways and other industrial activities. Industrial capitalists insisted on various forms of state aid, a cheap labour force, and a stable economy. The form of state aid in Quebec changed from direct subsidies to favourable investment, tax, and labour laws.

Fernand Dumont has shown how Quebec's baggage of minority status in Canada, its isolation, its poverty in the face of international capital, and its political and economic subjugation provided nationalists with strong ammunition (Dumont et Hamelin, 1971). On their right, politicians faced conservative Catholic and nationalist spokesmen like Jules-Paul Tardivel, Henri Bourassa, and Lionel Groulx. They attacked the provincial government for the hemorrhage of emigration, the failure of colonization, the inevitable minority position of Quebec in a federal state, and the moral disintegration that they perceived in an industrializing and urbanizing society. As early as the 1880s, provincial politicians had to compromise the reality of Canadian federalism with the vigorous arguments of nationalists like Tardivel.

> It should be obvious to anyone who thinks about it, that the French race in America will never have any real influence for good unless it is solidly based in the province of Quebec, as in a fortress. We must occupy the territory of this province, which belongs to us by every sort of title. We must develop and strengthen ourselves here, under the protection of the Church which watched over our beginnings and whose magnificent institutions are still our greatest strength (Tardivel, 1975: XXX).

The contradictions between provincial rights and "sunny ways", between federal and provincial forums, between traditional parties and third parties, can be perceived in the changing political alliances of Henri Bourassa's career. His ideology was rooted in conservatism, Catholicism, and French-Canadian nationalism. His attempt to integrate these principles with a larger Canadian ideal of mutual respect, biculturalism, pan-Canadian nationalism, and Canadian autonomy flew apart during the schools and conscription crises. Entering politics after the execution of Riel, Bourassa sat in both the federal (1890-1907, 1925-35) and provincial (1908-12) legislatures. He first sat as a Liberal but split with Laurier over the Boer War. He then sat as an Independent, was prominent in the establishment of a separate Nationalist party and the important Montreal newspaper *Le Devoir* (1910). Later he ran as a Conservative.

Nor were nationalists comfortable with their government's close relationship with the great trusts and industrial corporations. Once out of the premier's office, Lomer Gouin had moved to the board rooms of English Canadian companies like Sun Life and the Bank of Montreal. Concentrating particularly on electric power and transport monopolies, nationalists called for nationalization of waterpower sites, municipalization of Montreal transport and electric companies or, at the very least, an end to state subsidies to private companies. During the Depression, powerful nationalists like Groulx called for state action in the economy to protect Quebec culture. His speech still reflects the accepted ideology of Quebec governments.

> To be French is to remain French. More than our right, it is our duty and
> our mission. The state has an obligation to remember that the national
> good, our cultural heritage, is an integral part of the common good for
> which it is particularly responsible. And since the economic and the
> national are not without relationship, the state again has the obligation to
> remember that the national good imposes upon it certain duties, even of
> economic character (Jones, 1972: 50).

These attacks on the direction of Canadian federalism had important repercussions in the law, politics, and social legislation of the province. In 1918 Pierre-Basile Mignault was appointed to the Supreme Court of Canada. One of the province's foremost civil jurists, he rejected the federalism and pro-common law bias of early Quebec judges on the federal bench. He not only vigorously attacked the prevalence of common law principles in areas concerning the Quebec civil code but put his interpretation in the framework of a compact theory of Confederation (1891).

> The provinces were not created by this charter [the British North America
> Act]. Confederation is only the legalization of a pact concluded between the
> four provinces. It seems then that one can conclude *a priori* that the
> provinces acted like merchants who form a corporation. They put together
> a part of their property, but kept the rest (cited in Howes, 1987: 547).

Liberal provincial politicians, well-known for their sympathies with the federal government, found it in their interest to adopt the rhetoric of provincial rights. In 1927, when his government was protesting Ottawa's plan for Old

Age Pensions, Premier Taschereau outlined to a student audience his support of the compact theory of Confederation.

> Every Canadian must understand that sixty years ago we formed not a homogeneous country but a Confederation of different provinces for certain purposes, with the distinct understanding that each of these provinces should retain certain things which a people, like an individual, has no right to abdicate (cited in Vigod, 1986: 148).

This separateness was clearly evident in legislation on alcohol. Quebec refused the social values of Protestant Canada. In 1898 Quebec had been the only province to vote "no" in a prohibition referendum. In the next decades, Quebec, except for a short and theoretically dry period at the end of the First World War, continued to resist the prohibition movement. In 1919 alcohol was again being sold publicly in Quebec.

Traditionally, alcohol had been sold in Quebec by general merchants and grocers. With the establishment of the Quebec Liquor Commission in 1921, the state established a monopoly over the importation, transportation, and sale of alcoholic products (Figure 7.5). The disparity between the public sale of alcohol in Quebec and prohibition in nearby Canadian and American jurisdictions led to widespread smuggling. Revenues of the Quebec Liquor Commission in 1929-30 were $20 million; with depression conditions and the lifting of American prohibition in 1933, Commission revenues dropped to $5 million (*La Presse*, November 29, 1986).

Figure 7.5 Quebec Liquor Commission Permit. Church concerns for temperance were reflected by government liquor regulations. Liquor stores were characterized by shaded windows and bottles stored behind counters. During the war, liquor permits were needed and coupons controlled consumption.

No 271664 C

Ce Permis autorise le(a) soussigné(e)
This Permit authorizes the undersigned

M. *R. Charette*

(Nom en lettres carrées)—(Name in block letters)

Domicilié(e) à *21-26e ave*
Residing at *Lachine*

qui déclare être âgé(e) de 20 ans ou plus, à acheter de l'alcool et des spiritueux, aux magasins de la Commission des Liqueurs de Québec, conformément aux conditions mentionnées au verso.

who declares being of the full age of 20 years, to buy alcohol and spirits from the Quebec Liquor Commission, in accordance with regulations mentioned on the other side.

Emis ce *6* jour de *sept* 194 *5*
Issued this — day of

Magasin No *04* Par
Store No. — By

(Initiales de l'employé(e))
(Employee's initials)

René Charette

(Signature du détenteur) — (Signature of Permitholder)

NUL SI DÉTACHÉ — VOID IF DETACHED

REMARQUES

Ce permis est personnel et non transférable.

Il confère à son détenteur le droit d'acheter, en une ou plusieurs fois, une quantité maxima d'alcool et de spiritueux de 40 onces par quinzaine.

Le coupon inutilisé au cours de la quinzaine est nul après cette période.

Lors d'un achat, le commis détachera ou annulera lui-même les coupons requis.

La Commission confisquera tout permis émis à la suite de renseignements inexacts ou erronés.

REGULATIONS

This permit is personal and not transferable.

The holder of this permit may purchase, on one or several occasions, a quantity of alcohol and spirits not exceeding a total of 40 ounces per fortnight.

The unused coupon becomes void at the expiration of the fortnight.

At every purchase, the necessary coupons must be detached or cancelled by the store clerk himself.

The Commission will confiscate any permit which has been issued on incorrect information.

DATE	ONCES - - OUNCES				
Quinzaine commençant 16 Avril April 16	10	10	10	1	1
Half Month beginning	2	2	2	1	1
Quinzaine commençant 1 Avril April 1	10	10	10	1	1
Half Month beginning	2	2	2	1	1
Quinzaine commençant 16 Mars March 16	10	10	10	1	1
Half Month beginning	2	2	2	1	1
Quinzaine commençant 1 Mars March 1	10	10	10	1	1
Half Month beginning	2	2	2	1	1
Quinzaine commençant 16 Fév. Feb. 16	10	10	10	1	1
Half Month beginning	2	2	2	1	1
Quinzaine commençant 1 Fév. Feb. 1	10	10	10	1	1
Half Month beginning	2	2	2	1	1

The Era of Gouin and Taschereau

The Liberal administrations of Lomer Gouin (1905-1920) and Louis-Alexandre Taschereau (1920-36) tried to conciliate the interests of both conservative nationalists and the industrial capitalists. Strong support for industrial "progress" was what they described as the bedrock of their three decades of provincial power. Specifically, this meant the rapid exploitation of natural resources, low taxes, minimal state interference with business and a paternalistic attitude to labour. They were particularly anxious to attract American capital which, as Taschereau explained, they saw as essential to the province's development: "We still don't have enough American capital interested in our enterprises. It would be difficult to get $75 for an undertaking like that at Caron Falls if we relied solely on Canadians. We need to develop ourselves with the gold of our neighbours" (Jones, 1972: 28-29).

The alliance between successive Liberal provincial governments and the major financial and industrial corporations was cemented with cronyism, directorships, legal business, sinecures, and political contributions. Even native peoples, increasingly marginal to the power structure, felt the impact. The Huron Indians of the Lorette reserve, for example, saw part of their reserve expropriated and their traditional way of life threatened when the Quebec and Lake St. John Railway was built.

At the same time, Gouin and Taschereau worked to maintain Cartier's and La Fontaine's tradition of good political relations with the church hierarchy. In their commitment to industrial expansion, regional economic growth, and social peace, officials of both church and state usually shared a common ideology. This ideology was reinforced by social contact and systematic consultation between the hierarchy of church and state: "You know on what terms of friendship I was with your predecessor", Archbishop Bruchési wrote to Premier Taschereau in 1920. "We always got along well in all matters. I have no doubt it will be the same with you, Mister Premier, especially in questions which interest the Church. For a long time I have known your feelings. I will act with you as a friend and I urge you to be the same with me."

For his part, Premier Taschereau assured a 1933 banquet for the province's leading cleric, Cardinal Jean-Marie-Rodrigue Villeneuve, that the church was an ally in maintaining social order by its teaching of: "obedience to authority, respect for law and property, the sanctity of the home, the sovereignty of the father of the family in his little kingdom [and] the assurance that death is not an end but a beginning" (Vigod, 1986: 201).

The church proved a reliable force in maintaining social order; indeed it was Premier Taschereau's uncle, Cardinal Elzéar-Alexandre Taschereau, who had condemned the Knights of Labour in 1885 (Ryan, 1966: 201). In 1907 Cardinal Louis-Nazaire Bégin founded the newspaper *l'Action sociale*, a persistent supporter of industrial development. In Montreal, Archbishop Paul

Bruchési responded to a rash of strikes in 1903 with a pastoral letter rejecting a labour theory of value and calling on workers to be moderate in their wage demands. Strikes, he contended, forced capital to flee and resulted in cheap immigrant labour replacing striking francophone workers.

Nor was it just the church hierarchy that favoured industrial development. In 1913, when government officials inquired as to the needs of 270 parishes, 116 local priests replied by inviting industries into their parishes (Ryan, 1966: 198). Despite orders from the hierarchy that they not serve on the boards of industrial companies, many priests continued the entrepreneurial tradition of curé F-X-A Labelle of Saint-Jérôme. In Lake Mégantic, for example, the local curé built the town's first electrical generating station and served as its electrician until his death.

Church-state collaboration was clear in education. The Education Act of 1875 gave every bishop in the province an automatic seat on the Catholic committee of the Council of Public Instruction. Louis-Philippe Audet summed up the significance of this clerical power in the organization of the provincial education bureaucracy:

> [The law] resulted in a considerable growth of clerical influence to the
> point, that, after this date, most Catholic leaders in the francophone sector
> bowed gracefully before the combined power of the Catholic hierarchy,
> clergy, and religious communities. Conscious of the power which it held,
> the Church in Quebec considered its role—which historic circumstances
> had temporarily confided it with—as a 'mission de droit' (Audet, 1969: 37).

Despite some state centralization of education to oversee financing and inspection, the church successfully opposed demands for formation of a Ministry of Education. It continued to control curriculum and textbooks and resisted compulsory education. In 1908 the provincial education budget was less than $0.50 for each child enrolled in elementary school (Ryan, 1966: 216). A major factor in these low costs was the cheap labour of the nuns and brothers who made up 48.3 percent of elementary teachers and 85 percent of secondary and classical college teachers. The labour of clerics ensured that the salaries of lay teachers, largely female, would remain low. Despite its low expenditures, Quebec's literacy and its attendance rate was comparable to that of other provinces.

State participation was also evident in the social sector. While not challenging clerical control, the Public Assistance Law of 1921 recognized institutions of public utility and established a statutory system of subsidies.

This church-state collaboration did not mean an absence of friction. State authorities faced new exigencies of financing, new demands for curriculum change, and pressure from their Protestant and Jewish constituencies. As early as 1830 classical colleges received subsidies and a 1922 provincial law permitted each college to receive up to $10 000 from the state. The state assumed financing of male elementary education in 1897, while female elementary education remained a preserve of the church. In 1900 the province's fifty female boarding schools received the equivalent state aid of one classical college. Permission was granted to the Congrégation de Notre-Dame to open the province's first female school of higher learning in 1908, although it was not given the status of a classical college until 1926 when it became the Collège Marguerite-Bourgeoys (Dumont and Fahmy-Eid, 1986: 21; Heap, 1987).

The same tension was evident in the social sector, where clerical control and Catholic ideology were often at odds with the imperatives of an urban society. Quebec's reported illegitimacy rate varied between 2.9 and 3.4 percent of live births and was slightly lower than the Canadian average. Twenty percent of Quebec's reported illegitimate births took place in Montreal's Miséricorde Hospital (Figure 7.6).

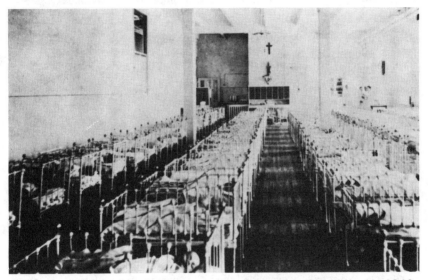

Figure 7.6 The Sisters of Miséricorde Hospital (1900). Established in 1840, this maternity hospital was part of a wider social control network. Young domestic servants between the ages of eighteen and twenty-two formed the majority of expectant mothers. Mothers forced to abandon their babies often sent money, asked for photographs, and wrote with instructions and wishes for their infant's care: "Let her take fresh air outside. I would so like her to enjoy good health." Most babies were sent for adoption or to the Grey Nuns orphanage. In 1933 the overcrowded institution began turning pregnant women away, accepting only local women who were at least in the seventh month of pregnancy (Lévesque, 1984: 179).

With the evolution of work and family patterns in industrial capitalist society, the vocation of many Catholic institutions changed. From the mid-nineteenth century, day-care centres had been an increasingly important element of the family strategy of working class families (Table 7.3). The number of children in the Grey Nuns' day-care centres peaked at the turn of the century and then declined, causing Micheline Dumont to speculate that centres were converted into hospices for the children of the poor. Sylvie Côté argues that while social control was evident in Sacré-Coeur hospice's curriculum and organization, it served as an element in the family strategy of the Sherbrooke proletariat. Faced with unemployment, wartime separation, or the imprisonment, illness, or alcoholism of the family head, parents interned their children at the hospice. Both parents of 63 percent of children at the school were alive.

Table 7.3 Number of Children in the Grey Nuns' Day-Care Centres, 1858-1922

Institution	Period	Number of Children	Daily Average
Saint-Joseph	1858-1899	9793	242
Nazareth	1861-1914	14 925	?
Bethléem	1868-1903	12 853	350
Saint-Henri	1885-1920	16 700	450
Sainte-Cunégonde	1889-1922	6000	?

(Dumont, 1980: 40)

State financial participation in social affairs involved the government in questions touching nationalist and religious sensitivities. In 1924, the Taschereau government passed a Child Adoption Act designed to relieve crowding in orphanages, to find homes for illegitimate children, and to give legal safeguards to adopting parents. Clerics, supported by Henri Bourassa and other conservatives, protested vigorously against the act, particularly the provision that Roman Catholic children could be placed in non-Catholic families. With the bogey of the French Revolution and the secularism of France always handy, clerical speakers described the bill as part of an anticlerical campaign aimed at "the successful elimination and systematic displacement of the church's maternal influences" (Vigod, 1986: 118).

Populism in Montreal

The proletarianization of Montreal that we observed in Chapter 6 resulted in urban populism. In the 1880s popular-class communities like Hochelaga (1893) and Saint-Jean-Baptiste (1885) to the east of Montreal were annexed to the city. This added francophone weight to Montreal's proletariat. Popular class francophones became an increasingly important political factor in a city faced with rapid industrialization, private monopolies in municipal utilities such as electric power and tramways, persistent strikes in the transport sector and dire public health conditions.

The smallpox epidemic of 1885 with its 2500 victims led to riots. In 1913 a sixty-foot crack in the city's water conduit cut off the water supply for four days. In the 1918 influenza epidemic Quebec was the worst-hit province with 530 000 cases and 14 000 deaths (McGinnis, 1977: 128). Impure milk and the resulting tuberculous and diarrheal diseases gave the city the highest infant mortality rate in North America. Perhaps the disaster that shocked the public the most was the Laurier Palace Theatre fire of January 9, 1927.

The 1000-seat Laurier Palace Theatre was located in east-end Montreal in a working-class neighbourhood. During a Sunday showing of a children's film, fire broke out. Seventy-eight children died. Almost all of them died of asphyxiation on the stairs of the four exits. An inquiry showed that the theatre was operating without a permit, that inspection was lax, that exit doors were blocked by ropes and snow, and that safety laws had been disobeyed. By law, parents were to accompany children under seventeen, but not one of the victims was over sixteen.

Until 1914 Montreal's tradition of a mayoralty alternating between francophones and anglophones continued. Anglophone reformers like shoe manufacturer Herbert Ames published *The City Below the Hill* and Hugh Graham's Montreal *Star* used yellow journalism to expose the living conditions of the city's popular classes. Given their strong class and ethnic affiliations, these calls for an end to municipal patronage and its replacement with reform in the "City Beautiful" tradition did not attract support from the popular classes.

While labour party candidates with class interpretations of industrial capitalist society were largely ignored, charismatic leaders with bases in the popular-class neighbourhoods of Montreal dominated local politics. Populists like Médéric Martin and Camilien Houde were able to capture strong support by using patronage effectively, and by attacking the big corporations and traditional patrician leadership.

In 1914 Médéric Martin ran against establishment candidate George Washington Stephens. While Martin was a cigar maker from the popular class neighbourhood of Saint-Marie, Stephens was a McGill University graduate and the dominant shareholder of the Canadian Rubber Company; he lived permanently in the Ritz-Carlton Hotel. Although supported by almost all Montreal newspapers and the Trades and Labour Council, Stephens' campaign for the City Beautiful, for a just and efficient city, for female suffrage, and for library and sewage facilities, was defeated by Martin whose campaign contrasted his worker background against "the millionaires and rich men pretending to be working in the public interest".

Martin never forgot his origins. Instead of appealing to progressive sentiments, he promised pavement, patronage, and public works projects in popular neighbourhoods. This formula, along with his skills as an orator and his image as an "east-end boy" who rubbed shoulders with princes and kings kept him in office for a decade. In 1927, the Laurier Palace fire, a typhoid epidemic caused by lax pasteurization procedures of local milk producers, and his promotion of a local beer called "la bière Martin" led to his defeat by Camilien Houde. Like Martin, Houde was a product of the popular classes, a store clerk who had advanced to bank clerk and ultimately bank inspector.

Houde was able to exploit the fears and conservative impulses of the Montreal proletariat with a millennial message that linked the monopoly interests of the great banks and tramway and electrical companies to paganism: "I believe that the limited liability company, both from the moral and material standpoints, is the most serious error of our century. It is driving us straight to paganism which will, if it continues, lead to the disappearance of our western civilization" (1934). Houde also emphasized what he saw as the profound social and sexual implications of women's participation in the paid labour force: "The man at home in a bathrobe while the woman is in a factory in pyjamas, the husband taking care of the children while the wife is out fighting for their daily bread and perhaps her honor, that is the world upside down" (Taylor, 1981: 7).

Women's Rights in Industrial Capitalist Quebec

Chapter 6 emphasized the participation of working women in labour's organization and resistance to industrial capitalism. Women's participation in wage labour had not alleviated their mothering and domestic duties. Earlier examples of day-care, maternity hospitals, hospices for the offspring of the poor, and the economic implications of widowhood emphasize the particular social dimensions of industrial society for women. In the church, convents at one level symbolized female subordination to male supervision and male concepts of Marianism. However, they also served to protect female autonomy and provided legitimate and economically-viable alternatives to domestic life and mothering. While their institutions acted as elements of social control, we have also observed the adaptation of their day-care and hospice institutions to the family strategies of the popular classes.

Bourgeois women, disenfranchised and blocked from power in the state, the professions, and corporations, were handicapped in their efforts to take social and political action. In 1911 there were no female architects or engineers in Quebec and fewer than one percent of the 17 787 civil servants in Quebec were women. Of Quebec's 2000 doctors, twenty-one were women, none of whom had studied medicine in Quebec (Danylewycz, 1987: 57). Women were admitted to the practice of law in 1941 and to the notariat in 1956.

These restrictions on access to higher education and the professions were accompanied by strong ideological pressures concerning the symbolism of the female and her function within Quebec society (Figure 7.7). Marianism, with its emphasis on purity, humility, virtue, and subordination to males in public and private life, represented a strong countervailing weight to demands for female equality in politics, the law, the work place, and family. Henri Bourassa was a leading opponent of suffragist demands for the vote or legal equality, leading Susan Mann Trofimenkoff to dismiss him as "bitter, rigid, humourless, and pharisaic" (Trofimenkoff, 1983: 305). The vice-rector of Laval, an institution that finally permitted women to audit literature courses in 1904, explained his university's discrimination in the context of a social view in which women should be trained as "devoted companions" rather than "rivals" of men (Danylewycz, 1987: 146).

Figure 7.7 The Courtyard of the Ursuline Convent in Quebec. Girls of the elite were brought up with stern discipline and trained to do needlework and manage servants.

These values concerning the education of women as being directed essentially toward their larger motherly and domestic duties rather than a strict professional training was not limited to Catholic intellectuals. At the Montreal General Hospital, for example, entering student nurses in 1896 were reminded by a supervising doctor of their total subordination to male physicians.

> Your duty as a nurse in relation to the medical attendant of the patient is to quietly and thoroughly carry out the directions you may receive from him, to be an efficient and trustworthy aid to him in care of the sick, and not to constitute yourself in any way his censor or critic (Kenneally, 1983: 93).

At the end of the nineteenth century, Quebec women were active in a variety of women's organizations: the Montreal Local Council of Women, the Young Women's Christian Association, the Montreal Suffrage Association, and the Women's Christian Temperance Union. Run by women and with a strong influence from anglophones, these organizations were vigorous in their demands for social and legal reform and equality in the work place. They were soon surpassed in importance by the Fédération nationale Saint-Jean-Baptiste. With the approval of the archbishop, the federation was established in 1907 by Marie Gérin-Lajoie and Caroline Béique as a women's section of the Saint-Jean-Baptiste Society. Its Catholic and national perspective predominated over progressive feminism. It and journals such as *La bonne parole* called for extended civil rights for women, access to higher education for women, female suffrage, and protection for female workers. One of their most important campaigns was for reform of the Civil Code of 1866 with its blatant discrimination against women. While a husband could obtain separation from a wife on evidence of adultery, the wife could obtain separation only if the husband brought his concubine to live in the family home. In 1902 Marie-Gérin Lajoie published the *Traité de droit usuel*, a manual geared particularly to women, and which explained the law in lay terminology.

Despite the thrust of these reform demands, the federation was pressured to concentrate on sectors traditionally considered to be of female concern: children's hospitals, workers' housing, family courts, and alcohol abuse. At times, conservative rhetoric resurfaced such as in this Fédération nationale Saint-Jean-Baptiste pamphlet for nurses. It emphasized that hospital training

> ... prepared women admirably for their duties in family and in society.... After three years of work and struggle, when the student has completed her professional training, especially when, under the great law of duty, the woman can subjugate all the repugnances of her nature, all the whims of will, and all the feelings in her heart, when she is mature for the world that suffers, we call her a graduate" (Collectif Clio, 1982: 287).

Most nuns and rural women worked within a conservative framework of traditional Catholic attitudes. In rural newspapers, and then on radio, Françoise Gaudet-Smet encouraged women to retain their traditional artisanal skills in the face of consumerism and wage labour outside the home. In any case, the church had already perceived the relationship between home economics and social peace. As early as the 1880s nuns in rural regions were teaching domestic skills to girls destined to become farm wives. In 1905 the Ecole Ménagère agricole de Saint-Pascal de Kamouraska was established by the Congrégation Notre-Dame and a year later a school opened in Montreal.

During the First World War the emphasis on teaching women domestic skills shifted from rural to urban society. By 1917, under the patronage of parish priests and the Fédération nationale Saint-Jean-Baptiste, 10 000 Montreal women a year followed courses in sewing, cooking, and domestic skills. Night and summer courses were established for women working outside the home; between 1909 and 1922, 40 000 female workers took housekeeping courses in provincial schools.

Many women were not fooled by their circumstances. Telephone operator Juliette Richard, for example, had a lucid understanding of the nature of her employment and its implicit sexism. In 1921 she described her work in the "central" of the Kamouraska Telephone Company. Working from an office in the home of her employer for $15 a month, she had no choice but to remain in the home of her parents. She wrote:

> While it was men who invented the telephone, they called on women to operate them. This was done, since with the salaries offered, men were not interested; they served as a supplement to family revenues which the woman could contribute while still taking care of the family. Another determining factor in the employment of women as telephone operators, was that they were more patient, more intuitive, and their voices are softer than men's (Collectif Clio, 1982: 310).

Female campaigns for civil reforms were opposed by the state and clerical hierarchy, and largely dismissed by the Dorion Commission (1929). This provincial commission of enquiry rejected demands that married women have jurisdiction over their own salary, that there be equality between husband and wife in the control of community property, and that female members of a family be granted expanded rights of tutorship. The commission's findings were based on the principle that the individual rights of a married woman were subordinate to a "superior law" of the family.

> The state of marriage created for the woman—and for the man as well— obligations... One is free to establish a family or to retain one's full independence; when one has made one's choice, one is no longer free to reclaim individual rights that the superior law of the family has converted into duty (quoted in Casgrain, 1971: 89).

Although female suffrage had been granted in federal elections in 1918, women were not allowed to vote in Quebec provincial elections until 1940. In 1921 the Quebec suffrage movement was revived with the formation of a Provincial Franchise Committee. The committee found it politically advantageous to argue that the goal of women's suffrage was not to change the station of women in life but rather to raise and inspire social life in general.

After a schism in the movement in 1928, Thérèse Casgrain became president of the Ligue des droits de la femme and, for fourteen years, she led the fight for equality of political and civil rights. Quebec lagged far behind other North American constituencies in this regard, maintaining, in the words of Jennifer Stoddart, "the almost complete exclusion of women from the exercise of public rights and the severe curtailment of civil capacity for married women" (Stoddart, 1981: 325).

The suffrage campaign faced hostility from both clerical and political leaders. In 1922 Episcopal authorities asked the Premier to oppose female suffrage that would represent "an attack against the fundamental traditions of our race and of our faith" (Hamelin et Gagnon, 1984: 327). Eighteen years later, the most important cleric in the province, Cardinal Villeneuve, reiterated his opposition, insisting that it would violate family unity and hierarchy, that it would tempt women with the passions and adventures of electoral politics, that most women did not really want the vote, and that most of the social demands called for by women could be achieved by women's groups operating outside the elected parliamentary system.

For his part, Premier Taschereau called on Quebec women to "remain faithful to their ancestral conditions, with their status as queen of the household, to their works of charity and philanthropy, to their labours of love and denial" (Hamelin et Gagnon, 1984: 327). Female suffrage was finally granted by the Godbout government in 1940.

Conclusion

The dominant social characteristic of the industrial capitalist period was its conservatism. Both church and state were dominated by forces committed to the status quo and the reinforcement of traditional values. The voices of labour progressives, political reformers, and moderate Catholics were muffled by the power of conservatives controlling the state and church apparatus. For their part, female reformers across the period faced an uphill struggle for educational opportunity, legal equality, and the provincial vote.

Bibliography

Politics and Law
Liberal politics are treated in Bernard Vigod, *Quebec Before Duplessis: The Political Career of Louis-Alexandre Taschereau*. Bourassa and the nationalists are treated in Trofimenkoff, *The Dream of Nation* and in Joseph Levitt, *Henri Bourassa and the Golden Calf: The Social Program of the Nationalists of Québec (1900-1914)*, and his Canadian Historical Association pamphlet, *Catholic critic*. The most accessible statement of conservative nationalism in English is in Jules-Paul Tardivel, *For My Country: "Pour la Patrie"*. Urban reform is treated in Annick Germain, *Les mouvements de réforme urbaine à Montréal au tournant du siècle*. For the relationship of Quebec law to the Supreme Court of Canada, see James Snell and Frederick Vaughan, *The Supreme Court of Canada: History of the Institution*, and David Howes, "From Polyjurality to Monojurality: The Transformation of Quebec Law, 1875-1929".

The Church
The best treatment of twentieth-century Catholicism is in Jean Hamelin and Nicole Gagnon, *Histoire de catholicisme québécois*, and Nive Voisine, *Histoire de l'église catholique au Québec, 1608-1970*. There are several sociologi-

cal studies of the early twentieth century. In addition to Hughes and Miner, see Marcel Rioux, *Belle-Anse*, and Léon Gérin, *Léon Gérin et l'habitant de Saint-Justin*.

Women

For women, the best sources are Collectif Clio, *Histoire des femmes* and Marta Danylewycz's *Taking the Veil*. For male attitudes, see Trofimenkoff's "Henri Bourassa and 'The Woman Question'", 3-11, and "Les femmes dans l'oeuvre de Groulx". For the education of women see Micheline Dumont and Nadia Fahmy-Eid, *Les couventines: L'éducation des filles au Québec dans les congrégations religieuses enseignantes 1840-1960*. For feminism see Jennifer Stoddart, "Quebec's Legal Elite Looks at Women's Rights: The Dorion Commission 1929-31", Jean Baptiste and Marie Lavigne, Yolande Pinard and Jennifer Stoddart, "The Fédération Nationale Saint-Jean-Baptiste and the Women's Movement in Quebec". For single women of the popular classes see Andrée Lévesque, "Deviant Anonymous: Single Mothers at the Hôpital de la Miséricorde in Montreal, 1929-39".

Contemporary Quebec, 1933 to the Present

The fundamental characteristics of Quebec society have changed significantly since the 1930s. Periodization of contemporary Quebec poses serious problems, particularly since great overlapping of economic forms continues while the social changes initiated in the past half century remain incomplete. Many historians interpret the election of the Lesage government and the beginning of the Quiet Revolution in 1960 as the decisive turning point. We, however, perceive the emergence of contemporary Quebec in the crises of the Depression and the Second World War.

Perhaps the most significant feature of the period has been the growing secularization of Quebec society as manifested in education, hospitals, and trade unionism. This decline of the church and conservatism was accompanied by new importance for the ideologies of social democracy, Marxism, and particularly, changing forms of nationalism.

Statism, characterized by public ownership of important sectors of the economy such as electrical power and expansion of social and educational services, contributed to the growth of new social groups, especially francophone professionals who challenged the traditional imperatives of the clerical and anglophone elites. Employed as engineers, administrators, doctors, teachers, and journalists, professionals ridiculed the values of their classical college educations and demanded full participation in modern, consumer society. At the same time, a vigorous trade union movement and social-action groups inspired the popular classes to political action. Both of these social groups would be central players in the "national question".

In 1933 the total inadequacy of clerical institutions to cope with Depression conditions became evident; statism was the result. The year 1933 also coincided with a new coalition of liberal clerics, farm, co-operative, and union leaders who called for nationalization of electricity companies and demanded fundamental social reform. Statism, and the process of change unleashed in the Depression and the Second World War were stemmed but not stopped by the conservative regime of Maurice Duplessis.

In the postwar period, important social measures—family allowances, pensions, health care, and improved education—made up an increasing part of federal and provincial government expenditures. The state became a major force in the economy, with budgets escalating rapidly: from expenditures of $224 million in 1951-52, the Quebec government spent $24.5 billion in 1983-84.

Demographically, Quebec shared the experience of other western societies: a drop in the birth rate during the Depression and then a postwar baby boom. Since then, Quebec's birth rate has fallen dramatically and the province faces a rapidly aging population. Immigration and demographic evolution have made Montreal's non-francophone population more cosmopolitan while the rest of the province has become more homogeneously francophone. The part of the anglophone population whose origin is Great Britain has continued to decline and to be concentrated in western parts of Montreal.

Despite the boom in the Second World War and postwar period, the contemporary period is characterized by the decline of the industrial sector in favour of the tertiary or service sector, which in the 1980s provides 70 percent of all jobs in Quebec. Metropolitan dominance of the Canadian economy, formerly shared by Montreal and Toronto, has passed to the latter. Montreal's pan-Canadianism was increasingly replaced by a regional and francophone perspective.

As in other industrial societies, Quebec has had to cope with shifts in economic health: desperate poverty and unemployment in the Depression, prosperity and employment in the war and postwar period; and a sharp recession in the early 1980s. Quebec's population has also had to adjust to the changing nature of work: part-time work, rapid technological change, increased work in the public sector until the early 1980s, and privatization since.

The role of women in contemporary Quebec society is changing. Women are increasingly important in all sectors of the work force, from professional and corporate levels to part-time work in the service sector. The decline of conservative ideology and clerical restrictions, the impact of feminism and changing family and social mores in the areas of divorce and abortion have led to strong political demands: equality before the law and in the work place; improved facilities for day care and health care; removal of forms of sexual violence.

Development of northern Quebec has given new political significance to the province's native peoples who occupied and who had legal rights to much of the territory needed for the state's energy development projects.

Nationalism and the State

The "national question", as it is called in Quebec, has dominated political debate in the province and has been a major factor in reshaping Canadian federalism. As late as the 1920s, Quebec nationalists usually perceived themselves as defending their vision of a bicultural Canada against British imperialism. In the Depression, however, nationalists moved away from this pan-Canadian perspective to focus on Quebec's specific problems. They waged campaigns to boycott anglophone (particularly Jewish) businesses (Figure 8.1), demanded greater government action and, in some cases, proposed independence to solve Quebec's socio-economic problems (Hamelin et al., 1976: 432-33).

In 1933 a coalition of social activists from the Ecole sociale populaire, the Caisses Populaires, the Catholic farmers' union, and the Catholic labour unions published a reform program, le programme de restauration sociale. These groups were inspired by their experience in co-operatives and agreed on the need for increased state action. They called for state-sponsored relief

Figure 8.1   Although Jews in Lower Canada were granted full civil rights in 1832, antisemitism in Quebec can be dated from 1807-09 with the attempt to stop Ezekiel Hart from taking his seat in the Legislative Assembly. In the 1920s and 1930s antisemitism became virulent in Quebec with the "Achat chez nous" campaign illustrated in the cartoon, and with Adrien Arcand's Nazi-type movement that attracted 700 members. Recurrent struggles between Jews and Montreal's Protestant School Board, and restrictive admissions policy at McGill University are reminders that antisemitism was not restricted to francophones.

programs, breakup of the great electric trusts, and election, labour, and agricultural reforms. Progressive Liberals like Paul Gouin, son of the former Premier, and nationalists like Philippe Hamel and René Chalout were attracted to this program and in 1934 a new political group, the Action Libérale Nationale (ALN), was established.

In the same period the Conservative Party, out of power since 1897, was being revitalized under Maurice Duplessis who became leader in 1933. Son of a Conservative politician, Duplessis was a Trois-Rivières lawyer whose forte was his understanding of rural and small-town Quebec. Although Gouin and the progressives were suspicious of Duplessis' reform credentials, the Action Libérale Nationale and the Conservative Party united into the Union Nationale in 1935, and adopted the ALN program.

The Taschereau government was weakened by charges of corruption, tired leadership and complicity with the electric trusts. In the elections of November 1935, sixteen Conservative and twenty-six ALN members were elected to challenge Taschereau's forty-eight Liberals. In the months that followed, Duplessis established his dominance over both the ALN and the Liberals. In June 1936, he broke with Gouin and, as undisputed leader of the Union Nationale, forced an election in August. Campaigning for a breakup of the trusts and for rural revitalization, Duplessis overwhelmed the Liberals and won a majority.

The Union Nationale quickly established its colours as a conservative party. Breaking with nationalists and Liberals who wanted to nationalize the electric trusts, Duplessis emphasized finances and provincial autonomy. He built up his political base in rural Quebec with extended agricultural credit, creation of agricultural schools, rural electrification, and improvement of rural roads. He capitalized on rural Quebec's traditional suspicions of urban life, and took an anti-labour stance, denied the closed shop, passed anti-labour bills, and sided with owners in the textile strike of 1937.

His sustained campaign against communism gained him conservative and clerical support. The infamous Act Concerning Communist Propaganda (1937) was particularly repugnant to civil libertarians. Better known as the Padlock Act, this measure permitted the police to lock any building used for "Communism or Bolshevism". Politicians and the police took advantage of this broad definition and used the act against unions, political groups, and religious minorities such as the Jehovah's Witnesses. Despite decades of resistance by civil libertarians, the law was declared unconstitutional by the Supreme Court of Canada only as recently as 1957 (Sarra-Bournet, 1986).

With the outbreak of war in 1939, Duplessis called an election on the issue of possible conscription. With support from federal Liberals who threatened to resign if Duplessis was reelected, Adélard Godbout and the Liberals were elected. Faced with the wartime crisis, Godbout left centralized economic planning to the federal government and, when Ottawa created the Family Allowance Program (commonly known as the baby bonus) in 1944, he did not fight vigorously to preserve exclusive provincial jurisdiction in social services.

On other fronts, however, Godbout did respond to reform demands. In 1940 Quebec women were finally granted the right to vote in provincial elections. Labour relations were regulated by a new law that recognized workers' rights to join an accredited union and to negotiate collective agreements. Schooling was made mandatory for children between the ages of six and fourteen in 1943. Finally, and very symbolically, Hydro-Québec was created in 1944 by the nationalization of Montreal Light, Heat and Power.

Federal-Provincial Relations in the Duplessis Era

Although it won almost 40 percent of the vote compared to the Union Nationale's 36 percent, Godbout's Liberal government was defeated by Duplessis in the 1944 election. An important factor in the defeat was the association of Godbout with federal Liberals. Although francophone participation in the Second World War was greater than that in the First World War, many francophones felt betrayed by King's ambiguous stand on conscription and held a widespread, if generally unfounded, opinion that English officers used francophone troops as cannon-fodder. Duplessis capitalized on this resentment by portraying himself as a defender of provincial autonomy, language, and traditions.

Throughout the postwar period, federal-provincial conflicts over jurisdiction were prominent political issues. Centralization and the thrust for expanded federal participation in the social sector was reinforced by the 1940 report of the Royal Commission on Dominion-Provincial Relations (the Rowell-Sirois Report). It called for a pan-Canadian unemployment insurance plan and assumption by the central government of all the costs of old-age pensions.

In 1944, federal introduction of the Family Allowance signalled the coming of the welfare state. At the same time, expansion of federal cost-sharing programs, such as those for highways and universities, emphasized federal ambitions in social, regional, and educational sectors, prerogatives traditionally and constitutionally reserved for provincial authority. Federal power also intruded into culture. In 1929 a federal Royal Commission on Radio Broadcasting proposed a national broadcasting service capable of "fostering a national spirit and interpreting national citizenship", and in 1936 a federal crown corporation, the Canadian Broadcasting Corporation (CBC/Radio Canada) was created. Other federal actions such as the creation of Trans Canada Airlines (Air Canada) and the National Film Board reinforced the sense of federal expansionism.

This federal intrusion into provincial domains was difficult to resist because of the structure of government finances. In 1933, 47.7 percent of taxes in Quebec were collected by the federal government, 10 percent by the provincial government, and 42.3 percent by municipalities. The Second World War accelerated this tendency and in 1945 the federal government collected 82.8 percent of taxes in Quebec, while the province had slipped to 7.3 percent and municipalities to 9.9 percent (Linteau, Durocher, Robert, Ricard, 1986: 152). While most provinces accepted these federal funds and programs, Quebec resisted in the name of autonomy.

In the same manner as the federal government used commissions and the support of intellectuals to justify its programs, Quebec began marshalling ideological and statistical support for provincial autonomy. Most important was the 1954 provincial Royal Commission of Enquiry on Constitutional Problems (Tremblay Report), which defined Confederation as a compact in which the federal government had been a creation of the provinces. The commission maintained that provinces had the right to impose direct taxation to finance programs in their exclusive jurisdiction (Kwavnick, 1973). The Quebec government used the report to justify the establishment of a provincial income tax in 1954. This enabled provincial finance ministers to shape independent fiscal policy geared to specific provincial objectives.

The Emergence of the Independence Movement

The 1960 defeat of the Union Nationale government by Jean Lesage's Liberals is usually cited as the beginning of the Quiet Revolution, a movement which radically changed Quebec society and politics. However, this period may have been less pivotal than earlier developments. Clerical influence was on the decline by the Second World War, while in the 1930s the union movement was challenging employers and the state. With radio, the automobile, and other elements of consumer society, the popular classes had been undergoing a long process of integrating American values to their culture. With all these developments, a more aggressive form of nationalism emerged. Using the slogan "Maîtres chez nous"—Masters in our own House—the Lesage government implemented education and health-care reforms. It actively intervened in the economy through the nationalization of the remaining private electricity companies and the creation of new crown corporations.

To many nationalists, the Lesage government refused the logical implications of its own policy, for underlying these reforms was the desire to improve the economic position of francophones in Quebec. Foremost among the doubters was René Lévesque (1922-1987), a key member of the Lesage government and the minister largely responsible for the nationalization of electricity. Born in the Gaspé, Lévesque studied law and was a war correspondent and a popular television journalist before he entered politics in 1960. His effective political style and nationalist message captured the public imagination.

> We in Quebec feel it is essential that the responsibility for resources must
> rest with us at the provincial level. It is of vital importance to French
> Canadians that the day-to-day handling of economic affairs such as
> planning and policy making, whatever their nature, be left to us. And we
> Québécois are the only ones who can do this. Otherwise we will never get
> on our feet (1961).

The inferior position of francophones in Canada was clearly documented by the federal Royal Commission on Bilingualism and Biculturalism (1966). It revealed that unilingual anglophones in Quebec earned an average annual salary of $6049. This was more than bilingual anglophones ($5929) and much more than bilingual ($4523) or unilingual ($3107) francophones. These statistics emphasized the low status of French in business and the necessity for francophone professionals to work in English. The reality of the francophones' situation contributed to a deepening hostility toward the anglophone elite (Figure 8.2).

Figure 8.2 Grafitti on the Sun Life Building, 1978. When Sun Life decided to move its head office to Toronto in 1978, nationalists wrote "good riddance" on the entrance of the building. Hostility to Sun Life was fueled by its refusal to communicate in French and to integrate effectively into Quebec society. In addition, the company's refusal to hire francophone professionals and, finally, the transfer of head offices and economic power out of Quebec added to the antagonism.

This economic inferiority in the private sector contrasted sharply with francophone pride in state-owned enterprises like Hydro-Québec. At the same time, the weak political and cultural position of francophones outside Quebec, along with ongoing federal intrusion into provincial jurisdiction and the emergence of an expanding and ambitious francophone bourgeoisie in Quebec, contributed to the independence movement. The first parties committed to independence, the Ralliement National (RN) and the Rassemblement pour l'Indépendance Nationale (RIN), won 8 percent of the popular vote but no seats in the 1966 elections.

In 1968, when Lévesque left the Liberal Party and formed the Mouvement Souveraineté Association, he was joined by RN and RIN members. Together they formed the Parti Québécois in 1969. With Quebec independence as a banner unifying its diverse political elements, the Parti Québécois won 24 percent of the popular vote and seven seats in what, since 1968, is called the National Assembly.

Revolutionary elements in the popular classes rejected the democratic process as a means to obtain independence. Embittered by unemployment, foreign control of the Quebec economy, and conflicts over the language of education, many turned to Marxist ideologies and Third World national liberation models.

One of the leading marxist figures of the 1960s was Pierre Vallières, product of a Montreal working-class family. He sought to politicize Québécois in his influential *White Niggers of America* by comparing them to other colonized peoples. This ideology took practical form with the formation in 1963 of the Front de Libération du Québec (FLQ). Committed to overthrowing "medieval catholicism and capitalist oppression" through revolution, the FLQ took particular aim at the federal government and anglophone bourgeoisie. They threatened to destroy

> a) all colonial symbols and institutions, in particular the RCMP and the armed forces;
> b) all the information media in the colonial language which hold us in contempt;
> c) all commercial establishments and enterprises which practise discrimination against Québécois and which do not use French;
> d) all plants and factories which discriminate against francophone workers.

Revolutionary activity through the 1960s culminated in the October crisis of 1970. The kidnapping of British consular official James Cross was followed by that of Quebec Labour Minister Pierre Laporte. Pierre Elliott Trudeau's federal government reacted strongly. It quickly subordinated the Quebec government and, instituting the War Measures Act, suspended civil liberties. Hoping to crush the independence movement in Quebec, the Trudeau government sent in the army. Hundreds of Quebec intellectuals, political activists, and labour leaders were imprisoned arbitrarily. At first, the Quebec populace was divided, with many attracted to the FLQ manifesto because of its powerful attacks on the church, corporate colonialism, and anglophone racism. However, the murder of Pierre Laporte discredited the revolutionary movement for independence.

Through the October crisis and the early 1970s, the Parti Québécois remained strong. It distanced itself from radicals and built a political base on a program of independence and social democracy. The Parti Québécois, benefiting from scandals concerning Robert Bourassa's Liberal government and a social climate poisoned by violent labour and linguistic disputes, took power in 1976. It moved quickly to institute its program, reinforcing earlier language legislation and making French the sole official language through Bill 101. Organized labour was given generous wage settlements and the labour code was reformed. Responding to social democratic demands for more state control, the government created a provincial auto insurance plan.

These policies and a strong, popular cabinet formed the background to the 1980 referendum in which Quebecers were asked to allow the government to negotiate a sovereignty association. According to the wording on the referendum ballot, "this agreement would enable Quebec to acquire the exclusive power to make its laws, levy its taxes and establish relations abroad—in other words, sovereignty—and at the same time, to maintain with Canada an economic association including a common currency."

Prime Minister Trudeau was a powerful force in the campaign. A wealthy Montreal intellectual from a mixed anglophone-francophone background, Trudeau had established reform credentials as a leader of the opposition to Duplessis. A strong believer in liberal democracy and federalism as protective forces for minorities, he was blunt in his assesment of both ethnic groups.

> Historically, French Canadians have not really believed in democracy for themselves; and English Canadians have not really wanted it for others.
> Such are the foundations upon which our two ethnic groups have absurdly pretended to be building democratic forms of government. No wonder the ensuing structure has turned out to be rather flimsy (1958).

As Prime Minister, Trudeau implemented one recommendation of the Bilingualism and Biculturalism Commission pushing through the Official Languages Act (1969), which made Canada officially bilingual. Through the 1970s he fought hard to maintain federal authority. Trudeau actively campaigned for the "No" side, pointing to the federal government's presence in Quebec, and he promised to renew Canadian federalism if the "Yes" vote was defeated. Although a majority of francophones supported the "Yes", non-francophone votes went overwhelmingly against, and the referendum was defeated with 59.6 percent of voters opting for the "No".

The Changing Role of the State

The alliance of the Quebec state and industrial capitalists dominated government actions until the 1960s. To provide capitalists with the necessary infrastructures for economic growth, the state played an active role, investing more than a quarter of its total budget in the construction of transportation systems: first, railways in the late 1800s and then a network of highways after the First World War. At the same time, the rationale of laissez-faire liberalism and reliance on religious orders to provide hospital administration, nursing services, and teachers led to limited expenditures on health care and education.

By 1933, however, traditional Catholic social services such as the Saint-Vincent de Paul Society had been overwhelmed by the scale of public relief needed in Montreal, and the municipal government was obliged to step in. Despite Taschereau's concern for provincial autonomy and exaggerated state welfare measures, he was forced to accept Old Age Pensions under the Depression conditions of 1936.

Total provincial government expenditures in 1933-34 were just over $60 million and rose slowly but continuously throughout the Duplessis years to reach almost $600 million in 1959-60. With the arrival of the Lesage government in 1960, expenditures increased rapidly, passing the $1 billion mark in 1963-64 and reaching over $3 billion by 1970. Increased spending and the inflation of the 1970s and early 1980s pushed government spending over the $25 billion level.

Table 8.1 Quebec Government Expenditures, 1934-1985 (in thousands of dollars)

1934-35	66 308
1939-40	108 195
1944-45	104 433
1949-50	198 196
1954-55	356 379
1959-60	598 397
1964-65	1 437 715
1969-70	3 234 744
1974-75	7 208 600
1979-80	15 123 200
1984-85	25 895 000

(Bernier and Boily, 1986: 349).

The growth in the Quebec budget emphasized the changing role of the state in the province's social and economic life. After 1960 the state progressively took responsibility from the church for the greatly expanded programs in education and health care. Secondary education became free and secular. In 1968 a system of secular community colleges, Collèges d'enseignement général et professionnel, was created. These CEGEPs provided post-secondary training in the arts and sciences for those entering university, and technical and professional degrees for those directly entering the job market. The province's universities and student population expanded greatly, particularly with the establishment of the University of Quebec in 1968 which has campuses in seven cities.

As well as offering traditional programs, the University of Quebec has a particular mandate toward mature students to provide special programs, evening classes, and courses in remote regions or on television. These reforms have had dramatic influences on the educational level of the population. Whereas only 3 percent of Quebec students went to university in 1951-52, 8 percent attended university in 1971-72 and 13.5 percent in 1985-86. Despite this increase in attendance, university education still remains a preserve of the children of the elite. As a result of these reforms, expenses related to education make up about one-quarter of the provincial budget.

In public health, Quebec rapidly followed the lead of the federal government and subsidized hospitalization in the early 1960s and adopted a universal program of free health care in 1970. Quebec went even further than other Canadian provinces by paying for dental care for children under fourteen years. Health-care spending represents 40 percent of provincial spending.

In both its provincial and federal dimensions, by the 1970s the mature welfare state addressed the problem of the unequal distribution of wealth. Federal unemployment insurance, old age and disability pensions, and provincially administered social welfare payments were key elements in guaranteeing a minimum family income. These are complemented by family allowances and diverse federal and provincial tax credits and deductions.

Several programs, particularly those of the federal department of regional economic expansion, have been designed to reduce regional disparities by favouring economic development in outlying regions. Despite these government programs, regional disparities in income distribution (Table 8.2) and unemployment remain high. In the Gaspé, the Saguenay, and Abitibi, unemployment is normally twice the Montreal level. In the 1980s high costs, a prevailing conservatism, and the growth of support for privatization have put many of these programs in jeopardy.

Table 8.2 Per Capita Income in Quebec Administrative Regions, 1961 and 1981 (in dollars)

Administrative region	1961	1981
Lower St. Lawrence—Gaspé	707	7 228
Saguenay—Lac Saint-Jean	1 070	8 150
Quebec City	1 070	9 104
Trois-Rivières	1 082	8 550
Eastern Townships	1 093	8 609
Montreal	1 586	10 456
Ottawa Valley	1 166	8 802
Abitibi—Témiskamingue	1 041	8 734
North Shore	1 550	8 729
New Quebec	1 547	4 586
Provincial average	1 341	9 658

(Bernier et Boily, 1986: 237)

The Quebec state was increasingly seen as a vehicle to assert francophone rights. With justification, francophone professionals believed that the anglophone corporate elite blocked their access to power in the private sector. The expanding population of francophone university graduates looked to the state for opportunities: Hydro-Québec and its massive development projects provided work for engineers and managers; rapid expansion and secularization of secondary and post-secondary education brought new teaching positions; expanded health-care services created demand for health and social service professionals; the expansion of the government bureaucracy (the number of civil servants grew from 28 302 in 1955 to 150 333 in 1985) offered employment to professionals and clerical workers (Figure 8.3). The same trend was evident in the federal civil service where bilingualism has aided the recruitment of francophones since 1969.

Figure 8.3 Daniel Johnson Dam on the Manicouagan River. This dam, the biggest in the world when it was inaugurated in 1968, symbolized the economic power of the state for many Quebecers and proved that francophone engineers could rival those of any other country.

By the 1960s, the state was increasingly active in modernizing Quebec's economy and in giving francophones more economic power. With the increase of state expenditures, government purchasing policies were developed to favour Quebec-based suppliers. Both federal and provincial governments have used direct subsidies, tax incentives, and interest-free loans to attract and to modernize industries. Nationalization and the creation of crown corporations have been important strategies.

The most dramatic and successful nationalization was that of the private hydroelectric companies in 1962, which gave Hydro-Québec a monopoly of the production and distribution of electricity. Megaprojects, first along the North Shore and then in the James Bay region, made Hydro-Québec an important motor in Quebec's industrial growth.

The Quebec government increased its presence in industrial activities by creating public companies to undertake mineral exploration (SOQUEM for mining, SOQUIP for oil and gas, and the Société nationale de l'amiante for asbestos) and production (SIDBEC). It also created companies in forestry management and marketing (REXFOR), processing and marketing of agricultural products (SOQUIA), and the Société général de financement (SGF) holding company to finance industrial expansion.

Capital generated in Quebec often went to large anglophone institutions such as Sun Life, and was not reinvested in the province. The creation of the Caisse de dépôt et de placement du Québec to invest funds generated by the Quebec pension plan aimed at making Quebecers' capital serve them and gave the government power on the boards of many important Canadian companies. Despite the positive effects of many of these ventures, the neo-conservative policies of the Quebec Liberals and the Parti Québécois have brought statism into question.

Demographic change

After declining significantly during the Depression, Quebec's birth rate rose above thirty per thousand and continued into the years of the "baby boom". This level was maintained until the beginning of the 1960s when birth-control devices became more widely accessible. This and the opening of Canada's first abortion clinics in the early 1970s had important demographic and social implications.

Family strategies have changed with married women remaining in the labour force; day-care has become a major priority of the women's movement. Although birth rates across Canada declined in the same period, the drop in Quebec has been more severe since 1966 and, at 13.4 in 1984, is well below the Canadian average. Quebec's share of the Canadian population has declined from 29 percent in the 1940s and 1950s to just over 26 percent in the 1980s.

Besides the declining birth rate, immigration has contributed to the changing population profile. Heavy postwar immigration to Quebec has given way since the mid 1960s to net emigration away from the province. Out-migration climaxed in the three years following the election of the Parti Québécois government in 1976 when emigrants outnumbered immigrants by more than 80 000. Although Quebec still has a negative balance, this trend had slowed by the 1980s.

The declining birth rate and a drop in the mortality rate have combined to increase the average age of Quebec's population. Whereas male life expectancy at the beginning of the Second World War was only about sixty years, it lengthened to 70.7 years in the 1980s; in the same period the rate for women has gone from sixty-three years to 78.5. This profile has important implications for Quebec society. The school-age population has been decreasing steadily since the 1960s and the number of young people entering the work force has slowed since the mid 1970s.

At the same time, demands for health care and pensions have been rising. Although a higher standard of living has offset some of the negative effects of this evolution in terms of demand for housing and consumer goods, Quebec's potential market is shrinking with deleterious effects on employment (Figure 8.4).

Changes in the structure of the family are a striking feature of contemporary Quebec demographics. With the sharp decline in religious practice since 1960, marriage is no longer the norm for many Quebecers. In 1981, 242 345 couples (including 9330 homosexuals) declared themselves to be living in common law relationships in Quebec and 13 percent of the female population aged twenty to twenty-four were living in concubinage. In 1951 the province's 85 000 monoparental families were made up mostly of widows, while in 1981 the 208 435 monoparental families were mainly headed by single or divorced women. The structure of the family changed for married couples as well; in 1951 35 percent of families had five or more children, whereas in 1981 only 16 percent were this size and most had two or fewer children. Of the people who bought homes in 1986, 42 percent were childless.

Heavy immigration right after the Second World War—over 420 000 immigrants settled in Quebec in the period 1945-1961—significantly altered the ethnic composition of Quebec's non-francophone population (Table 8.3). The vast majority settled in the Montreal region; 87.3 percent of all people whose mother language is other than French or English lived on Montreal Island in 1981. Over two-thirds of these immigrants opted to educate their children in English. They did this for two main reasons: English was necessary to be eligible for the better paying jobs and they perceived Quebec as part of a North American whole in which English was identified with the elite and material success.

At the same time, the concentration of Quebec anglophones in the Montreal region continued, a process that had been going on for decades. While just under two-thirds of Quebec anglophones lived on the Montreal Island in 1941, this proportion had increased to three-quarters by 1981. The concentration of non-francophones in Quebec's metropolis caused linguistic tension and gave a Montreal focus to the struggle for French language rights.

Immigration to Canada has been declining since 1974 and Quebec's share of this immigration has also been decreasing. The ethnic origin of immigrants has undergone dramatic change: in the postwar years most immigrants were Europeans, but in the 1970s and 1980s most came from the Caribbean (Haiti), South America (Chile and El Salvador) and Southeast Asia. Many of these immigrants are refugees and, because of Quebec government policy favouring francophones, a growing number speak French. The concentration of these immigrants in particular Montreal neighbourhoods has resulted in racial tension, and immigrants are poorly represented in municipal services such as the police.

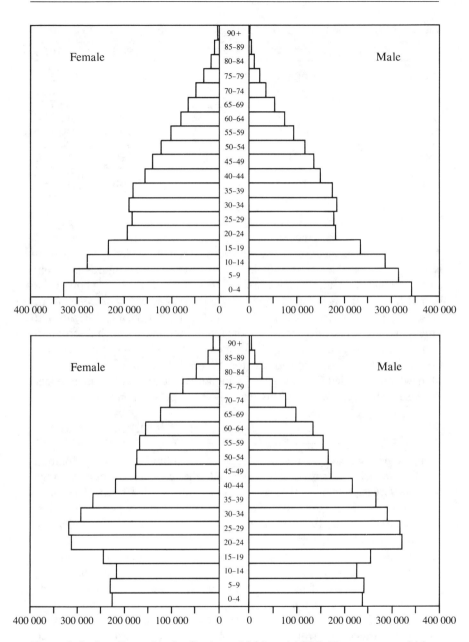

Figure 8.4 Age Pyramids for Quebec, 1961 and 1985. The age pyramid for 1961 shows the decline in births during the Depression (20- to 29-year age groups) and the baby boom after the war. By 1985 the baby boomers were in their twenties and thirties and were followed by a much smaller generation.

Table 8.3 The Ethnic Origin of the Population of Quebec, 1941-1981

	1941	1951	1961	1981
French	2 695 032	3 327 128	4 241 354	5 105 665
British Isles	452 887	491 818	567 057	487 385
German	8 880	12 249	39 457	33 770
Greek	2 728	3 388	19 390	49 420
Italian	28 051	34 165	108 552	163 735
Jewish	66 277	73 019	74 677	90 355
Polish	10 036	16 998	30 790	19 755
Asian	7 119	7 714	14 801	64 415
Indian and Inuit	13 641	16 620	21 343	46 855

During the 1940s native people in Quebec regained their precontact population and have since been increasing at a greater rate than the Quebec average. Access to better medical services, especially in remote regions of the North, is mainly responsible for this evolution. As well, census figures probably underestimate their total numbers since women who married whites were barred from tribal membership by the Indian Act, and Métis descendants of these marriages have no Indian status. The Canadian Charter of Rights and Freedoms (1982) and amendments to the Indian Act prohibit such discrimination and a growing number of native women are returning to live on reserves. (Mary Two-Axe Early who fought for 50 years to regain her status as a Mohawk and founded Equal Rights for Indian Women in 1967 is an excellent example.) This trend will probably increase the population on reserves.

The Quebec Economy

From the beginning of the nineteenth century until the Depression, Montreal was the financial metropolis of Canada with the most active stock exchange and the largest number of important corporate head offices. The city's dominance slipped in the 1930s—the Toronto stock exchange became the most active in 1933. By the 1960s Montreal was rapidly falling behind the Ontario capital. The exodus of corporate head offices accelerated in the 1970s and, despite misguided government policies such as the construction of Mirabel Airport, Montreal has lost much of its former prominence in Canada.

After the downturn of the Depression and the controlled economy of the war, Quebec, like the rest of Canada, experienced economic expansion from 1945 to 1957 in response to consumer demand to make up for wartime privations. A recession from 1957 to 1962 was followed by growth that lasted until the oil crisis of 1973. Crude oil prices rose from $2 to $30 a barrel by 1980 fueling inflation and causing slow economic growth. Slow growth, high unemployment and interest rates, and growing inequalities in wealth characterized the Quebec economy in the 1980s.

Postwar reconstruction in Europe, consumerism and demand for steel in the United States during the Korean and Vietnam wars created strong demand for Quebec raw products, particularly for minerals. This prompted the rapid development of resources along the North Shore region of Quebec and gave new life to other peripheral regions such as Abitibi which had severely suffered during the Depression. New company towns like Schefferville and Gagnon grew up in Northern Quebec to exploit iron ore deposits. The Iron Ore Company constructed a railway linking these mines to Sept-Iles, which became one of Quebec's busiest ports, especially after the 1957 completion of the St. Lawrence Seaway gave the region improved access to the mid-western American market.

The aluminum and asbestos industries also profited from high demand. The net value of production in the mining industry rose from $59 million in 1945 to over $246 million in 1960. However, apart from aluminum smelting, which relies on cheap electricity, this sector suffered during the 1980s. Recession in the United States; competition from international corporations locating in Third World countries to benefit from their cheaper labour; and health hazards associated with asbestos fibres have led to the closing of copper and asbestos mines and the complete shutting down of operations at Schefferville and Gagnon.

Quebec came out of the Second World War with an industrial structure inherited from both the transition and the industrial capitalist phases. On the one hand, traditional industrial establishments in the food, clothing, textile, leather, wood, and tobacco industries continued to rely on cheap immigrant and rural labour. This sector accounted for 4.2 percent of Quebec's industrial labour force and 48.6 percent of the total value of industrial production in 1950. In 1983 this sector still represented 43.1 percent of industrial labour and 35.7 percent of industrial output (Bernier et Boily, 1986). This emphasizes not only the continuity in Quebec's industrial structure but the threat to these industries from cheap labour in developing Asian countries.

Industries created in the second phase of Quebec's industrialization and reliance on hydroelectric power continue to occupy an important role in the economy. The pulp-and-paper and chemical industries were a central part of postwar industrial growth. The most dramatic expansion, however, occurred in the petroleum industry. Consumerism in the form of the family car and suburban living created new demand for petroleum products from the refineries of Montreal East. Since Montreal area refineries used imported rather than Canadian crude, they were severely affected by the energy crises of the 1970s and 1980s that benefited Ontario refineries, particularly those at Sarnia. With the purchase of foreign companies by Petro Canada, most of the refineries in Montreal closed in the 1980s.

On the other hand, the oil crisis benefited the aluminum industry as automobile manufacturers turned to lighter metals to improve fuel efficiency.

Quebec's hydroelectric resources contributed to maintaining the province's world leadership in aluminum production. Despite leadership in this industry, Quebec has not emerged as a leading producer of transportation equipment. Although there is a large General Motors plant just north of Montreal, automobile production remains centred in Ontario as does the auto-parts industry.

Despite the success of some individual models such as the Canadair water bomber and the Challenger executive jet, the aeronautics industry never regained the importance it held during the war. Bombardier, on the other hand, has become a leader in rail and mass transit technology. Consumer electronics benefited from consumerism but, despite such companies as Ogivar, Quebec did not fare well in the field of high technology and in the computer revolution.

Table 8.4 Percentage of the Gross Value of Quebec's Industrial Production, 1945-83 (Thirteen Most Important Industries in 1945)

	1945	1955	1965	1975	1983	Rank in 1945	1983
Food and drink	15.5	16.0	18.0	18.5	17.7	1	1
Clothing	10.7	8.5	9.1	8.3	5.6	2	7
Iron and steel	10.0	7.8	7.9	7.1	7.5	3	4
Paper	9.6	11.6	10.7	9.6	9.6	4	3
Transport material	9.4	4.8	4.7	6.6	7.2	5	6
Textiles	8.1	6.7	7.7	5.1	5.1	6	9
Chemicals	7.6	5.6	5.1	5.6	7.4	7	5
Other metals	7.4	11.1	6.5	6.2	5.2	8	8
Wood	4.9	4.8	4.8	3.2	3.8	9	12
Leather	3.1	1.7	1.7	1.1	0.8	10	18
Tobacco	3.0	2.6	2.2	1.5	1.3	11	17
Petroleum	2.5	6.5	4.0	7.2	10.1	12	2
Electrical appliances	2.5	4.2	5.1	4.9	5.0	13	10

The construction industry is often seen as a barometer of Quebec's economic health. Fifteen years of steady growth was fueled by demand for housing, office, and retail space until 1966 when the industry entered a five-year slowdown. Rapid growth resumed in 1971. After 1976, however, the industry entered a period of sluggish performances that lasted until the 1980s. Large government-sponsored projects—Expo '67 (1965-67), hydroelectric developments on the North Shore (1962-68) and in the James Bay drainage basin (1971-80), the Olympic Games (1974-76), the construction of Mirabel Airport (1974-77), and housing programs such as Quebec's corvée habitation or Montreal's opération 100 000 logements—have been largely responsible for maintaining the industry since the mid-1960s when Montreal lost its position as the corporate headquarters of Canada.

The growing dominance of the tertiary sector (from 45.9 percent of Quebec's gross domestic production in 1951 to 70.7 percent in 1983) is the key element in Quebec's postwar economic development. Consumerism created new demand for retail outlets, consumer credit and insurance institutions, advertising, and the expansion of the entertainment, tourism and recreation industries. Although most automobiles are not manufactured in Quebec, motor vehicle registrations provide a good measure of consumer spending (Table 8.5). New state services in the health and education sector, and the expansion of government bureaucracy to administer the welfare state also contributed to the growth of the service sector. In 1933 there were 2.51 civil servants for every 1000 people in Quebec; by 1960 this rate had reached 7.13; in 1985 it stood at 22.8 with a total of 150,333 civil servants.

Table 8.5 Motor Vehicle Registrations in Quebec, 1940-1982

Year	Total Registrations	Family Cars	Snowmobiles
1940	225 152	174 761	N/A
1960	1 096 053	820 152	N/A
1982	2 826 150	2 376 745	84 215

Within this sector there has been increasing concentration, which is illustrated by the retail trade. Based on the convenience of the shopping plaza with its numerous services and large parking lot, Quebec-owned supermarket chains such as Steinberg and Provigo with their own canning, baking, and transportation networks used price wars to eliminate the small independent grocers. To protect themselves, the latter used the same techniques in forming the Métro chain. Government protection in the form of a monopoly on the sale of beer and the right to sell certain Quebec bottled wines and lottery tickets kept small outlets in business as convenience stores. However, during the 1980s the large chains have been allowed to sell beer and wine and have set up affiliated chains of convenience stores. Eaton's and The Bay have consolidated their hold over large department store outlets in an attempt to fight competition from small boutiques and catalogue counters.

The postwar prosperity kept unemployment rates low until the recession of the late 1950s. In 1960 the unemployment rate peaked at over 10 percent before dropping off. However, unemployment started to rise after 1966 as the baby boomers started to enter the job market. The situation was not dramatic for those born between 1946 and 1955, but for young people born thereafter, finding a job has been a major preoccupation as unemployment rates soared to well over 10 percent.

The increased importance of the tertiary sector and of the number of women in the labour market has been marked by a heavy reliance on part-time labour and by high seasonal unemployment. Although the Montreal region has an unemployment rate close to the Canadian average, other regions have been hit particularly hard. The closing down of Iron Ore's operations at Schefferville left that town with only a small native population. The mining town of Gagnon disappeared from the map. Sept-Iles' shipping activity was severely curtailed causing massive unemployment.

Although foreign capital continued to play an important role in the Canadian and Quebec economies throughout the postwar period, government policies and native investment have reduced the proportion of foreign capital in the economy from a high of 38 percent in 1968 to 26 percent in 1982. Within Quebec the emergence of a strong francophone bourgeoisie has been one of the most important developments. Paul Desmarais, director of Power Corporation, and Pierre Péladeau of Québécor are examples of this new bourgeoisie which has joined the Simard and Bombardier families at the apex of Canadian business. Francophone companies have risen to new prominence in banking (National Bank), engineering (Lavalin), and food processing and distribution (Culinar) both in Canada and in international markets.

Agriculture

Agriculture has undergone dramatic transformation since the Second World War. The farming population declined dramatically after 1951, as did agriculture's importance in the Quebec economy. Mechanization in the forest industries eliminated seasonal employment on which farmers who relied on the old agro-forestry system depended. With that source of income unavailable, many people deserted their farms in peripheral areas such as the clay belt of Abitibi, the Laurentians, and the Eastern Townships. In the Montreal plain and close to Quebec City, urban sprawl encroached on some of the best farm lands until a 1978 law protected agricultural land from urban developers. As a result of these factors and the consolidation of family farms into larger units—the average farm grew from forty-seven hectares in 1941 to 78.5 hectares in 1981—the number of farms dropped sharply from over 154 000 in 1941 to under 50 000 in 1981 (Figure 8.5).

With greater capitalization, the remaining farms that are concentrated in the St. Lawrence Lowlands are able to take full advantage of mechanization. Quebec agriculture rapidly modernized in the 1940s and 1950s as tractors replaced draught animals. Only 4 percent of farms had tractors in 1941, 23 percent in 1951, 63 percent in 1961, and virtually all farms had tractors by 1971. Rural electrification programs of the Duplessis government enabled most farms to install refrigeration and mechanical milking machines between 1945 and 1960. Use of chemical fertilizers increased yields, and with

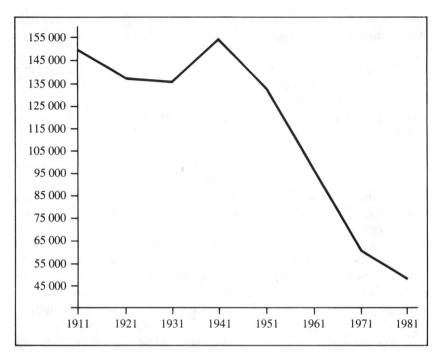

Figure 8.5 Number of Farms in Quebec, 1911-1981. The number of farms started to decline slowly after 1911, but colonization movements during the Depression account for the rise in 1941. The sharp decline occurred in the postwar period.

specialization in dairy farming, pork, and poultry production, productivity more than tripled between 1950 and 1970. Despite these gains, agricultural production stagnated between 1950 and 1965. However, in the period from 1971 to 1983 the value of agricultural production rose from $305 million to $1.5 billion.

Modernization had important consequences for the capitalization of farming. In 1951 the average Quebec farm had $9334 invested in land, equipment, and livestock. This figure rose to $18 606 in 1961, $35 390 in 1971, and $197 594 in 1981. As capital requirements grew, large corporations entered the agricultural sector and an increasing percentage of farmers rented all or part of their land. In 1941 only 6.8 percent of farmers leased land, whereas in 1981 21.8 percent did so. Greater capital requirements also caused debt loads to rise, making farmers vulnerable to price and interest rate fluctuations.

At the end of the war, farms were still small, relatively independent production units. By 1960 they were small capitalist enterprises dependent on tractors, electricity, fertilizers, outside supplies of feed, and large corporations to market their production. Accounting and marketing were increasingly important. Government programs in the 1950s established marketing boards and promoted education. Farmers used tools developed during the first half of the century to try to obtain some freedom of action. Agricultural co-operatives prospered but as they became large concerns the original participatory democratic principles fell before the needs of sound management. Farmer unionism became more radical as the Union catholique des cultivateurs (UCC) evolved into the Union des producteurs agricoles (UPA), which used its collective strength to lobby government for marketing programs, subsidies, and production quotas.

Labour

Labour has played an important role in the modernization of Quebec's economic, political, and administrative structures. Until the 1960s, Quebec labour organizations were divided between lay organizations (the Fédération provinciale du travail du Québec, affiliated with the international union movement and independent industrial unions affiliated with the Canadian Labour Congress) and the Catholic labour movement (the Confederation of Catholic Trade Unions for industrial workers, the Union catholique des cultivateurs for farmers, and the Corporation des instituteurs et institutrices catholiques for teachers).

Quebec governments, and particularly that of Maurice Duplessis, had long vaunted the docility and cheapness of Quebec's labour force as a means of attracting foreign investment. They had reinforced this image with legislation designed to curb workers' rights to associate and to strike. At the same time, labour militancy in Quebec had been present since the beginning of the industrial capitalist period in the late nineteenth century. The Second World War stimulated organized labour and the Godbout government passed a more equitable labour code in 1944. The number of unionized workers doubled to over 29 percent of the industrial work force in 1946 and the Catholic unions, rejecting the social program of the church, admitted non-Catholics and adopted more democratic practices and a more pragmatic stance on the needs of their membership. After a period of numerical stability, organized labour expanded again in the 1960s, particularly with the unionization of the public sector. As of the last decades, Quebec has one of Canada's highest rates of unionization and the most militant labour movements (Rouillard, 1983).

Labour was not docile in the Duplessis years as witnessed by the important strikes in the textile industry (1937), at Asbestos (1949), Louiseville (1952), and Murdochville (1957). The state suppressed labour by appointing pro-employer mediators, by refusing accreditation to unions, by using the provincial police to escort scabs and intimidate strikers, and by using repressive legislation such as the Padlock Act to restrict free assembly.

In the 1930s and 1940s Catholic unions moved to the forefront of labour resistance. This action placed the Catholic hierarchy in a difficult position because traditionally, the church had collaborated with the Quebec government in supporting corporatist and conservative concepts of labour organization. There was also some paranoia about communism in the church. Catholic union militancy, however, led some bishops to speak out. During the Asbestos strike in 1949, Mgr. Joseph Charbonneau of Montreal condemned police brutality, stating that "the working class is the victim of a conspiracy which aims at crushing it". Across the province, parishes demonstrated the extent of working class solidarity by holding special collections to support the strikers.

The adoption of a new labour code in 1964 gave new guarantees to unions, ensured their financial independence, and, most important, gave public sector employees the right to strike. Unions affiliated with the international unions became more nationalistic and obtained a greater degree of independence. Louis Laberge, leader of the Fédération des travailleurs du Québec (FTQ) since 1964, became a prominent spokesman for the union movement and was deeply involved in politics through his support particularly for the Parti Québécois. Catholic unions ended their religious affiliation in 1960, becoming the Confédération des syndicats nationaux (CSN).

The CSN greatly benefited from unionization in the public sector, and under leaders like Marcel Pepin they used union power to fight for fundamental social and economic change in Quebec. Unlike the FTQ, which supported traditional political action through established political parties, the CSN adopted a Marxist ideology of class struggle, interpreting the union movement as part of a larger struggle to overthrow the capitalists who controlled the Quebec economy and state. From here, it was a short ideological step to transforming conservative nationalism into an arm for bringing about an independent socialist state. In the 1970s, the teachers union, the Corporation des enseignants du Québec (CEQ) strongly supported the CSN and its principles (Rouillard, 1981: 226-235).

Fired up with growing membership (the rate of unionization peaked in 1971 at 42.1 percent) and intellectual support from the changing nationalist movement, unions took the forefront of political opposition to the liberal state in the period 1970-1976. Their challenge was epitomized by the Common Fronts in 1972 and 1975-76, which grouped all unionized workers in the public sector. The bitter strike in 1972 ended with government injunctions against the unions, a legislated settlement, and the jailing of union leaders Marcel Pepin, Louis Laberge, and Yvon Charbonneau who became martyrs for the workers' cause.

Not all workers shared the ideological stance of their leadership, however, and a new organization, the Centrale des syndicats démocratiques, was formed in 1972 to protest the increasingly radical politics of the CSN. The destruction of an important James Bay hydro project site where workers drove bulldozers through buildings before setting them on fire (Figure 8.6), along with the disruption of essential services especially in health care, alienated public opinion and tarnished the image of the union movement. After 1974 the rate of unionization started to fall and union influence declined.

Figure 8.6 The Destruction of LG2. In March 1974, union activists destroyed most of the camp that housed several thousand workers building the dam and generating station on the Grande River near James Bay. This, along with other violent labour conflicts such as that of Montreal fire fighters during which dozens of buildings burned, and the 1971 strike at Montreal's most important francophone paper, *La Presse*, which left one person dead and hundreds injured, contributed to a lessening of public support for organized labour.

The coming to power of the Parti Québécois in 1976 brought a respite from the violent social confrontations of the Bourassa years. René Lévesque's Parti Québécois government seemed to share many of the social democratic goals of the union movement and included important reformers such as Robert Burns, Claude Charron, Jacques Couture, and Pierre Marois.

The province's extremely progressive labour code of 1977 outlawed strike-breaking, and instituted the Rand formula for deducting union dues at source. Legislation in 1979 regulated working conditions in non-unionized sectors and allowed workers to refuse work that endangered their health. It regulated minimum wages, maternity leave, and annual vacations. Always torn between its conservative and social democratic origins, the PQ was forced to make difficult political choices during the recession that started in 1981. Harmony between labour and the PQ ended in 1982 when the government, facing a rapidly growing deficit, legislated a pay reduction for all public-sector employees. This alienated labour support and contributed to the PQ defeat in 1985.

Women

A result of Quebec's changes in demographics, family structures and social and work-place conditions has been the emergence of a vigorous women's movement. Family planning, control over their bodies, equality in the work place and greater political power have been major goals (Figure 8.7).

Figure 8.7   A Demonstration in Favour of Legalized Abortions, 1970. Although Quebecers are often divided along language lines, the women's movement has recruited support from both francophones and anglophones. While Quebec has been a leader among Western countries in providing free abortions, the system has been under persistent attack from Catholic conservatives, and throughout the 1970s abortion was a key issue. In the 1980s, day-care, economic equality, pornography and other violence to women have become rallying points.

Quebec has been strong in guaranteeing women legal equality but has lagged in providing day-care. Divorce laws have been liberalized but women have had to fight for adequate child support. The women's movement has also had to battle against violence to women: pornography, rape, wife beating, sexual harassment on the job, and other sexual assaults.

Women have been asserting their presence in the Quebec labour force; while 26 percent were active in 1950, 47.9 percent were active in 1983. Role stereotypes remain, however. Less educated women enter jobs in clerical work or in the service sector as cashiers and salespersons; more educated women seem to choose teaching and nursing. Their position in the lower paying and least skilled sectors leaves them vulnerable to technological change and the syndrome of part-time work. Although law, medical, and university careers are accessible, professional and university hierarchies are still male dominated; technical professions have been slower to open their doors to women, and management positions remain a largely male preserve both in the public and private sectors.

Table 8.6 Fifteen Occupations Employing the Largest Number of Women, 1981

Occupations	Number of Employees	Rank by Number of Employees in 1971
Secretaries	113 000	1
Book-keepers	75 000	7
Salespeople	61 000	23
Cashiers	57 000	8
Seamstresses	52 000	5
Waitresses	44 000	6
Nurses	38 000	9
Primary school teachers	36 000	2
Office workers	29 000	3
Cooks	22 000	18
Typists	22 000	15
Secondary school teachers	21 000	11
Receptionists	21 000	19
Domestic and office cleaners	19 000	24
Nursing assistants	18 000	12

(Brunelle and Drouilly, 1986: 281)

Wage discrimination remains characteristic of the Quebec work force. In 1971, salaries for full-time male employees were almost double those of their female counterparts, and although the gap had narrowed by 1981, it still remained substantial (Table 8.7). Given the importance of part-time labour for women, this wage gap is even greater for the labour force as a whole.

Table 8.7 Wage Spreads between Men and Women, 1971 and 1981 (in dollars)

Profession	1971		1981	
	Men	Women	Men	Women
Directors	14 802	8 184	29 068	18 599
Professionals	10 888	6 816	26 887	20 016
Manual workers				
white collar	7 249	4 259	17 720	11 860
blue collar	6 631	3 609	17 504	10 188
Farmers	4 207	2 787	12 643	7 714
Army, police, fire	8 345	5 953	23 227	16 083
Quebec Average	7 759	4 711	20 561	13 935

(Brunelle and Drouilly, 1986: 282)

Women have entered politics in increasing numbers: in 1961 Claire Kirkland-Casgrain became the first woman elected to the Quebec Assembly; in 1985 eighteen women were elected. In addition, both federal and provincial portfolios have been created to deal specifically with the status of women. However, women are still underrepresented and misrepresented in politics, and at the highest levels of the civil service.

Culture

The decline in the influence of the church has been the dominant change in Quebec culture. This has been accompanied by two distinct and perhaps contradictory trends: Americanization and the affirmation of a distinct francophone identity.

The power, influence, and numerical strength of the Roman Catholic church peaked in the 1950s. With over 8000 priests and 50 000 members of religious communities, the church was a daily presence in the lives of Quebecers through its control over Catholic education and health-care institutions. Its strong alliance with the Duplessis government ensured a favourable legal and financial climate for religious institutions. But, despite this apparently secure position, the church was vulnerable.

By the 1950s there was movement for change from within the church. The new spirit symbolized by the liturgy introduced by Vatican II in the 1960s did not go far enough for some, but alienated others who clung to traditional certainties. Attendance at non-obligatory services declined dramatically; the rosary and the adoration of saints became practices unknown to the young; Sunday attendance at mass dropped from 61.2 percent of all Montreal Catholics in 1961 to 30 percent a decade later. Young people, affected by secular values, deserted the church almost entirely with only between 12 and 15 percent practising their religion.

In addition to the dramatic decrease in religious practice, the state progressively took control of education and health care (Figure 8.8). With the struggle between progressives and traditionalists over liturgy, celibacy, and the church's social role in the aftermath of Vatican II, many clerics left the church and ordinations dropped off dramatically. By 1975, there were only 3148 priests in Quebec, a number barely sufficient for pastoral needs.

At the same time, the rising standard of living, the effect of advertising and the media, along with the automobile, caused a homogenization of Quebec culture and weakened regional variations. The establishment of the state-owned Canadian Broadcasting Corporation/Radio-Canada in 1936, which produced much of the popular entertainment first in radio and, after 1952, in television, had a distinctive Montreal accent and flavour. For their part, anglophones lived in the same cultural universe as their American and Ontario neighbours and shared tastes for fast foods, for rock and roll, for American network television programs and for Hollywood movies.

Figure 8.8 The Université du Québec à Montréal Campus. Perhaps nothing is more symbolic of the decline of religious influence than this campus where a church and a convent were torn down to build new university buildings. Parts of the church's facade were integrated into the new structure.

Although perhaps less subject to Americanization than their anglophone counterparts, popular-class francophones also have adopted many of these tastes and the same passion for American sports such as baseball. These factors helped to create an outlook that emphasized consumerism and the American way of life. The francophone and anglophone intellectual elites, on the other hand, looked to Europe and developed tastes for international cuisine, European cars, cinema and music.

This decline in religious influence and the growing Americanization made retaining a francophone identity difficult within the North American world. As the certainties linked with Catholicism and the idealization of rural values were replaced by a new nationalism, francophones sought a new basis for their distinct culture. The result was the affirmation of a new Québécois identity that turned its back on francophone minorities outside Quebec.

Between 1933 and 1945 Quebec authors had produced masterpieces with rural themes that effectively reflected rural traditions: Claude-Henri Grignon's *Un homme et son péché* (1933), Félix-Antoine Savard's *Menaud maître-draveur* (1938), Ringuet's (Philippe Panneton) *Trente arpents* (1938), and Germaine Guevremont's *Le survenant* (1945). But these novels were not in pace with urban, industrial Quebec. The postwar generation of writers such as Gabrielle Roy, André Langevin, Roger Lemelin, Gérard Bessette, and Anne Hébert turned to the city to portray French-Canadian life and won recognition in international literary circles.

Many of these books, Claire Martin's autobiographical novels on her childhood, for example, criticized the authoritarian and religious climate that prevailed in Quebec society. Martin's bitter portrayal of her mother said volumes about the idealization of traditional Quebec family life: "In July, Mother became pregnant with her fifth child. What can have been the state of mind of that poor woman, so gentle and frail, when she found herself on her way to producing yet another little misery, a part of whose life, as she well knew, would be abominable."

The most severe attack on the traditional order came from Jean-Marie Desbiens who, under the pseudonym Frère Untel, published his famous *Insolences du frère Untel* in 1960. He attacked clerical control of education, particularly the anachronistic curriculum and the teaching of French, which he felt was menaced by its insistence on ultra-conservative Catholic authors. Over 100 000 copies sold in four months and the book generated a debate that was a powerful factor in the establishment of the Parent Royal Commission to study education.

Throughout the 1960s and 1970s Quebec culture was extraordinarily dynamic in literature, theatre, and music. Although some performers—Robert Charlebois and Diane Dufresne, for example—gave rock and roll a francophone flavour, the strongest impact came from the chansonniers. Félix Leclerc and Gilles Vigneault are examples of singers whose ballads stressed the uniqueness of the Québécois identity. Emphasis on the distinct character of Quebec also influenced literature and theatre and fueled the debate over *joual*—Montreal popular language—as a viable means of expression. Many authors like Michel Tremblay felt that *joual* was necessary to express the true nature of Quebec whereas others fought to preserve an international French.

The question of joual underlines the major theme of Quebec cultural consciousness in the post-1960 era: the primacy of the French language in Quebec. The large anglophone corporations used English, which was also widespread in advertising and on many work sites. Pierre Vallières reflects the frustration felt by many young nationalists: "Spring 1951. I was soon going to leave primary school for good. To go where? To the long, dark rooms of the Raymond canneries, to hull strawberries all day long? To the city streets to work as a drawer of water [...] or to be one of the unemployed? To the collège in Longueil, to study for a job as an office clerk—bilingual if possible?".

Francophones, especially in the Montreal region where anglophone presence was the strongest, resented not being able to get service in their language in stores and restaurants, and being forced to speak English at work. During the 1960s unions fought for contracts written in French and mounted movements to boycott anglophone stores, and nationalists fought to transform McGill University into a French institution.

Conflict over language crystallized in the field of education. As the birth rate declined and statistics showed francophones being assimilated, nationalists became increasingly worried about the status of French in Quebec. Immigrants had to be assimilated into francophone rather than anglophone society through education. When the Saint-Léonard school board, supported by the Mouvement pour l'intégration scolaire, tried to replace bilingual classes with unilingual French ones, parents of Italian origin resisted and violence broke out in 1969.

The Union Nationale government of Jean-Jacques Bertrand responded with Bill 63 guaranteeing freedom of choice and provoked the ire of nationalists. Although Robert Bourassa's Liberal government made French the official language and tried to promote French in the work place in 1974, its granting of freedom of choice in the language of education was bitterly attacked by nationalists. Law 101, adopted by the Lévesque government in 1977, went much further; it restricted English education to children whose parents were educated in English in Quebec, prohibited bilingual signs, and restricted use of English in business and government. Despite protests from the anglophone community, this law satisfied the aspirations of the great majority of francophones.

While the primacy of the French language was being strengthened within Quebec, francophone minorities in the rest of Canada were undergoing assimilation. Nationalists like Henri Bourassa at the beginning of the twentieth century had sought to protect minorities, but by 1960 there was a growing feeling that "outside Quebec there was no salvation".

Despite federal government efforts to provide services in both official languages throughout the country after the adoption of the Official Languages Act in 1969, official bilingualism is largely a myth. Although growing numbers of anglophone children outside Quebec are enrolled in French immersion courses, francophone minorities have had to fight (sometimes unsuccessfully) to obtain control of French schools, particularly in Ontario. The result is that outside northern New Brunswick and the Ontario counties bordering on Quebec, rapid assimilation is taking place.

Cultural revival in Quebec depended on the expansion of a cultural infrastructure that had been sadly lacking. In 1960 only 45 percent of the population had access to one of the seventy-one municipal libraries in Quebec.

By 1984, 83 percent of the population had access to a lending library. New concert halls and auditoriums (Place des Arts in Montreal (1967) and the Grand Théâtre in Quebec City (1971) are the finest examples) introduced classical music, opera, and theatre to wider audiences. New galleries such as the Museum of Contemporary Art (1965), and the Saidye Bronfman Centre (1967), along with the expansion of Montreal's Museum of Fine Arts gave the visual arts new prominence. Much of this cultural infrastructure benefited mainly members of the Montreal and Quebec elites, but cultural centres were built throughout the province in conjunction with the centenary celebrations in 1967, which gave most regions access to a hall for concerts and theatre.

While theatre and music are strongly supported by all segments of Quebec society, a 1979 poll indicated that 77 percent of Quebecers never go to a public library; 50 percent never go to a bookstore; and 44 percent never read a book or magazine. Art museums are visited only by about a quarter of the population (Linteau, Durocher, Robert, Ricard, 1986: 692-95). Americanization continues to concern nationalists. Many of the programs on French language television are dubbed versions of popular American series such as *Dallas*, and pop stars such as Madonna draw huge crowds.

Native Peoples

In southern Quebec, native groups such as the Mohawk of Kahnawake and the Huron of Lorette have shared the same work experiences as their neighbours for over a century. Among native peoples, the increase in the population and a growing awareness of their heritage, along with land claims outstanding since the end of the French regime, produced a greater degree of politicization and community solidarity. On the Kahnawake reserve south of Montreal, for example, Mohawks established the Kahnawake Survival School in 1977. This school aims at giving children an education based on tribal tradition with emphasis on the Mohawk language, history and culture. It also tries to prepare them for work in North American society by giving courses in computing and science.

In the North, hunting and trapping remained the main activities for the Montagnais, Cree, and Inuit until the 1960s and 1970s when resource development, and particularly hydroelectric developments such as the Manicouagan and James Bay complexes, changed life in their homelands. The James Bay agreement of 1975 was a landmark in Quebec native land claims. By this agreement the Cree received $137 million as compensation for giving up their claims to the territory.

In the past, the federal Department of Indian Affairs usually managed the proceeds of such agreements. But capital from the James Bay settlement is administered by a holding company, Cree Regional Economic Enterprises (CREECO), which is controlled by the Cree band council. CREECO controls a construction company, a skate sharpening franchise, an airline serving northern Quebec (Air Creebec), and real estate in the Abitibi region. It was instrumental in having the new settlement of Chisasibi built along plans drawn to meet the needs of Cree social organization.

The autonomy and economic position of the Cree are, however, exceptional. Most native people in Quebec continue to suffer from discrimination in employment, even in areas where they predominate, and 60 percent live on unemployment insurance or welfare. The traditional livelihood of many natives in the North has been hurt by international campaigns against fur clothing. In 1981 the average annual income of non-native Canadians was $13 100 but the average native income was only $8600. Quebec, like other Canadian provinces, has failed to resolve this low standard of living, which causes serious health problems: infant mortality rates are double the Canadian average, and suicide, alcoholism and drug abuse are widespread.

Conclusion

The writing of this conclusion coincides with the burial of René Lévesque on November 5th 1987. His passing symbolizes the end of a generation that fought for social, economic, and political liberation. This generation has left Québécois more confident to assert their distinct identity, but uncertain of their economic future. Greater justice for women, social problems caused by an aging population, the place of the French language in North America, the nature of the Canadian state and Quebec's place in it, control of a rapidly changing economy, and native peoples' rights remain on the agenda for the future.

Bibliography

Contemporary Quebec

The best overview of contemporary Quebec is Paul-André Linteau, René Durocher, Jean-Claude Robert and François Ricard, *Histoire du Québec contemporain: le Québec depuis 1930*. Apart from census returns and the annual Quebec Yearbook, Gérard Bernier and Robert Boily's collection of historical statistics, *Le Québec en chiffres de 1850 à nos jours*, is useful.

The Taschereau regime has been treated by Bernard Vigod, *Quebec before Duplessis. The Political Career of Louis-Alexandre Taschereau*, while the Union Nationale has been treated by Herbert F. Quinn, *The Union Nationale. A Study in Quebec Nationalism*, and by Michael Behiels' *Prelude to the Quiet Revolution*. The period since 1960 has yet to be studied in depth but political biographies (Peter Desbarats' *René. A Canadian in Search of a Country* or Ian Macdonald's *Bourassa*) give a feeling for political life during this period.

The Independence Movement

The independence movement cannot be understood without reading Pierre Vallières' *White Niggers of America* and René Lévesque's *An Option for Quebec*. Richard Jones' *Community in Crisis. French Canadian Nationalism in Perspective* is also useful.

Ideologies in French Canada

On ideologies in French Canada, see Susan Mann Trofimenkoff's *Abbé Groulx. Variations on a Nationalist Theme* and the two-volume collection of articles edited by Fernand Dumont and Jean Hamelin, *Les idéologies au Canada Français, 1939-1974.*

Francophones Outside Quebec

The problems of francophones outside Quebec have been treated by Richard Joy, *Languages in Conflict*, and most poignantly by the Fédération des francophones hors Québec in *The Heirs of Lord Durham. Manifesto of a Vanishing People.*

Bibliography

This bibliography is weighted in favour of the socio-economic perspective of the text. For certain well-published authors such as Fernand Ouellet, Jean-Pierre Wallot and others, only the most important works have been cited.

The most extensive bibliographies of Quebec history are in Paul Aubin and Louise-Marie Coté's six volume *Bibliographie de l'histoire du Québec et du Canada/Bibliography of the History of Quebec and Canada* (Québec, Institut québecois de recherche sur la culture, 1981-7) and ongoing bibliographies in the *Revue d'histoire de l'Amérique française*. Also of importance both for their articles and bibliographical material are the *Revue d'histoire de l'Amérique française, Histoire sociale/Social History, Recherches sociographiques, Labour/Le Travail*, and the *Urban History Review/Revue d'histoire urbaine*.

The most important source for biographical data is the *Dictionary of Canadian Biography* (Toronto and Quebec, University of Toronto Press and Presses de l'Université Laval, 1964-ongoing).

Abella, Irving, "Portrait of a Jewish Professional Revolutionary: The Recollections of Joshua Gershman", *Labour/Le travailleur* 2 (1977): 185-213.

Akenson, Donald, *The Irish in Ontario: A Study in Rural History* (Kingston and Montreal, McGill-Queen's University Press, 1984).

Allaire, Gratien, *Les engagés de la fourrure, 1701-1745: une étude de leur motivation* (Unpublished Ph.D. thesis, Concordia University, 1982).

Allaire, Gratien, "Officiers et marchands: les sociétés de commerce des fourrures, 1715-1760", *Revue d'histoire de l'Amérique française*, 40,3 (hiver 1987): 409-428.

Anctil, Pierre et Gary Caldwell, *Juifs et réalités juives au Québec* (Québec, Institut québécois de recherche sur la culture, 1984).

Armstrong, Christopher and H.V. Nelles, *Monopoly's Moment: The Organization and Regulation of Canadian Utilities, 1830-1930* (Philadelphia, Temple University Press, 1986).

Armstrong, Robert, *Structure and Change: An Economic History of Quebec* (Toronto, Gage, 1984).

Audet, Louis-Philippe et Armand Gauthier, *Le système scolaire du Québec* (Montréal, Beauchemin, 1969) 2 vol.

Audet, Pierre, *Apprenticeship in early 19th Century Montreal 1790-1812*, (Unpublished M.A. thesis, Concordia University, 1975).

Axtell, James, *The Invasion Within. The Contest of Cultures in Colonial North America* (New York, Oxford, 1985).

Baribeau, Claude, *La seigneurie de la Petite-Nation, 1801-1854: le rôle économique et social du seigneur* (Hull, Asticou, 1983).

Bates, Réal, "Les conceptions prénuptiales dans la vallée du Saint-Laurent avant 1725", *Revue d'histoire de l'Amérique française*, 40,2 (automne 1986): 253-272.

Behiels, Michael, *Prelude to Quebec's Quiet Revolution: Liberalism versus Neo-Nationalism, 1945-1960* (Kingston and Montreal, McGill-Queen's University Press, 1985).

Bélanger, Jules, Marc Desjardins, et Yves Frenette, *Histoire de la Gaspésie* (Montréal, Boréal Express, 1981).

Bernard, Jean-Paul, *Les Rouges: libéralisme, nationalisme et anticlericalisme au milieu du XIXe siècle* (Montréal, Les Presses de l'Université du Québec, 1971).

Bernard, Jean-Paul, Paul-André Linteau, et Jean-Claude Robert, "La structure professionelle de Montréal en 1825", *Revue d'histoire de l'Amérique française*, 30,3 (décembre 1976): 383-415.

Bernard, Jean-Paul, *Les rébellions de 1837-1838* (Montréal, Boréal Express, 1983).

Bernier, Gérald et Robert Boily, *Le Québec en chiffres de 1850 à nos jours* (Montréal, Association canadienne-française pour l'avancement des sciences, 1986).

Bilson, Geoffrey, *A Darkened House: Cholera in Nineteenth-Century Canada* (Toronto, University of Toronto Press, 1980).

Bluteau, M-A., Charland, J-P., Thivierge, M., Thivierge, N., *Les cordonniers, artisans du cuir* (Montréal/Ottawa, Boréal Express/Musée national de l'Homme, 1980).

Bouchard, Gérard, "Family Structures and Geographic Mobility of Laterrière, 1851-1935", *Journal of Family History*, 4 (Winter 1977): 350-369.

Bouchard, Gérard, "Les systèmes de transmission des avoirs familiaux et le cycle de la société rurale au Québec du XVIIe au XXe siècle", *Histoire sociale/Social History*, 16,31 (May 1983): 35-60.

Bradbury, Bettina, "The Family Economy and Work in an Industrializing City: Montreal in the 1870s", Canadian Historical Association *Historical Papers* (1979): 71-96.

270

Bradbury, Bettina, "The Fragmented Family: Family Strategies in the Face of Death, Illness and Poverty, Montreal, 1860-1885", in Joy Parr, ed., *Childhood and Family in Canadian History* (Toronto, McClelland & Stewart, 1982).

Bradbury, Bettina, *The Working Class Family Economy: Montreal, 1861-1881* (Unpublished Ph.D. thesis, Concordia University, 1984a).

Bradbury, Bettina, "Women and Wage Labour in a Period of Transition: Montreal, 1861-81", *Histoire sociale/Social History*, 17,33 (May 1984b): 115-132.

Bradbury, Bettina, "Pigs, Cows and Boarders: Non-wage forms of Survival among Montreal Families", *Labour/Le Travail*, 14 (Fall 1984c): 9-48.

Brière, François, "Pêche et politique à Terre-Neuve au XVIIIe siècle: la France véritable gagnante du traité d'Utrecht", *Canadian Historical Review*, 64,2 (June 1983): 168-187.

Brière, François, "Le commerce triangulaire entre les ports Terre-Neuviers français, les pêcheries d'Amérique du Nord et Marseille au 18e siècle: nouvelles perspectives", *Revue d'histoire de l'Amérique française*, 40,2 (automne 1986): 193-214.

Brierley, John, "Quebec's Civil Law Codification Viewed and Reviewed", *McGill Law Journal*, 14 (1968): 521-589.

Brunelle, Dorval et Pierre Drouilly, "La structure socio-professionnelle de la main-d'oeuvre", in Gérard Boismenu, Laurent Mailhot et Jacques Rouillard, eds., *Le Québec en textes*, 2e édition (Montréal, Boréal Express, 1986).

Burgess, Joanne, "L'industrie de la chaussure à Montréal: 1840-1870—le passage de l'artisanat à la fabrique", *Revue d'histoire de l'Amérique française*, 31,2 (septembre 1977): 187-210.

Burgess, Joanne, *Work, Family, and Community: Montreal Leather Craftsmen, 1790-1831*, (Unpublished Ph.D. thesis, Université du Québec à Montréal, 1986).

Cairns, John W., "Employment in the Civil Code of Lower Canada: Tradition and Political Economy in Legal Classification and Reform", *McGill Law Journal*, 32,3 (July 1987): 673-711.

Caldwell, Gary and Eric Waddell, *The English of Québec: from Majority to Minority Status* (Québec, Institut québécois de recherche sur la culture, 1982).

Campeau, Lucien, *Les finances publiques de la Nouvelle-France sous les Cent-Associés, 1632-1665* (Montréal, Bellarmin, 1975).

Campeau, Lucien, *La mission des Jésuites chez les Hurons, 1634-1650* (Montréal, Bellarmin, 1987).

Cardin, Martine, *Jean Leroux dit Provençal, marchand à Sorel au XVIIIe siècle* (Unpublished M.A. thesis, Université de Montréal, 1987).

Careless, J.M.S., *The Union of the Canadas: The Growth of Canadian Institutions 1841-1857* (Toronto, McClelland & Stewart, 1967).

Casgrain, Thérèse, *Une femme chez les hommes* (Montréal, Editions du Jour, 1971).

Caulier, Brigitte, *Les confréries de dévotion à Montréal du 17e au 19e siècles* (Unpublished Ph. D. thesis, Université de Montréal, 1986).

Chabot, Richard, *Le curé de campagne et la contestation locale au Québec de 1791 aux troubles de 1837-38* (Montréal, Hurtubise HMH, 1975).

Charbonneau, Hubert, ed., *La population du Québec: études rétrospectives* (Montréal, Boréal Express, 1973).

Charbonneau, Hubert, *Vie et mort de nos ancêtres* (Montréal, Les Presses de l'Université de Montréal, 1975).

Charland, Jean-Pierre, *Histoire de l'enseignement technique et professionel* (Québec, Institut québécois de recherche sur la culture, 1982).

Charpentier, Alfred, *Les mémoires d'Alfred Charpentier* (Québec, Les Presses de l'Université Laval, 1971).

Clement, Wallace, *The Canadian Corporate Elite: An Analysis of Economic Power* (Toronto, McClelland & Stewart, 1975).

Clermont, Norman, "L'hiver et les indiens nomades du Québec à la fin de la préhistoire", *Revue de Géographie de Montréal*, 29 (1974): 447-452.

Cliche, Marie-Aimée, "Les attitudes devant la mort d'après les clauses testamentaires dans le gouvernement de Québec sous le Régime français", *Revue d'histoire de l'Amérique française*, 32,1 (juin 1978): 57-94.

Cliche, Marie-Aimée, *La religion populaire dans le gouvernement de Québec sous le Régime français d'après la pratique des actes surérogatoires* (Unpublished Ph.D. thesis, Université Laval, 1985).

Cohen, Marjorie, "The Decline of Women in Canadian Dairying", *Histoire sociale/Social History*, 17,34 (November 1984): 307-334.

Collectif Clio, *L'histoire des femmes au Québec depuis quatre siècles* (Montréal, Les Quinze, 1982).

Cook, Ramsay, *French-Canadian Nationalism: an anthology* (Toronto, Macmillan, 1969).

Cook, Ramsay, *The Maple Leaf Forever* (Toronto, Macmillan, 1971).

Copp, Terry, *Anatomy of Poverty: The Condition of the Working Class in Montreal 1897-1929* (Toronto, McClelland & Stewart, 1974).

Courville, Serge, "La rente agricole au Bas-Canada: éléments d'une reflexion géographique", *Cahiers de géographie du Québec*, 24,62-3 (septembre-décembre 1980): 193-223.

Courville, Serge, "Esquisse du dévoloppement villageois au Québec: le cas de l'aire seigneuriale entre 1760 et 1854", *Cahiers de géographie du Québec*, 28, 73-4 (avril-septembre 1984): 9-46.

Courville, Serge, "Villages and Agriculture in the Seigneuries of Lower Canada: Conditions of a Comprehensive Study of Rural Quebec in the First Half of the Nineteenth Century" in Donald Akinson, *Canadian Papers in Rural History*, Vol. 5 (Gananoque, Langdale Press, 1986): 121-149.

Craven, Paul and Tom Traves "Canadian Railways as Manufacturers, 1850-1880", Canadian Historical Association *Historical Papers* (1983): 254-281.

Creighton, Donald, *The Empire of the St. Lawrence* (Toronto, Macmillan, 1956).

Cross, Michael, "The Shiners' War", *Canadian Historical Review*, 54,1 (March 1973): 1-26.

Cross, Suzanne, "The Neglected Majority: The Changing Role of Women in Nineteenth Century Montreal", *Histoire sociale/Social History*, 6,12 (November 1973): 202-23.

Crowley, Terence, "'Thunder gusts': Popular Disturbances in Early French Canada", Canadian Historical Association *Historical Papers* (1979): 11-32.

Cuthbert-Brandt, Gail, "Weaving it Together: Life Cycle and the Industrial Experience of Female Cotton Workers in Quebec, 1910-1950", *Labour/Le Travailleur*, 7 (Spring 1981): 113-125.

Dales, John H., *Hydroelectricity and Industrial Development. Quebec 1898-1940* (Cambridge, Harvard University Press, 1957).

Danylewycz, Marta and Alison Prentice, "Teacher's Work: Changing Patterns and Perceptions in the Emerging School Systems of Nineteenth and Early Twentieth Century Central Canada", *Labour/Le Travail*, 17 (Spring 1986): 59-82.

Danylewycz, Marta, *Taking the Veil: An Alternative to Marriage, Motherhood and Spinsterhood in Quebec, 1840-1920* (Toronto, McClelland & Stewart, 1987).

Davis, Ralph, *The Rise of the Atlantic Economies* (London, Wiedenfeld & Nicolson, 1973).

Dechêne, Louise, "L'évolution du régime seigneurial au Canada: le cas de Montréal aux XVIIe et XVIIIe siècles", *Recherches sociographiques*, 12,2 (mai-août 1971): 143-183.

Dechêne, Louise, *Habitants et marchands de Montréal au XVIIe siècle* (Paris, Plon, 1974).

Dechêne, Louise et Jean-Claude Robert, "Le choléra dans le Bas-Canada, mesure des inégalités devant la mort", in Hubert Charbonneau et André Larose, eds., *Les grandes mortalités* (Liège, Ordena, 1979): 229-57.

Dechêne, Louise, "La rente du faubourg Saint-Roch à Québec, 1750-1850", *Revue d'histoire de l'Amérique française*, 34,4 (mars 1981): 569-596.

Dechêne, Louise, "Observations sur l'agriculture du Bas-Canada au début du XIXe siècle", in Joseph Goy et Jean-Pierre Wallot, eds., *Evolution et éclatement du monde rural, France-Québec, XVIIe–XXe siècles*, (Montréal et Paris, Les Presses de l'Université de Montréal et l'Ecole des Hautes Etudes en Sciences Sociales, 1986): 189-202.

DeLottinville, Peter, "Joe Beef of Montreal: Working Class Culture and the Tavern, 1869-89", *Labour/Le Travailleur*, 8-9 (1981-2): 9-40.

Desbarats, Peter, *René. A Canadian in Search of a Country* (Toronto, Seal Books, 1977).

Desrosiers, Claude, *L'analyse du livre de comptes (1794-1797) du marchand général Joseph Cartier: premiers résultats d'un traitement informatisé* (Unpublished M.A. thesis, Université de Montréal, 1984).

Dessureault, Christian, *Les fondements de la hierarchie sociale au sein de la paysannerie: le cas de Saint-Hyacinthe, 1760-1815* (Unpublished Ph.D. thesis, Université de Montréal, 1986).

Dever, Alan, "Economic Development and the Lower Canadian Assembly, 1828-40" (Unpublished M.A. thesis, McGill University, 1976).

DeVries, Jan, *The Economy of Europe in an Age of Crisis, 1600-1750* (Cambridge, Cambridge University Press, 1976).

Dickason, Olive Patricia, *The Myth of the Savage and the Beginnings of French Colonialism in the Americas* (Edmonton, University of Alberta Press, 1984).

Dickinson, John A., "Un aperçu de la vie culturelle en Nouvelle-France: l'examen de trois bibliothèques privées", *Revue de l'Université d'Ottawa*, 44,4 (octobre-décembre 1974a): 453-466.

Dickinson, John A., "La justice seigneuriale en Nouvelle-France: Le cas de Notre-Dame-des-Anges", *Revue d'histoire de l'Amérique française*, 28,3 (décembre 1974b): 323-346.

Dickinson, John A., "La guerre iroquoise et la mortalité en Nouvelle-France, 1608-1666", *Revue d'histoire de l'Amérique française*, 36,1 (juin 1982a): 31-54.

Dickinson, John A., *Justice et justiciables. La procédure civile à la Prévôté de Québec, 1667-1759* (Québec, Les Presses de l'Université Laval, 1982b).

Dickinson, John A., "Les Amérindiens et les débuts de la Nouvelle-France", *Canada Ieri e Oggi* (Bari, Schena editore, 1986a): 87-108.

Dickinson, John A., "La législation et les travailleurs québécois, 1894-1914", *Relations Industrielles*, 41,2 (juin 1986b): 357-380.

Dickinson, John A., "Réflexions sur la police en Nouvelle-France", *McGill Law Review*, 32,3 (July 1987): 496-522.

Drolet, Antonio, *Les bibliothèques canadiennes, 1604-1960* (Ottawa, Cercle du livre de France, 1965).

Dumas, Evelyn, *The Bitter Thirties in Québec* (Montreal, Black Rose Books, 1975).

Dumont, Fernand et Jean Hamelin, *Les idéologies au Canada Français, 3 Vols.* (Québec, Les Presses de l'Université Laval, 1971-1981).

Dumont, Micheline, "Des garderies au XIXe siècle: Les salles d'asile des Soeurs Grises à Montréal", *Revue d'histoire de l'Amérique française*, 34,1 (juin 1980): 127-56.

Dumont, Micheline et Nadia Fahmy-Eid, *Les couventines: L'éducation des filles au Québec dans les congrégations religieuses enseignantes 1840-1960* (Montréal, Boréal Express, 1986).

Easterbrook, W. T. and M. H. Watkins, *Approaches to Canadian Economic History* (Toronto, McClelland & Stewart, 1967).

Eccles, William John, *Canada Under Louis XIV* (Toronto, McClelland & Stewart, 1964).

Eccles, William John, *The Canadian Frontier* (New York, Holt, Rinehart & Winston, 1969).

Eccles, William John, "The Social, Economic and Political Significance of the Military Establishment in New France", *Canadian Historical Review*, 52,1 (March 1971): 1-22.

Eccles, William John, "A Belated Review of Harold Adams Innis's *The Fur Trade in Canada*", *Canadian Historical Review*, 60,4 (December 1979): 419-441.

L'église de Montréal. Aperçus d'hier et d'aujourd'hui (Montréal, Fides, 1986).

Fahmy-Eid, Nadia, *Le clergé et le pouvoir politique au Québec: Une analyse de l'idéologie ultramontaine au milieu du XIXe siècle* (Montréal, Hurtubise HMH, 1978).

Fahmy-Eid, Nadia and Micheline Dumont, *Maîtresses de maison, maîtresses d'école: Femmes, famille et éducation dans l'histoire du Québec* (Montréal, Boréal Express, 1983).

Fecteau, Jean-Marie, "Régulation sociale et répression de la déviance au Bas-Canada au tournant du 19e siècle (1791-1815), *Revue d'histoire de l'Amérique française*, 38,4 (printemps 1985): 499-522.

Fecteau, Jean-Marie, "Prolégomènes à une étude historique des rapports entre l'Etat et le droit dans la société québécoise, de la fin du XVIIIe siècle à la crise de 1929", *Sociologie et sociétés*, 18,1 (avril 1986): 129-138.

Fecteau, Jean-Marie, "Mesures d'exception et règle de droit: Les conditions d'application de la loi martiale au Québec lors des rébellions de 1837-1838", *McGill Law Journal*, 32,3 (July 1987): 465-495.

Fédération des francophones hors Québec, *The Heirs of Lord Durham. Manifesto of a Vanishing People* (Toronto, Burns & MacEachern, 1978).

Ferland, Jacques, *Evolution des rapports sociaux dans l'industrie canadienne du cuir au tournant du 20e siècle* (Unpublished Ph.D. thesis, McGill University, 1985).

Ferland, Jacques, "Syndicalisme 'parcellaire' et syndicalisme 'collectif': Une interprétation socio-technique des conflits ouvriers dans deux industries québécoises (1880-1914)", *Labour/Le Travail*, 19 (Spring 1987): 49-88.

Ferretti, Lucia, "Mariage et cadre de vie familiale dans une paroisse ouvrière montréalaise: Sainte-Brigide", *Revue d'histoire de l'Amérique française*, 39,2 (automne 1985): 233-251.

Francis, Daniel and Toby Morantz, *Partners in Furs. A History of the Fur Trade in Eastern James Bay, 1600-1870* (Kingston and Montreal, McGill-Queen's University Press, 1983).

Frégault, Guy, *Canadian Society in the French Regime* (Ottawa, Canadian Historical Association, Historical Booklet 3, 1964).

Gadoury, Lorraine, *Le comportement démographique et les alliances de la noblesse de la Nouvelle-France* (Unpublished Ph.D. thesis, Université de Montréal, 1988).

Gaffield, Chad, *Language, Schooling and Cultural Conflict: The origins of the French-Language Controversy in Ontario* (Kingston and Montreal, McGill-Queen's University Press, 1987).

Gagnon, Serge, "Pour une conscience historique de la révolution québécoise", *Cité Libre*, 16,83 (1966): 4-16.

Gagnon, Serge, *Quebec and its Historians: 1840 to 1920* (Montreal, Harvest House, 1982).

Gagnon, Serge et Louise Lebel-Gagnon, "Le milieu d'origine du clergé québécois 1775-1840: mythes et réalités", *Revue d'histoire de l'Amérique française*, 37,3 (décembre 1983): 373-398.

Galarneau, Claude, *Les collèges classiques au Canada français* (Montréal, Fides, 1978).

Gérin, Léon, *Léon Gérin et l'habitant de Saint-Justin* (Montréal, Les Presses de l'Université de Montréal, 1968).

Gervais, Gaetan, *L'expansion du reseau ferroviaire québecois, 1875-1895* (Unpublished Ph.D. thesis, Université d'Ottawa, 1979).

Gossage, Peter, *Abandoned Children in Nineteenth-Century Montreal,* (Unpublished M.A. thesis, McGill University, 1983).

Grant, Hugh M., "One Step Forward, Two Steps Back: Innis, Eccles and the Canadian Fur Trade", *Canadian Historical Review*, 62,3 (September 1981): 304-322.

Greenwood, Murray, "The Chartrand Murder Trial: Rebellion and Repression in Lower Canada, 1837-1839", *Criminal Justice History*, 5 (1984): 129-159.

Greer, Allan, "The Pattern of Literacy in Quebec, 1745-1899", *Histoire sociale/Social History*, 11,22 (November 1978): 295-335.

Greer, Allan, "Rebels and Prisoners: The Canadian Insurrections of 1837-8", *Acadiensis*, 14,1 (Autumn 1984): 137-145.

Greer, Allan, *Peasant, Lord and Merchant. Rural Society in Three Quebec Parishes, 1740-1840* (Toronto, University of Toronto Press, 1985).

Griffiths, Naomi, *The Acadians: Creation of a People* (Toronto, McGraw-Hill Ryerson, 1973).

Groulx, Lionel, *Michel Barrin de la Galissonière* (Toronto, University of Toronto Press, 1970).

Hamelin, Jean et Yves Roby, *Histoire économique du Québec, 1851-1896* (Montréal, Fides, 1971).

Hamelin, Jean et al., *Histoire du Québec* (Toulouse, Privat, 1976).

Hamelin, Jean et Nicole Gagnon, *Histoire de catholicisme québécois* (Montréal, Boréal Express, 1986).

Hanna, David, *Montreal: a City built by Small Builders, 1867-1880* (Unpublished Ph.D. thesis, McGill University, 1986).

Hanna, David, *The New Town of Montreal: Creation of an Upper Middle Class Suburb on the Slope of Mount Royal in the Mid-Nineteenth Century* (Unpublished M.A. thesis, University of Toronto, 1977).

Hardy, Jean-Pierre, et Thierry Ruddel, *Les apprentis artisans à Québec, 1660-1815* (Montréal, Les Presses de l'Université du Québec, 1977).

Hardy, Jean-Pierre, "Quelques aspects du niveau de richesse et de la vie matérielle des artisans de Québec et de Montréal, 1740-1755", *Revue d'histoire de l'Amérique française*, 40,3 (hiver 1987): 339-372.

Hardy, René et Normand Séguin, *Forêt et société en Mauricie* (Montréal, Boréal Express, 1984).

Harney, Robert F., "Montreal's King of Italian Labour: A Case Study of Padronism", *Labour/Le Travailleur*, 4, (1979): 56-84.

Harris, Richard Colebrook, *The Seigneurial System in Early Canada* (Québec and Madison, Les Presses de l'Université Laval and University of Wisconsin Press, 1966).

Harris, Richard Colebrook and John Warkentin, *Canada before Confederation* (New York, Oxford University Press, 1974).

Harris, Richard Colebrook, "Of Poverty and Helplessness in Petite Nation", in J. Bumsted, ed., *Canadian History Before Confederation* (Georgetown, Irwin Dorsey, 1979): 329-354.

Harris, Richard Colebrook, ed., *Historical Atlas of Canada* (Toronto and Montréal, University of Toronto Press and Les Presses de l'Université de Montréal, 1987).

Harvey, Fernand, *Le mouvement ouvrier au Québec* (Montréal, Boréal Express, 1980).

Heap, Margaret, "La grève des charretiers à Montréal, 1865", *Revue d'histoire de l'Amérique française*, 31,3 (décembre 1977): 371-395.

Heap, Ruby, "Urbanisation et éducation: la centralisation scolaire à Montréal au début du XXe siècle", Canadian Historical Association *Historical Papers* (1985): 132-155.

Heap, Ruby, *L'église, l'état et l'enseignement primaire public catholique au Québec, 1897-1920* (Unpublished Ph.D. thesis, Université de Montréal, 1987).

Heidenreich, Conrad, *Huronia. A History and Geography of the Huron Indians, 1600-1650* (Toronto, McClelland & Stewart, 1971).

Helm, June, ed., *Handbook of North American Indians*, Vol. 6, *Subarctic* (Washington, Smithsonian Institution, 1981).

Henripin, Jacques, *La population canadienne au début du XVIIIe siècle* (Paris, Institut national d'études démographiques, 1954).

Hopes and Dreams: the Diary of Henriette Desaulles, 1874-1881 (Toronto, Hounslow Press, 1987).

Hoskins, Ralph, *Original Acquisition of Land in Montreal by the Grand Trunk Railway of Canada* (Department of Geography, McGill University, "Shared Spaces", no.7, 1987).

Howes, David, "From Polyjurality to Monojurality: The Transformation of Quebec Law, 1875-1929", *McGill Law Journal*, 32,3 (July 1987): 523-558.

Igartua, José, *The Merchants and Négociants of Montréal, 1750-1775: A Study in Socio-Economic History* (Unpublished Ph.D. thesis, Michigan State University, 1974).

Igartua, José, "A Change in Climate: The Conquest and the *Marchands* of Montreal", Canadian Historical Association *Historical Papers* (1974): 115-134.

Innis, Harold, *The Fur Trade in Canada* (Toronto, University of Toronto Press, 1956).

Jaenen, Cornelius, *Friend and Foe. Aspects of French-Indian Cultural Contact in the Sixteenth and Seventeenth Centuries* (Toronto, McClelland & Stewart, 1976a).

Jaenen, Cornelius, *The Role of the Church in New France* (Toronto, McGraw-Hill Ryerson, 1976b).

James, William C., *A Fur Traders Photographs. A. A. Chesterfield in the District of Ungava, 1901-4*, (Kingston and Montreal, McGill-Queen's University Press, 1985).

Jones, Richard, *Community in Crisis. French Canadian Nationalism in Perspective* (Toronto, McClelland & Stewart, 1972)

Jones, Richard, *Duplessis and the Union Nationale Administration* (Ottawa, Canadian Historical Association Booklet 35, 1983).

Joy, Richard, *Languages in Conflict* (Toronto, McClelland & Stewart, 1972).

Kenneally, Rhona, *The Montreal Maternity Hospital, 1843-1926* (Unpublished M.A. thesis, McGill University, 1983).

Kesteman, Jean-Pierre, *Une bourgeoisie et son espace: Industrialisation et développement du capitalisme dans le district de Saint-François (Québec), 1823-1879* (Unpublished Ph.D. thesis, Université du Québec à Montréal, 1985).

Kolish, Evelyn, *Changements dans le droit privé au Québec/Bas-Canada entre 1760 et 1840: attitudes et réactions des contemporains* (Unpublished Ph.D. thesis, Université de Montréal, 1980).

Kolish, Evelyn, "Le Conseil législatif et les bureaux d'enregistrement (1836)", *Revue d'histoire de l'Amérique française*, 35,2 (septembre 1981): 217-30.

Kolish, Evelyn, "Imprisonment for Debt in Lower Canada, 1791-1840", *McGill Law Journal*, 32,3 (July 1987): 602-635.

Kreech III, Shepard, *Indians, Animals and the Fur Trade* (Athens, University of Georgia Press, 1981).

Lacelle, Claudette, *Urban Domestic Servants in 19th-Century Canada* (Ottawa, Parks Canada, 1987).

Lachance, André, *La justice criminelle du roi au Canada au XVIIIe siècle. Tribunaux et officiers* (Québec, Les Presses de l'Université Laval, 1978).

Lachance, André, *Crimes et criminels en Nouvelle-France* (Montréal, Boréal Express, 1984).

Lachance, André, *La vie urbaine en Nouvelle-France* (Montréal, Boréal Express, 1987).

Lacroix, Benoît et Jean Simard, *Religion populaire, religion de clercs* (Québec, Institut québécois de recherche sur la culture, 1985).

Lamonde, Yvan et Raymond Montpetit, *Le parc Sohmer de Montréal, 1889-1919. Un lieu de culture urbaine* (Québec, Institut québécois de recherche sur la culture, 1986).

Lapointe-Roy, Huguette, *Charité bien ordonnée: Le premier réseau de lutte contre la pauvreté à Montréal au 19e siècle* (Montréal, Boréal Express, 1987).

Lauzon, Gilles et Lucie Ruelland, *1875/Saint-Henri* (Montréal, Société historique de Saint-Henri, 1985).

Lauzon, Gilles, *Conditions économiques de la production et de l'usage des espaces d'habitation populaire et ouvrière en période d'industrialisation: le village St-Augustin (St-Henri), en périphérie de Montréal, 1850-1875* (Unpublished M.A. thesis, Université du Québec à Montréal, 1987).

Lavigne, Marie et Yolande Pinard, *Travailleuses et féministes: les femmes dans la société québécoise* (Montréal, Boréal Express, 1983).

Lavigne, Marie, Yolande Pinard and Jennifer Stoddart, "The Fédération Nationale Saint-Jean-Baptiste and the Women's Movement in Quebec", in Linda Kealey, *A Not Unreasonable Claim: Women and Reform in Canada 1880s-1920s* (Toronto, Women's Press, 1979).

Lavoie, Yolande, *L'émigration des Canadiens aux Etats-Unis avant 1930* (Montréal, Les Presses de l'Université de Montréal, 1972).

Leacock, Eleanor, "Montagnais Women and the Jesuit Program for Colonization", in Veronica Strong-Boag and Anita Clair Fellman, *Rethinking Canada. The Promise of Women's History* (Toronto, Copp Clark Pitman, 1986): 7-22.

Lee, David, *The Robins in Gaspé, 1766 to 1825* (Toronto, Fitzhenry & Whiteside, 1984).

Lemieux, Lucien, *L'établissement de la première province ecclésiastique au Canada, 1783-1844* (Montréal, Fides, 1968).

Lépine, Daniel, *La domesticité juvénile à Montréal pendant la première moitié du XVIIIe siècle* (Unpublished M.A. thesis, Université de Sherbrooke, 1982).

Lévesque, Andrée, "Deviant Anonymous: Single Mothers at the Hôpital de la Miséricorde in Montreal, 1929-39", Canadian Historical Association *Historical Papers* (1984a): 168-184.

Lévesque, Andrée, *Virage à gauche interdit: les communistes, les socialistes et leurs ennemis au Québec, 1929-1939* (Montréal, Boréal Express, 1984b).

Lévesque, René, *An Option for Quebec* (Toronto, McClelland & Stewart, 1968).

Levitt, Joseph, *Henri Bourassa and the Golden Calf: The Social Program of the Nationalists of Québec (1900-1914)* (Ottawa, University of Ottawa Press, 1972).

Levitt, Joseph, *Henri Bourassa, Catholic critic* (Ottawa, Canadian Historical Association Booklet 29, 1976).

Linteau, Paul-André and Jean-Claude Robert, "Land Ownership and Society in Montreal: an Hypothesis", in G. Stelter and A. Artibise, eds., *The Canadian City: Essays in Urban History* (Toronto, McClelland & Stewart, 1977).

Linteau, Paul-André, *Maisonneuve: Comment des promoteurs fabriquent une ville* (Montréal, Boréal Express, 1981).

Linteau, Paul-André, René Durocher, and Jean-Claude Robert, *A History of Contemporary Quebec, 1867-1930* (Toronto, Lorimer, 1983).

Linteau, Paul-André, René Durocher, Jean-Claude Robert et François Ricard, *Histoire du Québec contemporain: le Québec depuis 1930* (Montréal, Boréal Express, 1986).

Little, Jack, "The Social and Economic Development of Settlers in two Quebec Townships, 1851-1870", in Donald Akenson, *Canadian Papers in Rural History*, Vol. 1 (Gananoque, Langdale Press, 1978): 89-113.

Little, Jack, "Watching the Frontier Disappear: English-Speaking Reaction to French Canadian Colonization in the Eastern Townships, 1844-1890", *Journal of Canadian Studies*, 15 (1980-1): 98-103.

Little, Jack, "Colonization and Municipal Reform in Canada East", *Histoire sociale/Social History*, 14,27 (May 1981): 93-122.

Lowe, Graham S., "Mechanization, Feminization, and Managerial Control in the Early Twentieth-Century Canadian Office", *On the Job: Confronting the Labour Process in Canada* (Kingston and Montreal, McGill-Queen's University Press, 1986): 177-209.

McCallum, John, *Unequal Beginnings: Agriculture and Economic Development in Quebec and Ontario until 1870* (Toronto, University of Toronto Press, 1980).

McCann, L.D., *Heartland and Hinterland: A Geography of Canada* (Scarborough, Prentice Hall, 1982).

Macdonald, Ian, *From Bourassa to Bourassa* (Montreal, Harvest House, 1984).

McGinnis, Janice P. Dickin. "The Impact of Epidemic Influenza, Canada 1918-1919", Canadian Historical Association *Historical Papers* (1977): 120-141.

McInnis, Marvin and Frank Lewis, "The Efficiency of the French Canadian Farmer in the Nineteenth Century", *Journal of Economic History*, 40 (1980): 497-514.

McInnis, Marvin, "A Reconsideration of the State of Agriculture in Lower Canada in the First Half of the Nineteenth Century", in D. Akenson, *Canadian Papers in Rural History*, Vol. 3 (Gananoque, Langdale Press, 1982): 9-49.

McNally, Larry, *Water Power on the Lachine Canal, 1846-1900* (Ottawa, Parks Canada, 1982).

Magnuson, Roger, *A Brief History of Quebec Education* (Montreal, Harvest House, 1980).

Marsan, Jean-Claude, *Montréal en évolution* (Montréal, Fides, 1974).

Martin, Calvin, *Keepers of the Game: Indian-Animal Relationships and the Fur Trade* (Berkeley, University of California Press, 1978).

Massicotte, Daniel, *Le marché du logement locatif à Montréal de 1731 à 1741* (Unpublished M.A. thesis, Université de Montréal, 1987).

Mathieu, Jacques, *La construction navale royale à Québec, 1739-1759* (Québec, Société historique de Québec, 1971).

Mathieu, Jacques, *Le commerce entre la Nouvelle-France et les Antilles au XVIIIe siècle* (Montréal, Fides, 1981).

Metcalfe, Alan, "The Evolution of Organized Physical Recreation in Montreal, 1840-1895", *Histoire sociale/Social History*, 11,21 (May 1978): 144-166.

Michel, Louis, "Un marchand rural en Nouvelle France: François-Augustin Bailly de Messein, 1709-1771", *Revue d'histoire de l'Amérique française*, 33,2 (septembre 1979): 215-262.

Michel, Louis, "Varennes et Verchères, des origines au milieu du XIXe siècle: état d'une enquête", in Joseph Goy et Jean-Pierre Wallot, eds., *Evolution et éclatement du monde rural, France-Québec, XVIIe–XXe siècles* (Montréal et Paris, Les Presses de l'Université de Montréal et l'Ecole des Hautes Etudes en Sciences Sociales, 1986): 325-340.

Miquelon, Dale, *Society and Conquest. The Debate on the Bourgeoisie and Social Change in French Canada, 1700-1850* (Toronto, Copp Clark, 1977).

Miquelon, Dale, *Dugard of Rouen. French Trade to Canada and the West Indies, 1729-1770* (Kingston and Montreal, McGill-Queen's University Press, 1978).

Miquelon, Dale, *New France, 1701-1744* (Toronto, McClelland & Stewart, 1987).

Monet, Jacques, *The Last Cannon Shot: A Study of French-Canadian Nationalism 1837-1840* (Toronto, University of Toronto Press, 1969).

Moogk, Peter, *The Craftsmen of New France* (Unpublished Ph.D. thesis, University of Toronto, 1973).

Nahuet, Robert, *Une experience canadienne de Taylorisme. Le cas des usines Angus du Canadien Pacifique* (Unpublished M.A. thesis, Université du Québec à Montréal, 1984).

Neatby, Hilda, *Québec: The Revolutionary Age 1760-1791* (Toronto: McClelland & Stewart, 1966).

Niosi, Jorge, "La Laurentide (1887-1928): pionnière du papier journal au Canada", *Revue d'histoire de l'Amérique française*, 29, no.3 (décembre 1975): 375-415.

Nish, Cameron, *The French Canadians, 1759-1766: Conquered? Half-Conquered? Liberated?* (Toronto, Copp Clark, 1966).

Nish, Cameron, *François-Etienne Cugnet. Entrepreneur et entreprises en Nouvelle-France* (Montréal, Fides, 1975).

Noel, Françoise, *Gabriel Christie's Seigneuries: Settlement and Seigneurial Administration in the Upper Richelieu Valley, 1764-1854* (Unpublished Ph.D. thesis, McGill University, 1985).

Noel, Françoise, "Chambly Mills, 1774-1815", Canadian Historical Association *Historical Papers* (1985): 102-116.

Noel, Jan, "New France: Les femmes favorisées", in Veronica Strong-Boag and Anita Clair Fellman, eds., *Rethinking Canada. The Promise of Women's History* (Toronto, Copp Clark Pitman, 1986).

Ouellet, Fernand, *Louis Joseph Papineau: A Divided Soul* (Ottawa, Canadian Historical Association, 1964).

Ouellet, Fernand, *Eléments d'histoire sociale du Bas-Canada* (Montréal, Hurtubise HMH, 1972).

Ouellet, Fernand, *Lower Canada, 1791-1840: Social Change and Nationalism* (Toronto, McClelland & Stewart, 1980).

Ouellet, Fernand, *Economic and Social History of Quebec* (Toronto, Macmillan, 1981).

Palmer, Bryan, *Working-Class Experience: the Rise and Reconstitution of Canadian Labour, 1800-1980* (Toronto and Vancouver, Butterworth, 1985).

Paquet, Gilles et Jean-Pierre Wallot, *Patronage et pouvoir dans le Bas-Canada (1794-1812)* (Montréal, Les Presses de l'Université du Québec, 1973).

Paquet, Gilles et Jean-Pierre Wallot, "Sur quelques discontinuités dans l'expérience socio-économique du Québec: une hypothèse", *Revue d'histoire de l'Amérique Française*, 35,4 (mars 1982): 483-521.

Paquet, Gilles et Jean-Pierre Wallot, "Stratégie foncière de l'habitant: Québec (1790-1835)", *Revue d'histoire de l'Amérique française*, 39,4 (printemps 1986): 551-582.

Paquette, Lyne et Réal Bates, "Les naissances illégitimes sur les rives du Saint-Laurent avant 1730", *Revue d'histoire de l'Amérique française*, 40,2 (automne 1986): 239-252.

Pendergast, James and Bruce Trigger, *Cartier's Hochelaga and the Dawson Site* (Kingston and Montreal, McGill-Queen's University Press, 1972).

Pentland, H. C., *Labour and Capital in Canada* (Toronto, Lorimer, 1981).

Piédalue, Gilles, *La bourgeoisie canadienne et le problème de la réalisation du profit au Canada, 1900-1930* (Unpublished Ph.D. thesis, Université de Montréal, 1976).

Plamondon, Lilianne, "A Businesswoman in New France: Marie-Anne Barbel, the Widow Fornel", in Veronica Strong-Boag and Anita Clair Fellman, eds., *Rethinking Canada. The Promise of Women's History* (Toronto, Copp Clark Pitman, 1986).

Pomfret, Richard, *The Economic Development of Canada* (Toronto, Methuen, 1981).

Posgate, Dale and Kenneth McRoberts, *Quebec: Social Change and Political Crisis* (Toronto, McClelland & Stewart, 1980).

Potvin, Damase, *La baie des Hahas* (Port Alfred, Chambre de commerce de la Baie des Hahas, 1957).

Poutanen, Mary Anne, *For the Benefit of the Master: The Montreal Needle Trades During the Transition 1820-1842* (Unpublished M.A. thesis, McGill University, 1985).

Pouyez, Christian and Yolande Lavoie, *Les Saguenayens: Introduction à l'histoire des populations du Saguenay XVIe-XXe siècles* (Québec, Les Presses de l'Université du Québec, 1983).

Pritchard, James, "The Pattern of French Colonial Shipping to Canada before 1760", *Revue française d'histoire d'outre-mer*, 63,231 (1976): 189-210.

Quinn, Herbert, *The Union Nationale: A Study in Quebec Nationalism* (Toronto, University of Toronto Press, 1963).

Ramirez, Bruno and Michael Del Balso, *The Italians of Montreal: From Sojourning to Settlement* (Montreal, Editions du courant, 1980).

Ramirez, Bruno, "Brief Encounters: Italian Immigrant Workers and the CPR, 1900-30", *Labour/Le Travail*, 17 (Spring 1986): 9-28.

Ramsden, Peter G., "Rich Man, Poor Man, Dead Man, Thief. The Dispersal of Wealth in 17th Century Huron Society", *Ontario Archaeology*, 35 (1981): 35-40.

Rioux, Marcel, *Belle-Anse* (Ottawa, National Museum of Canada, 1961).

Rioux, Marcel and Yves Martin, *French-Canadian Society* (Toronto, McClelland & Stewart, 1964).

Roback, Leo, "Quebec Workers in the Twentieth Century", in W. J. C. Cherwinski and G. S. Kealey, *Lectures in Canadian Labour and Working-Class History* (St. John's, Committee on Canadian Labour History, 1985): 165-182.

Robert, Jean-Claude, "Un seigneur entrepreneur, Barthélemy Joliette, et la fondation du village d'Industrie (Joliette)", *Revue d'histoire de l'Amérique française*, 26,3 (décembre 1972): 375-396.

Robert, Jean-Claude, "Aperçu sur les structures socio-professionelles des villages de la région nord de Montréal durant la première moitié du XIXe siècle", *Cahiers de geographie du Québec*, 28, 73-4 (avril-septembre 1984): 63-72.

Roby, Yves, *Alphonse Desjardins et les caisses populaires, 1854-1920* (Montréal, Fides, 1964).

Roby, Yves, *Les Québécois et les investissements américains (1918-1929)* (Québec, Les Presses de l'Université Laval, 1976).

Rouillard, Jacques, *Les syndicats nationaux au Québec de 1900 à 1930* (Québec, Les Presses de l'Université Laval, 1979).

Rouillard, Jacques, *Histoire de la CSN (1921-1981)* (Montréal, Boréal Express, 1981).

Rouillard, Jacques, "Le militantisme des travailleurs au Québec et en Ontario, niveau de syndicalisation et mouvement de grève (1900-1980)", *Revue d'histoire de l'Amérique française*, 37,2 (septembre 1983): 201-226.

Rudé, George, *Protest and Punishment: The Story of the Social and Political Protesters Transported to Australia, 1788-1868* (Oxford, Oxford University Press, 1978).

Rudin, Ronald, *The Forgotten Quebecers: A History of English-Speaking Quebec 1759-1980* (Québec, Institut québécois de recherche sur la culture, 1985a).

Rudin, Ronald, *Banking en français: The French Banks of Quebec, 1835-1925* (Toronto, University of Toronto Press, 1985b).

Rudin, Ronald, "Bankers' Hours: Life Behind the Wicket at the *Banque d'Hochelaga*, 1901-21", *Labour/Le Travail*, 18 (Fall 1986): 63-76.

Ryan, William, *The Clergy and Economic Growth in Quebec (1896-1914)* (Québec, Les Presses de l'Université Laval, 1966).

Ryerson, Stanley, *Unequal Union: Confederation and the Roots of Conflict in the Canadas, 1815-1873* (Toronto, Progress Books, 1968).

Samson, Roch, "Une industrie avant l'industrialisation: le cas des forges du Saint-Maurice", *Anthropologie et Sociétés*, 10,1 (1986): 85-107.

Sarra-Bournet, Michel, *L'affaire Roncarelli. Duplessis contre les Témoins de Jéhovah* (Québec, Institut québécois de recherche sur la culture, 1986).

Savoie, Sylvie, *Les couples en difficulté aux XVIIe et XVIIIe siècles: les demandes en séparation en Nouvelle-France* (Unpublished M.A. thesis, Université de Sherbrooke, 1986).

Schulze, David, "Rural Manufacture in Lower Canada: Understanding Seigneurial Privilege and the Transition in the Countryside", *Alternate Routes*, 7 (1984): 134-167.

Séguin, Maurice, *L'idée d'indépendance au Québec. Genèse historique* (Trois-Rivières, Boréal Express, 1968).

Séguin, Maurice, *La nation "canadienne" et l'agriculture (1760-1850)* (Trois-Rivières, Boréal Express, 1970).

Séguin, Normand, *La conquête du sol au 19e siècle* (Montréal, Boréal Express, 1977).

Séguin, Normand, *Agriculture et colonisation au Québec* (Montréal, Boréal Express, 1980).

Senior, Elinor Kyte, *British Regulars in Montreal: An Imperial Garrison, 1832-1854* (Kingston and Montreal, McGill-Queen's University Press, 1981).

Senior, Elinor Kyte, *Redcoats and Patriotes: the Rebellions in Lower Canada, 1837-38* (Ottawa, Canada's Wings, 1985).

Silver, A.I., *The French-Canadian Idea of Confederation* (Toronto, University of Toronto Press, 1982).

Smith, Françoise, *The Establishment of Religion in the Eastern Townships, 1799-1851* (Unpublished M.A. thesis, McGill University, 1975).

Snell, James and Frederick Vaughan, *The Supreme Court of Canada: History of the Institution* (Toronto, The Osgoode Society, 1985).

Steedman, Mercedes, "Skill and Gender in the Canadian Clothing Industry, 1890-1940", in C. Heron and R. Storey, eds., *On the Job: Confronting the Labour Process in Canada* (Kingston and Montreal, McGill-Queen's University Press, 1986): 152-176.

Stevens, G.R., *History of the Canadian National Railways* (New York, Macmillan, 1973).

Stoddart, Jennifer, "Quebec's Legal Elite Looks at Women's Rights: The Dorion Commission 1929-31", in David Flaherty, *Essays in the History of Canadian Law* (Toronto, University of Toronto Press, 1981), vol. 1, 323-357.

Sweeny, Robert, *A Guide to the history and records of selected Montreal businesses before 1947* (Montréal, Centre de recherche en histoire économique du Canada français, 1978).

Sweeny, Robert, *Internal Dynamics and the International Cycle: Questions of the Transition in Montreal, 1821-28* (Unpublished Ph.D. thesis, McGill University, 1985).

Tardivel, Jules-Paul, *For My Country: "Pour la Patrie"* (Toronto, University of Toronto Press, 1975).

Tétreault, Martin, "Les maladies de la misère—aspects de la santé publique à Montréal—1880-1914", *Revue d'histoire de l'Amérique française*, 36,4 (mars 1983): 507-526.

Thivierge, Marîse, "La syndicalisation des institutrices catholiques, 1900-1959", in N. Fahmy-Eid et M. Dumont, *Maîtresses de maison, maîtresses d'école* (Montréal, Boréal Express, 1983): 171-189.

Thivierge, Nicole, *Ecoles ménagères et instituts familiaux: un modèle féminin traditionel* (Québec, Institut québécois de recherche sur la culture, 1982).

Thwaites, Reuben Gold, *The Jesuit Relations and Allied Documents* (Cleveland, Burrows Brothers, 1896-1901), 72 vols.

Tousignant, Pierre, "Problématique pour une nouvelle approche de la constitution de 1791", *Revue d'histoire de l'Amérique française*, 27,2 (1973): 181-234.

Tousignant, Pierre, "The integration of the Province of Quebec into the British empire", *Dictionary of Canadian Biography* (Toronto and Québec, University of Toronto Press and Les Presses de l'Université Laval, 1979), Volume IV: xxxii-xlix.

Tremblay, Louise, *La politique missionnaire des Sulpiciens au XVIIe et début du XVIIIe siècles* (Unpublished M.A. thesis, Université de Montréal, 1981).

Tremblay, Robert, "Un aspect de la consolidation du pouvoir d'Etat de la bourgeoisie coloniale: La législation anti-ouvrière dans le Bas-Canada, 1800-1850", *Labour/Le Travailleur*, 8/9 (Autumn/Spring 1981-2): 243-52.

Tremblay, Robert, "La grève des ouvriers de la construction navale à Québec (1840)", *Revue d'histoire de l'Amérique française*, 37,2 (septembre 1983): 227-240.

Trigger, Bruce, "Order and Freedom in Huron Society", *Anthropologica*, 5,2 (1963): 151-169.

Trigger, Bruce, *The Children of Aataentsic. A History of the Huron People to 1660* (Kingston and Montreal, McGill-Queen's University Press, 1976), 2 volumes.

Trigger, Bruce, ed., *Handbook of North American Indians*, Volume 15, *Northeast* (Washington, Smithsonian Institution, 1978a).

Trigger, Bruce, *Indians and the "Heroic Age" of New France* (Ottawa, Canadian Historical Association, Booklet 30, 1978b).

Trigger, Bruce, *Natives and Newcomers. Canada's "Heroic Age" Reconsidered* (Kingston and Montreal, McGill-Queen's University Press, 1985).

Trofimenkoff, Susan Mann, "Henri Bourassa and 'The Woman Question'", *Journal of Canadian Studies*, 10 (1975): 3-11.

Trofimenkoff, Susan Mann, *Abbé Groulx. Variations on a Nationalist Theme* (Toronto, Copp Clark, 1978a).

Trofimenkoff, Susan Mann, "Les femmes dans l'oeuvre de Groulx", *Revue d'histoire de l'Amérique française*, 32,3 (décembre 1978b): 385-98.

Trofimenkoff, Susan Mann, *The Dream of Nation: A Social and Intellectual History of Quebec* (Toronto, Gage, 1983).

Trudel, Marcel, *The seigneurial regime* (Ottawa, Canadian Historical Association, Booklet 6, 1956).

Trudel, Marcel, *An Introduction to New France* (Toronto, Holt, Rinehart & Winston, 1968).

Trudel, Marcel, *The Beginnings of New France, 1524-1663* (Toronto, McClelland & Stewart, 1973).

Trudel, Marcel, *Histoire de la Nouvelle-France* (Montréal, Fides, 1966-1983), 4 vols.

Tulchinsky, Gerald J.J., *The River Barons: Montreal Businessmen and the Growth of Industry and Transportation, 1837-53* (Toronto, University of Toronto Press, 1977).

Turgeon, Laurier, "Pour une histoire de la pêche: le marché de la morue à Marseille au XVIIIe siècle", *Histoire sociale/Social History*, 14,28 (November, 1981): 295-322.

Turgeon, Laurier, "Pour redécouvrir notre 16e siècle: les pêches à Terre-Neuve d'après les archives notariales de Bordeaux", *Revue d'histoire de l'Amérique française*, 39,4 (printemps 1986): 523-549.

Urquhart, M.C. and K.A.H. Buckley, *Historical Stastistics of Canada* (Toronto, Macmillan, 1965).

Vachon, André, "The Administration of New France", *Dictionary of Canadian Biography*, (Toronto and Québec, University of Toronto Press and Les Presses de l'Université Laval, 1969) Volume II: xv-xxv.

Vallières, Pierre, *White Niggers of America* (Toronto, McClelland & Stewart, 1971).

Vigod, Bernard, "Ideology and Institutions in Quebec. The Public Charities Controversy 1921-1926", *Histoire sociale/Social History*, 11,21 (May 1978): 167-182.

Vigod, Bernard, *Quebec before Duplessis. The Political Career of Louis-Alexandre Taschereau* (Kingston and Montreal, McGill-Queen's University Press, 1986).

Wade, Mason, *The French Canadians 1760-1967* (Toronto, Macmillan, 1968), 2 vols.

Wallerstein, Immanuel, *The Modern World System. Capitalist Agriculture and the Origins of the European World Economy in the Sixteenth Century* (New York, Academic Press, 1974).

Wallot, Jean-Pierre, "La religion catholique et les Canadiens au début du XIXe siècle" *Canadian Historical Review*, 52,1 (March 1971): 51-94.

Wallot, Jean-Pierre, *Un Québec qui bougeait: trame socio-politique au tournant du XIXe siècle* (Trois-Rivières, Boréal Express, 1973).

Weisz, George, "Origines géographiques et lieux de pratique des diplômés en médecine au Québec de 1834 à 1939", in Marcel Fournier, Yves Gingras et Othmar Keel, *Sciences et médecine au Québec: Perspectives sociohistoriques* (Québec, Institut québécois de recherche sur la culture, 1987): 129-170.

Willis, John, *The Process of Hydraulic Industrialization on the Lachine Canal 1840-80: Origins, Rise and Fall* (Ottawa, Environment Canada, 1987).

Wright, J.V., *Ontario Prehistory: An Eleven Thousand Year Archaeological Outline* (Ottawa, National Museums of Canada, 1981).

Wright, J.V., *Quebec Prehistory* (Ottawa, National Museums of Canada, 1980).

Young, Brian, *Promoters and Politicians: The North-Shore Railways in the History of Quebec 1854-85* (Toronto, University of Toronto Press, 1978).

Young, Brian, *George-Etienne Cartier: Montreal Bourgeois* (Kingston and Montreal, McGill-Queen's University Press, 1981).

Young, Brian, *In Its Corporate Capacity: the Seminary of Montreal as a Business Institution, 1816-76* (Kingston and Montreal, McGill-Queen's University Press, 1986).

Zoltvany, Yves, "Esquisse de la Coutume de Paris", *Revue d'histoire de l'Amérique française*, 25,3 (décembre 1971): 365-384.

Zoltvany, Yves, *Philippe de Rigaud de Vaudreuil. Governor of New France, 1703-1725* (Toronto, McClelland & Stewart, 1974).

Index

300

Acknowledgements

Fig. 1.2: Hudson's Bay Company Archives, HBCA Photograph Collection 1987/15 (A.A. Chesterfield, Album 14). Fig. 1.3: Illustration by Guy Lapointe, Recherches Amérindiennes au Québec, 1986. Fig. 1.5: Detail from *Traité général des pêches de Duhamel du Monceau*, Paris, 1772. Fig. 1.6: Detail of Herman Moll's *Map of North America, 1718*, Public Archives of Canada/C-3686. Fig. 1.9: Les Archives des Ursulines. Fig. 2.1: Public Archives Canada/C-355. Fig. 2.2: Public Archives Canada/C-15703. Fig. 2.3: B-962, Archives Nationales du Québec, 1688. Courtesy of J. Dickinson. Fig. 2.4: From The Seigneurial System in Early Canada by R. Cole Harris. Reproduced with the permission of University of Wisconsin Press. Fig. 2.6: Public Archives Canada/C-352. Fig. 3.2: *Lake of Two Mountains* (Oka), Steel engraving originally drawn by W.H. Bartlett, McCord Museum of Canadian History. Fig. 3.3: 74-12064, National Museum of Canada. Fig. 3.4: Attributed to George Seton, Public Archives Canada/ C-1241. Fig. 3.5: *A View of the Chateau Richer*, Watercolour by Thomas Davies, National Gallery of Canada. Fig. 3.6: Courtesy of Molson Breweries of Canada Limited. Fig. 3.7: Photo Livernois, 1958, 4666, Ste-Anne de Beaupré Archives, Galerie d'art de la Basilique. Fig. 4.1: Public Archives Canada/National Map Collection 19809, Reference code R-340, Montreal 1801 (1919). Fig. 4.4: 76310-I, Notman Archives. Fig. 4.5: Watercolour by Notman and Sandham, Notman Archives. Fig. 4.6: Courtesy of Redpath Sugar Museum. Fig. 4.7: Archives du Diminairi de Trois-Rivières. Fig. 4.8: Courtesy of Mississquoi Historical Museum. Fig. 4.9: Print by R.M.S. Bouchette in *British American Land Company: Views in Lower Canada*, London, 1836, Metro Toronto Public Library. Fig. 4.10: Société d'histoire régionale de Saint-Hyacinthe. Fig. 5.1: Public Archives Canada/C-15494. Fig. 5.2: Public Archives Canada/C-13392. Fig. 5.3: Public Archives Canada/C-40295. Fig. 5.6: 24027-II, Notman Archives. Fig. 5.7: Public Archives Canada/C-4733. Fig. 6.2: MP886(6), Notman Archives. Fig. 6.5: Université du Québec à Trois-Rivières, Hydro-Québec. Fig. 6.6: Public Archives Canada/C-55787. Fig. 6.7: Public Archives Canada/C-30811. Fig. 6.8: Public Archives Canada/DND/PA-24439. Fig. 7.1: Public Archives Canada/PA-43304. Fig. 7.2: 2698 View, Notman Archives. Fig. 7.3: Archives de la ville de Montréal. Fig. 7.4: Public Archives Canada/C-128063. Fig. 7.5: Société des alcools du Québec. Fig. 7.6: Sisters of Misericorde Archives. Fig. 7.7: Public Archives Canada/C-14394. Fig. 8.1: Canadian Jewish Congress, Gilbert to H.M. Caiserman, June 30, 1937. Fig. 8.2: Canapress. Fig. 8.3: Hydro-Québec. Fig. 8.6: Hydro-Québec Archives. Fig. 8.7: John Doggett/Public Archives Canada/PA-164027. Fig. 8.8: Université du Québec à Montréal.

1 2 3 4 5 4756-5 92 91 90 89 88